SPORT INDUSTRY
RESEARCH & ANALYSIS

AN APPROACH TO INFORMED DECISION MAKING

Jacquelyn Cuneen
BOWLING GREEN STATE UNIVERSITY

David A. Tobar
BOWLING GREEN STATE UNIVERSITY

Holcomb Hathaway, Publishers
Scottsdale, Arizona
HHP

Library of Congress Cataloging-in-Publication Data

Cuneen, Jacquelyn.
  Sport industry research and analysis : an approach to informed decision
making / Jacquelyn Cuneen, David A. Tobar.
      pages cm
  Includes index.
  ISBN 978-1-62159-017-0 (print) — ISBN 978-1-62159-018-7 (ebook)   1.
Sports administration—Research—Methodology.   2. Sports—Statistical
methods.   3. Microsoft Excel (Computer file) I. Tobar, David A.   II. Title.
  GV713.C84 2015
  796.06'9—dc23
                                                    2015001938

Please note: The authors and publisher have made every effort to provide current
website addresses in this book. However, because web addresses change constantly,
it is inevitable that some of the URLs listed here will change following publication
of this book.

Copyright © 2015 by Holcomb Hathaway, Publishers, Inc.

Holcomb Hathaway, Publishers, Inc.
8700 E. Via de Ventura Blvd., Suite 265
Scottsdale, Arizona 85258
480-991-7881
www.hh-pub.com

10 9 8 7 6 5 4 3 2 1

Print ISBN: 978-1-62159-017-0
Ebook ISBN: 978-1-62159-018-7

All rights reserved. No part of this publication may be reproduced, in any form
or by any means, without permission in writing from the publisher.

Printed in the United States of America.

Photo Credits:
Front cover: 06photo/123RF *(graph)*,
Sergey Nivens/123RF *(stadium)*,
sjenner13/123RF *(man). Back cover,*
Eric Broder Van Dyke123RF. *Page 1,*
Cathy Yeulet/123RF, yanlev/123RF,
nrey/123RF; *page 19,* Wavebreak
Media Ltd/123RF, Cameron Whit-
man/123RF, nrey/123RF; *page 81,*
Dmitriy Shironosov/123RF, Ruth
Peterkin/123RF, nrey/123RF.

Contents

PART TWO   INFORMATION PROCESSES: COLLECTING DATA   19

Approaches to Information Gathering   20

Descriptive Research Design and Methods   35

Historical and Philosophical Research Methods and Design   46

Qualitative or Naturalistic Inquiry   51

Delphi Study   57

Experimental Research
TESTING THE EFFECTS OF A VARIABLE   62

Case Studies
EXAMINING A SOLITARY ISSUE IN DETAIL   66

Feasibility and Profitability Studies
DETERMINING THE POSSIBLE   72

Grants and Contracts
FUNDED INVESTIGATIONS   76

PART THREE USING STATISTICS TO ANALYZE AND INTERPRET INFORMATION   81

Introduction to the Research Scenarios and the Data Analysis Software   82

Issues in Analyzing Data   94

Descriptive Statistics   103

Note on Protecting Participants and Research Data   216

Appendix

Appendix

Foreword

BY DIANNA P. GRAY

From popular lore . . .

One weekend Sherlock Holmes and Dr. Watson went camping. They pitched their tent under the stars and went to sleep. Sometime in the middle of the night, Holmes shook Watson awake and said, "Watson, look up at the sky, and tell me what you see."

Watson replied, "I see millions and millions of stars."

Holmes asked, "And what do you deduce from that?"

Watson answered: "Well, if there are millions of stars, and if even a few of those have planets, it's quite likely there are some planets like Earth out there. And if there are a few planets like Earth out there, there might also be life."

And Holmes said: "Watson, you idiot, it means that somebody stole our tent!"

Welcome to the introductory sport management research and analysis course, referred to by some as a "wonderfully uncomfortable" place to be, but more often referred to by students as "the *most* uncomfortable" class to take. However, as you read the numerous testimonials of sport professionals in this book regarding their daily use of the skills taught in such courses, the importance of collecting and interpreting data in the sport industry, and the degree to which research and analysis have enhanced or influenced their daily decision making and professional success, you might come to see that these skills are invaluable. In fact, many of those professionals would now admit that they wish they had paid more attention in class!

As you learn about research in sport enterprise, you will operate as a sort of Sherlock Holmes (or *Moneyball*'s Billy Beane, if you prefer). Except, unlike these "researchers," the problem to be investigated won't be determining who stole your tent or which players to select to assemble a winning team. Rather, you will learn systematic ways to explore and resolve problems that are an important part of the daily decision making sport industry professionals rely on for competitive success. The importance of data and information to sport managers is made exceedingly clear when we examine the many sport-specific decisions that must be made on a daily basis. Sport practitioners face such questions as: How can we attract and keep season ticket holders? What are the team's fan demographics and psychographics? What issues might deter families from attending certain games? What are our fans' media preferences? How can we increase merchandise sales? These are just a few of the many matters that are critical to business survival and success in sport. As you read, you will begin to appreciate that research and analysis constitute an ongoing creative activity through which we discover new ways of viewing and addressing problems.

This text differs from others in the field in that the authors deliver a clear, straightforward explanation of research processes: how to analyze and conduct research, how to analyze data by using readily available Microsoft Excel spreadsheets, and how to understand the data's meaning and usefulness. The book focuses on common research and analysis methodologies and techniques, presenting realistic sport industry settings and situations for which the methods and analytics will be useful. Given the extreme level of competition in sport and the growing acknowledgment of the benefits of statistical analysis, research skills are no longer a luxury for sport management graduates—they are a necessity.

The authors of this text have a combination of academic and professional experience that uniquely qualifies them to write this book. Their long tenure as university professors provides them with the insight and expertise to identify the research skills needed by current and future sport management professionals. In addition, their own research and associations with industry practitioners at all levels of sport have given them the ability to identify key sport industry trends and act as sleuths themselves, solving sport industry mysteries and challenges and preparing the next generation of sport management professionals.

I say, dear student, it's elementary that you should and will master sport management research!

Dianna P. Gray, Ph.D.
PROFESSOR, SPORT ADMINISTRATION
DIRECTOR, SPORT MARKETING RESEARCH INSTITUTE
UNIVERSITY OF NORTHERN COLORADO, GREELEY, COLORADO

Preface

Sport enterprise relies heavily on data-based decisions. Therefore, sport industry professionals must be able to judge the quality of the research processes and statistical procedures that produce the data. Sport managers who are not proficient in gathering and analyzing information risk making unsubstantiated decisions that adversely impact their organizational bottom lines. Even so, sport management students often underestimate the importance of research and statistics courses in their professional preparations, because they see no direct link between those topics and their dream jobs in sport.

As experienced professors who have taught graduate and undergraduate research and statistics to thousands of sport management students over the years, we understand the frustrations involved in convincing students that they need to know how to collect and interpret information without bias. Many sport management students, specifically those who do not plan to pursue a career in academe, fail to recognize that they may be dealing with information in the form of research and statistics every day of their working lives. Further, many students seem actually to fear research and statistics as a topical area of study. This book is intended to help students feel comfortable with and appreciative of research by providing them with an applied approach and a straightforward guide to make the study of research and statistics meaningful on a practical level.

In *Sport Industry Research & Analysis: An Approach to Informed Decision Making*, Parts One and Two rely as much as possible on a conversational model, outlining the practical uses and value of research and analysis in sport enterprise. This book is more or less a compilation of applied explanations to clarify the often-complicated descriptions offered by textbooks on academic research. Each chapter explains a part of the research process and guides readers through a specific form of inquiry or procedure, providing examples based on real-world issues to show how these research processes contribute to bottom-line decisions in the sport industry. We present testimonials from sport industry professionals periodically to reinforce the worth and value of research in the sport industry.

In addition, Part Three provides step-by-step instructions for solving statistical problems using Microsoft Excel, a software application familiar to most students. Students will be able to use statistical procedures in Excel to solve typical problems that arise in the sport industry. Because they are accustomed to Excel, students will likely find the process to be more meaningful and far less intimidating than if they were required to solve problems with an unfamiliar statistical software program. We provide Excel spreadsheets for the statistical processes addressed at the beginning and intermediate levels of study. Screenshots help to guide students through the problem-solving process. We discuss the statistical tests in the context of a common industry scenario (Minor League Baseball Research Scenario I) and include guidance in analyzing, interpreting, and presenting the results. Chapters end with a second scenario (Health Club Research Scenario II) that enables readers to practice performing the statistical test as well as analyzing, interpreting, and presenting the results. The data for both scenarios is available on the instructor ancillary website and in Appendices A and B. The ancillary website also offers the answers to the practice problems for Scenario II.

By providing a succinct, applied approach to research designs and statistical analyses that are useful for sport managers, our goal is to emphasize that sport industry professionals depend on research and data often and in a variety of settings. Students will, we hope, understand the importance of an information-based approach to decision making in sport enterprise and embrace the usefulness of research and statistics courses in their academic preparations. We also hope that instructors who teach research and statistics will find this book helpful for addressing crucial topics in a way that will be meaningful for the students in their courses. Further, we hope sport industry professionals will find this book to be a useful desktop reference tool and refresher guide as they continue to work with industry data.

ACKNOWLEDGMENTS

Many thanks to Dianna Gray and Bill Sutton for their support, as expressed in the Foreword and Afterword of this book. In addition, thanks to those professionals who contributed to our "In Practice" feature: Kathryn Bobel, Curtis Danburg, Simone Eli, Dick Irwin, Ray Schneider, Megan Valentine, and Sandy White provided readers with realistic examples of the essential role of research in sport management decisions. We also appreciate the support of our wonderful colleagues in the BGSU Sport Management program. And of course this book would not have been possible without the support and encouragement of our families, to whom we are grateful.

Finally, we would like to thank the following reviewers, who offered feedback on the manuscript at various stages of its development: Suzannah Armentrout, Minnesota State University, Mankato; Kimberly Bodey, Indiana State University; Michael Giardina, Florida State University; Brian Hickey, Florida A&M University; Kostas Karadakis, Southern New Hampshire University; Andreas Kavazis, Auburn University; J. C. Kim, Fairleigh Dickinson University; Eddie Lam, Cleveland State University; Heather Lawrence, Ohio University; Liette Ocker, Sam Houston State University; James T. Reese, Drexel University. The book is better as a result of their efforts, and we appreciate their help.

Jacquelyn Cuneen, Ed.D.
David A. Tobar, Ph.D.

About the Authors

Jacquelyn Cuneen, Ed.D., is Professor Emerita of Sport Management at Bowling Green State University, where she taught Sport and Event Promotion, Sport Finance, and Introduction to Research, and supervised sport management field experience students. Her research foci include sport-related advertising and professional preparation of sport managers. She has authored or co-authored more than 70 scholarly and professional articles for numerous journals, including *Journal of Sport Management, Sport Management Education Journal, Sport Marketing Quarterly, Sex Roles,* and others. Cuneen has served in various elected and appointed offices for the North American Society for Sport Management, the Sport Marketing Association, and the Ohio Association for HPERD. Prior to her academic career, she was Account Executive, Director of Women's Programming, and Educational Correspondent for two New York State–based ABC radio affiliates.

David A. Tobar, Ph.D., is an Associate Professor of Sport Management at Bowling Green State University, where he teaches Research Methods and Sport and Exercise Psychology, and supervises sport management field experience students. He earned his master's and doctoral degrees from the University of Wisconsin–Madison. He is a former Chair of the Sport Management, Recreation, and Tourism Division at BGSU. Tobar's research interests focus on personality and well-being in sport and exercise. He has published in peer-review journals such as *Sport Marketing Quarterly, International Journal of Sport and Exercise Psychology, Medicine and Science in Sports and Exercise,* and *Journal of Physical Activity and Health.* He also has presented his research at national and international meetings, including the North American Society for the Psychology of Sport and Physical Activity, the American College of Sports Medicine, Association of Applied Sport Psychology, and the International Society of Sport Psychology.

PART ONE

AN INFORMATION-BASED
APPROACH TO FINDING ANSWERS

1

Why We Need to Know About Research and Analysis . . .

AND WHAT THEY HAVE TO DO WITH A CAREER IN SPORT MANAGEMENT

EXECUTIVE SUMMARY Research and analysis have a mystique about them. We hear these words and may think of Madame Curie in her laboratory or Douglas McGregor's theories of management: Theory X and Theory Y. Yet research and analysis are far from mysterious. Sport industry professionals use research skills every day in solving substantial problems, such as decisions about the best ways to use scarce resources, which candidate to hire, or who should receive an end-of-year bonus. The key to good decisions is good research and analysis, and the key to good research and analysis is reliable data. Reliable data are assembled through a systematic process of planning. Research and analysis have an impact on organizational bottom lines, and sport managers must, therefore, be able to judge the quality of their research and the results it yields for their practical use.

SPORT MANAGERS USE RESEARCH AND ANALYSIS EVERY DAY

Research involves the systematic collection of data and study of materials to address a question or make a decision. **Analysis** is the exploration of data, especially through the use of statistics. *Ana-*

lytics is the process by which data are explored. **Statistics** is a way to interpret a collection of observations or data that is obtained from research. Professionals in the sport industry use research, analysis, and statistics every day to answer questions and make decisions. Consider the many questions sport managers must ask in a day. More importantly, think about the many answers they will need to find in order to make informed decisions.

Suppose a marketing director starts the day by interviewing five new sport management graduates for a sales position. The candidates' responses constitute data that the director will use in making the hiring decision. The director then attends a meeting where the current marketing staff presents findings on last season's game promotions and their effects on attendance. Those audience figures constitute data that the director and the sales team will use in determining the most efficient use of future resources to attract fans. The director then meets with the sport communications staff to discuss next year's 50th anniversary celebration of a team championship. She decides to look in the company's and local newspaper's archives to find out about the stadium signage from that era, in order to approach those same companies to sponsor the hallmark recognition event at the championship celebration. Finally, the director meets with the ticketing department staff to reach a consensus on the artwork that will be used on upcoming hard-copy and e-tickets and the corresponding graphics for the team's ticket office website.

All of the above situations are essentially analyses or research studies. For the interview, the director uses the *naturalistic method* to collect *qualitative data* that will be categorized to form a conclusion (Chapter 6). In the sales team meeting, the director is addressing *descriptive quantitative data,* likely collected via questionnaire (Chapter 4). As a result of the meeting to plan the anniversary celebration, the director will use primary and secondary sources to conduct *historical inquiry* (Chapter 5). Last, the session with the ticketing staff is a modified *Delphi study,* where a group of experts reaches consensus on a vital issue (Chapter 7).

As shown in these examples, research and analysis address critical questions such as

- whom to ask to get answers,
- what resources will be needed to find clear answers that can stand up to scrutiny,
- how the results should be interpreted, and
- what recommendations should be made.

Managers in any position—but particularly sport managers—benefit from research and analysis and, therefore, are obligated to understand it: to know the process by which they or others should conduct it, to have the savvy to interpret it, and to know what it can do for them.

IN PRACTICE

Research and Analysis in the Field

Sandy White, *Director of Operations & Chief Financial Officer, LPGA Marathon Classic*

When I was completing my research and statistics classes as a sport management undergraduate and master's student, I did not fully realize the extent to which I would be working with data in my career. I was not going to be a sport management researcher, and I did not fully appreciate those classes that seemed tailored to some of the other students who were planning to spend their careers in study and teaching. My dream was a career in the sport industry working in management, sponsorships, and finance, and the courses that focused on those topics were very meaningful and were really the most fun for me. I have to admit that I was glad when the research requirements were done.

My first sport management job was in ticket sales for a Major League Baseball team. We had sales meetings at least once a week, and many issues came up that reminded me of research studies that we had read for classes—such topics as how to attract and keep season ticket holders, important issues for families who attend games, couponing, and other matters that were critical to profits. I was using my research background already, and I was fortunate to understand the practicalities of useful research throughout my association with the team.

When the opportunity came for me to work in management, marketing, and finance for Toledo's LPGA tournament, I knew by then that good research was indispensable for decision making. I now use research conducted by others and actually help conduct it myself. I work with sport management students and professors from regional colleges in formulating questionnaires to collect fan demographics and psychographics, economic impact data, merchandising information, and work satisfaction levels of the hundreds of volunteers that help stage our annual tournament. In the long run, those research and statistics courses became more meaningful to me than I would have guessed.

In another turn of events that I could not have predicted, I often join the ranks of part-time faculty and teach marketing and management classes at nearby colleges. I never intended to use research or become a teacher who needed to have a research background, but those courses ended up playing much more of a role in my career than I could have imagined.

SCIENTIFIC METHOD: THE FOUNDATION OF THE RESEARCH AND ANALYSIS PROCESS

Although some sport industry issues might require a judgment call (e.g., hiring an established financial officer for a large salary or outsourcing accounting services to a local firm; purchasing a maintenance contract for a copier or paying higher fees when the machine needs prescribed service), most questions and problems that arise in the sport industry, as in any business, have to be addressed and solved without bias (e.g., audience assessment, economic impact). The **scientific method,** a centuries-old mainstay of scholarly inquiry, is a systematic, controlled process of information gathering and problem solving. Scholars employ the scientific method to generate theories (hypotheses), acquire new knowledge, test existing knowledge, and draw conclusions based on original data. The scientific method is also valuable for sport managers, who use it to determine solutions to practical issues in the workplace. Information collected through the scientific method tends to stand the test of repetition and time (i.e., it is **empirical research**). The information collected can be fundamental, essential knowledge (**basic research**), or it can be used in actual practice to solve problems (**applied research**).

The questions that scientists pose are similar in basic respects to the questions that arise in professional situations. In both cases, there is a relationship between two or more variables (this means that the question is one that does have an answer; we say that it possesses *feasibility*). Also, in both cases we have a clear question or unique problem that can be tested (we say that the question possesses *clarity*) and new facts that can be discovered to add to existing facts. In each setting, there is a problem or question to be solved or answered, an idea of what might be revealed, an observation to be made or data to be gathered, and a conclusion to be drawn.

Much of what we know about the sport management field and industry is the result of scientific inquiry. Information—whether it is called research, analysis, or a needs assessment—is indispensable to a sport organization's welfare. When information is lacking, unresolved major issues that could have been understood easily through simple analysis can blindside an organization and its strategic plan.

This book provides a straightforward explanation of research analysis processes—how to conduct research and analysis, how to treat data, and how to understand the meaning and usefulness of the results. With a focus on common research and analysis methodologies and techniques, we present realistic situations that illustrate how the methods will be useful in a sport industry setting. Following explanation of the methodologies, we present real-world accounts of statistical uses, including sample procedures and data sets, as well as instructions for using spreadsheet software to analyze the data. Throughout the book, industry professionals outline ways in which research and analysis have enhanced or influenced their decision making.

OVERVIEW OF RESEARCH AND ANALYSIS RESOURCES

The importance of information to sport managers becomes exceedingly clear when one examines the sport-specific analytics providers and professional associations that exist to contribute to the sport industry knowledge base. These organizations, which form a sector of the sport industry themselves, provide services ranging from interviewing (questionnaire construction; focus groups) to comprehensive consulting (research design, construction, coding, analysis, interpreting, reporting). Exhibit 1.1 is a partial listing of commercial information sources commonly used by sport managers.

EXHIBIT 1.1	Summary of commercial information providers and services.
PROVIDER	**SERVICES**
ESPN Sports Poll www.lukerontrends.com/aboutsportspoll/	Databases on trends, product usage and preferences, and fan interests. Poll results are often picked up by national media as newsworthy for the general public.
Joyce Julius & Associates www.joycejulius.com	Specialized firm measuring the outcomes of sponsorships and endorsements
Sport Business Research Network www.sbrnet.com	Data on participation, fan profiles, venues, finance, sporting goods industry, sponsorship and marketing, media
Nielsen Scarborough www.scarborough.com	Full-service audience assessment
Sports Economics www.sportseconomics.com	Provides consulting on various analyses related to sport business, finance, and marketing
Turnkey Sports & Entertainment turnkeyse.com	Provider of market research, data, and analytics related to sports and entertainment
Sport Marketing Association http://sportmarketingassociation.net	All segments of the sport marketing industries, through an annual conference and its journal, *Sport Marketing Quarterly*

Many other sources of reliable information regarding sport issues are available. Scholarly and other types of academic and specialized organizations provide continued professional learning to college and university faculty, as well as sport industry personnel. These are excellent sources of cutting-edge research, through their annual conferences and refereed (i.e., reviewed, adjudicated) journals. Exhibit 1.2 is a partial listing of academic societies and their associated journals.

In addition to scholarly journals, abstracts (brief summaries of original research) are usually available on the websites of the organizations listed in these exhibits. Finally, although they are journalistic rather than scholarly in context, trade journals such as *Street and Smith's Sports Business Journal* and *Team Marketing Report* are informative trade publications that contain up-to-date news, statistics, and views on sport enterprise. Information and data contained in these trade papers is highly regarded by the industry and often cited in scholarly works.

PRIMARY VERSUS SECONDARY DATA

rimary data are original and collected first-hand by researchers, through focus groups, interviews, surveys, field trials, and so forth. Although

Summary of academic societies and journals.

ACADEMIC SOCIETY	FOCUS
Association for Applied Sport Psychology www.appliedsportpsych.org	Issues associated with athletes, participation, and other psycho-social aspects of sport performance, through an annual conference and its publications, *Journal of Applied Sport Psychology* and *Journal of Sport Psychology in Action*
European Association for Sport Management www.easm.net	Study and research in sport management. Publishes *European Sport Management Quarterly*
North American Society for Sport Management www.nassm.com	Scholarship in sport leadership/management, media, finance, marketing, communication, venues, and legal and social aspects, through an annual conference and its publication, *Journal of Sport Management*
North American Society for the Sociology of Sport www.nasss.org	Sociological aspects of play, games, sport, and athletics, through an annual conference and its publication, *Sociology of Sport Journal*
Sport Management Association of Australia and New Zealand www.smaanz.org	Scholarly inquiry in sport management. Its publication is the *Sport Management Review*.
Sport Marketing Association http://sportmarketingassociation.net	All segments of the sport marketing industries, through an annual conference and its journal, *Sport Marketing Quarterly*

this book primarily focuses on methods for collecting and analyzing primary data, it will also assist readers in appraising the value of **secondary data**—information collected and reported by others through various research resources. In contrast to primary data, secondary data are previously gathered and made available, free or for purchase, by research houses, government organizations, or commercial agencies, such as chambers of commerce and local/regional business journals. These agencies can be good sources of information, but users should be cautious in applying the data to their specific needs. Secondary data may have resulted from a commissioned study, and thus the results may slant toward the individual or group that paid for the study (e.g., a sports brand commissions a study on equipment and reports only the good opinions of the gear); the information might be dated (for example, in government census reports); or the descriptions of the participants and the means that were used to collect the data might not be reported in detail.

Retail profiles (portrayals of businesses' market presence) are another common source of secondary data, providing dependable reports of commercial information. Retail profiles are periodically available in city or regional business journals, and they outline data such as the total population located within a 5-, 10-, and 25-mile radius of the business, household income, and monthly household spending on items such as clothing, groceries, and entertainment. The profiles are usually trustworthy sources of quality information, if they are presented in an unbiased report format. However, beware of retail profiles and other reports provided in the form of a printed or electronic infomercial, as they may not be research-based in the strictest sense and might reflect the biases of the advertisers.

Similar demographic figures are also available from the U.S. Census Bureau. That bureau provides information by city, county, or metropolitan statistical area. Its American Factfinder program (http://factfinder2.census.gov/faces/nav/jsf/pages/index.xhtml) provides information about gender, age, education level, income, and so forth for a city or county name or ZIP code.

TALKING POINTS

Research and Analysis in Sport Management

- Good information helps sport managers do their jobs more efficiently.
- Sport managers can purchase data from a commercial service, or they can collect it themselves, if they have expertise in how to conduct a sound study.
- Understanding the importance of research, judging the method by which data were collected, being aware of appropriate analysis and interpretation, and being able to explain the method and results to others are essential in the field.
- Sport managers need to be able to implement what they learn from research and analyses.

2

Reading and Understanding Existing Research

EXECUTIVE SUMMARY A systematic process exists for planning, conducting, and reporting the results of research. Research published in scholarly journals adheres consistently to a format that permits the researchers to report the details of their studies in a uniform manner that clearly communicates the purpose, existing facts, approach to data collection, and results. This format assists readers in understanding the study. When information is presented to a live audience, a standard process also exists for this form of dissemination.

WHERE TO FIND RELIABLE EXISTING INFORMATION

As indicated in Chapter 1, sport managers need information to guide their decision making. Theoretical (hypothetical) and applied (functional) research in sport management provides information to assist managers in planning and to inform their decisions. This research is readily available and easily accessible through scholarly and focus journals, as well as scholarly and professional societies and academies (discussed in Chapter 1). A number of first-rate proprietary journals are also available (these journals are not necessarily associated with a society but rather are privately owned and operated for profit). Research is often available in archival collections (e.g., sport halls of fame, public libraries), as well as in college and professional team annals. Additional information, although not always scholarly, may be found in trade journals and technical reports.

Most academic societies either sponsor or are associated with scholarly journals and, in addition, publish summaries of the studies that are presented at their annual conferences. The journals and societies generally adhere to the same processes for accepting and disseminating research through their channels. Information published in scholarly journals and most research and analyses that are presented through professional society conferences are refereed, adjudicated, or reviewed, meaning that a manuscript submitted to the journal or an abstract submitted for presentation will be read and accepted or rejected by members of the journal's editorial board or conference abstract review committee.

For those journals that operate for profit, the process is similar. Well-regarded proprietary journals have editorial boards comprising academic and, often, industry experts to review manuscripts.

HOW STUDIES GET PUBLISHED

All journals have guidelines that authors must follow as they prepare and submit manuscripts. Journal publication guidelines address the physical qualities of the manuscript, such as margin width, page length, and citation style requirements (e.g., American Psychological Association, *Chicago Manual of Style*), as well as statements regarding the journal's positions on such issues as plagiarism and originality of the manuscript data.

Upon submission of a manuscript, the journal's chief editor selects two or more established reviewers to evaluate the manuscript. Most journals and societies operate under a double-blind review system, meaning that the authors do not know the identities of the reviewers, and the reviewers do not know the identities of the authors.

The reviewers scrutinize the manuscript and make suggestions for improvement or recommend that the publication accept it as written; they may also reject the manuscript altogether. The editor then returns the manuscript to the author or, in the case of multiple authors, to the lead author or the collaborator who assumes leadership of the group. If the authors elect to revise the manuscript and resubmit it, the process begins anew. Again, the reviewers may offer additional suggestions for revision, may recommend accepting the manuscript, or may recommend rejecting it.

When a manuscript is accepted for publication, it joins a queue of articles awaiting print and is referred to as being "in press." A manuscript's wait in the queue may last several weeks or months, or even longer, because journals are typically published monthly, quarterly, or yearly.

CHARACTERISTICS OF PUBLISHED ARTICLES

Articles published in society-supported, proprietary, or focus journals characteristically adhere to a long-established, uniform format. Uniformity lends authority and trustworthiness to research reports and assists readers in understanding the research. Generally, published articles adhere to the following organization: abstract, introduction, review of literature and specific statement of the problem, methodology, results, and discussion, ending with conclusions and recommendations for future study.

The Abstract

An abstract or study summary precedes the main body of the article. The abstract provides an overview of the study and is usually between 75 and 250 words in length. Ingredients of the abstract include the purpose for the study and/or a statement of the problem; a description of the subjects (e.g., number, type, age, gender); procedures implemented to meet the purpose; an overview of the data analysis and results; conclusions, implications, or applications; and a statement of the significance of the research.

Introduction

Research is usually based on a relevant theory or guiding question. Starting with a theory or question helps guide investigators in examining what is already known about the topic and guides them as they form new concepts or reinforce existing concepts. This section of an article familiarizes readers with the theory and builds interest in the topic and issues associated with the topic.

The Review of Literature

In the review of literature, the authors summarize and discuss previous information that has been gathered on the topic. The literature review demonstrates how the current study is related to previous studies and presents a rationale for the current study. This section, usually several pages long, makes a case for the necessity of continued inquiry in the area. Some reviews, such as those contained in doctoral dissertations, exhaust the literature (i.e., they examine every available study conducted on the topic), but the majority of reviews limit their citations to essential or classic literature and vital recent studies. In essence, the literature review reports on what has already been discovered about a problem and offers a historical perspective.

Previous literature is routinely found in refereed journals, books, monographs (special-edition journals addressing one subject), technical reports, and unpublished materials such as dissertations, theses, and papers presented at conferences. Unless the review is intended to be exhaustive, researchers and analysts usually prefer to limit their citations to literature that has been published in the last seven to ten years. Ideally, all sources cited should be directly related to the study's topic; however, for sport management topics that are new or under-investigated, sufficient literature does not exist. A literature base is important because it establishes the actual need for a new study or indicates a need for future inquiry.

If literature is unavailable, researchers and analysts must base their work on studies that are as closely related as possible. For example, a sport manager attempting to discover if family ticket packages attract more families to National Basketball Association Development League (D-League) games may find that no previous research has been conducted on this topic. The alternative is to uncover related information that might help guide the study (see Exhibit 2.1). If no information is available for D-League, then perhaps similar data exist for family attendance in college basketball. Or, the analyst might investigate family attendance trends in the Women's National Basketball Association. Not finding enough information about family ticketing in the college game or the WNBA, the analyst's next target might be literature about amateur basketball. With little or no available literature on amateur basketball tickets, studies in high school basketball may offer guidance. In other words, studying other groups of fans that buy tickets to games could yield insight into fans' purchasing trends and their overall mindset.

Or, imagine that a parks and recreation director is investigating fundraising for community sport softball tournaments and does not find any previous studies in this area. The next step might be to find research on community sports tournament funding in general, and if he finds no satisfactory literature on that topic, his next move may be to investigate funding approaches for community recreational sports programs.

In actuality, researchers and analysts need not be deterred by a lack of literature. Linked literature can be effective, and, moreover, a lack of explicit literature can definitely provide a rationale for a currently useful and innovative study, such as the study mentioned in the last example.

The literature review commonly ends with a statement of the problem that indicates the specific purpose of the study. The problem statement clarifies the study's destination and purpose.

EXHIBIT 2.1   Example of alternative, related sources of data.

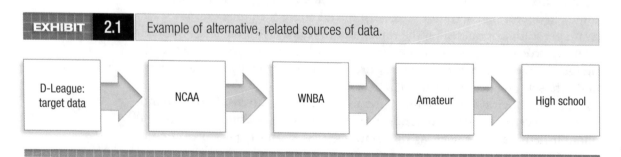

The Method

The method (or methodology) section explains, in meticulous detail, exactly how the study was conducted. The subjects are described in terms of how they were recruited and contacted, the number initially contacted or invited and the number subsequently participating, and other demographic information that helps readers understand who, precisely, was studied, such as gender, age, individual and/or household income, and education level. Other pertinent information in sport management studies is psychographic in nature, describing how subjects behave: how they hear about an event, how many times they attend, what they buy when they do attend, and what draws them to the event. A lack of detail about the subjects prevents readers from completely understanding a study's results and assessing its value. The method section should be so thoroughly detailed that other researchers and analysts wishing to replicate a study should have no questions about implementation.

In addition to describing the participants' characteristics, authors sometimes outline the steps taken to protect the subjects from harm and ensure their privacy. Usually, any researcher conducting a study involving human subjects has submitted a research proposal to a review board (e.g., Institutional Review Board, Human Subjects Review Board) consisting of a cross-section of individuals familiar with research procedures and processes (such as professors, physicians, and governmental officials). The board members represent the participants' best interests and demand a complete description of the precautions to be taken to shield them from maltreatment.

The Design

Design refers to the procedures used to collect information from the subjects or participants. This is the section of the article that identifies what, exactly, was required of the participants: did they respond to a survey, were they interviewed, or were they observed individually or in groups?

The design section also, often, details the instruments or materials (e.g., questionnaires, equipment) that were used to collect data from the participants. Some investigators prefer to disclose these elements in a separate section.

The Data Analysis

The data analysis section describes the techniques that were used to analyze the information obtained from the subjects. The study's purpose and design and the type of data that are collected determine the type of analysis a researcher performs. For quantitative data, this section can be a matter-of-fact outline of a mathematical model or a symbolic representation in numerical form of the logic used to analyze the information. For qualitative data, this section might go into great detail to describe the structure the investigators used to sort and categorize the information.

The Results

The results section conveys what the researchers found by conducting the study. The findings are usually presented in paragraph form, supported by tables, charts, or graphics. The results section is a technical report of the facts, free of any editorializing by the writers. That is, no opinions should be expressed in the results section. However, the researchers may state whether a hypothesis was supported or contradicted by the data.

The Discussion, Conclusions, and Recommendations

This section is where readers might find opinions and viewpoints. Investigators use the discussion section to report their nontechnical interpretations of the results. Here, researchers and analysts explain why they think they found what they found and either justify their original ideas about the problem under investigation or attempt to explain why the results were different from what they expected to find. They may also describe any limitations of the study—problems or issues such as a breakdown in design, subject dropout, or equipment difficulties. No matter how carefully a research design is planned and implemented, issues such as these can arise. When they do, the investigators should be sure to explain them and any effects they may have had on a study's outcome, in this section of the article. The following are common obstructions that may arise.

- **Systematic variance:** an inconsistency in a measure caused by known or unknown influences that skew the results in one direction or another. Systematic variance often happens when a study's participants have a bias against some aspect of the study. For instance, if a company with a new brand is surveying bowlers' preferences for shoes and gloves by providing the gear to them and recording their opinions after use, the company might not receive the bowlers' unbiased views, because the participants might have an unwavering loyalty to their current brand.

- **Extraneous variable:** a discrepancy in results traceable to unwanted effects that might affect the study's outcome. An extraneous variable is a variable that emerges during the study that is unrelated to the study's purpose. For instance, when a team is studying community support for a new arena, a finding that a new playground would be more beneficial would be considered an extraneous variable, as it was not part of the original problem statement.

- **Error (or random) variance:** a fluctuation of measures that is attributable to chance. Errors and random or unforeseen occurrences can hinder any study. For instance, whether fans indicate that they had a good or bad experience at a game might depend on the behavior of other fans who happen by chance to surround them in their seating section.

- **Lack of external validity:** In many instances, research results can be generalized to a population. Results can give a broad view of an issue. For instance, the results from a study of a representative sample of parents' reactions to Little League rules and regulations should apply to the general population of Little league parents, not just parents who participated in the study. If the parents who participated, however, were not representative of the population, then the results may not be generalizable. This might be the case if the participants were all from the same small, upper-middle-class community.

■ **History:** The longer a problem or specific participants are studied, the more likely it becomes that extraneous variables might affect the outcome of the study. Time affects responses. For instance, when sport managers' leadership qualities are measured, their records may show that they received mediocre evaluations as they eased into their jobs, bad evaluations after six months on the job, and good evaluations after 18 months because of the learning curve associated with any new experience.

■ **Maturation and mortality:** Participants can go through personal changes over time, and subjects may drop out of a study over time. Although these issues are mainly associated with longitudinal studies (studies that follow subjects over a long period of time), subjects in any study may rethink a position or become bored and drop out. For instance, officials and coaches participating in a study of home field advantage in high school football games over a single season might decide that the issue is too controversial to continue, or the subjects may lose interest in participating, due to the length of the inquiry.

■ **Selection bias:** A study's participants should be chosen randomly. Unless a study requires a purposefully chosen sample for a specific reason, participants should be selected at random so that the results can be generalized. For example, if investigators wish to find out why soccer fans attend away matches, and they select only fans who attend tournaments that are close by, the results will likely not answer the question of why the general population of soccer fans, who may or may not live close to tournaments, attends away matches.

■ **Bad instrumentation:** This obstruction occurs when measures are taken with an instrument that is not valid and reliable. (A *valid* instrument measures what it is supposed to measure; a *reliable* instrument gives consistent measurements over a period of time.) Statistical and other types of tests are available to help researchers ensure that instruments are designed to collect valid and reliable information. For instance, if investigators distribute a questionnaire to college students in order to find out their opinions on what constitutes an outstanding sport program, and the questionnaire was not based on literature or pilot tested for validity and reliability, the resulting data will not be useful.

At the end of the discussion section of an article, the authors state their conclusions, recommend avenues for further investigation, and acknowledge the limitations of their study.

References

Articles end with a complete list of references to the articles, reports, and books that the investigators used and cited. Each journal requires a specific reference style that is customary in its related academic disciplines. Most sport management journals require authors to use the currently updated reference style of the American Psychological Association (APA). Other styles that may be required are the Chicago, Campbell, or Harvard styles. Style requirements and submission guidelines are available from the journals, often on their websites.

HOW COMPLETED STUDIES ARE PRESENTED

For society conferences, authors submit an abstract for blind review by two to three experts appointed either by the conference program manager or by a content-area section head that the program manager has empowered to select reviewers. A presentation abstract is usually much longer than the abstracts that accompany a published research study; in some cases, they may be as long as two pages. Abstracts are generally accepted or rejected for presentation on the first round of review, with no option for revision. If an abstract is accepted for presentation, the authors present the entire study at the scholarly or professional conference.

Often, researchers and analysts will present their study to an audience of their peers prior to writing it in article form and submitting the manuscript to a journal. Questions posed by audience members are helpful to the authors as they prepare to write, and the audience's suggestions are often incorporated into the manuscript.

SPECIAL TOPIC RESEARCH REPORTS OR NON-PUBLISHED RESEARCH

Often, research that analysts undertake for sport enterprise will be unavailable for dissemination. Sport organizations employ their own analysts or contract with a commercial research house to collect information on their fan base, employee satisfaction or efficiency, and other essential operations. The organizations use the results of these inquiries privately, to inform their decision making. The reports, however, contain some of the same information as published research articles, in that they focus on the presentation and analysis of data from primary and secondary sources.

TALKING POINTS

Critiquing Research and Analysis

All published and presented research is subject to critique by peer reviewers prior to publication, as well as by readers after publication. All consumers of research should read with a critical eye before accepting the findings as trustworthy. Although specific issues are associated with particular designs, readers can consider several general points when assessing the overall quality of sport management research and analysis:

- The study should be based on a relevant theory or a practical problem.
- The problem under study should be significant and should be stated clearly.
- The authors should provide a well-developed rationale for conducting the inquiry.
- The relationship of the problem to previous research should be clear, and if no research exists that is directly related to the problem, the significance of the new problem should be apparent.
- The study should be guided by a clear and plausible hypothesis or research question.
- The subjects should be selected from the appropriate population for investigating the issue.
- The study design should be appropriate to the purpose and reported clearly.
- The article should be well organized and clearly written.

The research and analysis process is stringent and uniform, but it provides a fair and level playing field for information gathering, and it presents readers with a standardized investigative platform for learning. Studies should be conducted with great attention to detail and reported without bias, and the resulting articles often must be subjected to a peer review process.

PART TWO

INFORMATION PROCESSES: COLLECTING DATA

Approaches to Information Gathering

EXECUTIVE SUMMARY Knowledge exists in numerous forms, such as personal intuition, common knowledge, and expert opinions. However, the most reliable knowledge about problems comes from unbiased inquiry in the form of a needs assessment or a scientific/scholarly research study. Each method is designed to assist industry professionals and scholars in solving problems through a systematic process leading to reliable information and sound, logical decision making.

HOW SHOULD INFORMATION BE GATHERED TO MAKE AN INFORMED DECISION?

Nearly everyone who works in, or cheers for, a sport organization likely considers himself or herself to be knowledgeable about a team's operations and probably has a strong opinion to share. Insiders who work for the organization but do not have access to classified data may still believe that they have expert knowledge about the team's business. Fans and other individuals on the outside can be very certain of their beliefs yet have no inside information or any basis for an informed opinion. These examples of employees and fans involve common knowledge formed through everyday observations and interactions.

An example of a commonly accepted notion is that sport builds character. This concept is something many individuals believe to be true, because it has long been accepted that sport enhances the development of individuals' work ethic, teamwork, and persistence. Although this is true in many instances, many examples exist where athletes' behaviors on and off the playing field support a forceful argument that sport impedes the development of good character. Still, taxpayers more often than not support school athletics programs because of the prevailing notion that sport competition builds character. Taxpayers accept the sport–character relationship because it has always been stated as fact or because they intuitively believe that it is so, even though some evidence contradicts the concept.

Authoritative opinions are also usually accepted as true. When someone with authority states an opinion, it is apt to be accepted as fact or at least considered as a viable position. A sports journalist, for example, may express the opinion that women's basketball is much more fun to watch than men's basketball, because the women's game is based on strategy and skills, whereas the men's game is based on physicality and power. Yet television ratings and gate receipts often indicate that more fans prefer to watch men's basketball games, which would seem to refute the journalist's statement. However, when someone with authority states an opinion that women's basketball is more fun to watch, some people may accept it as fact.

In contrast to those who are informed only by common knowledge or the opinions of others, sport industry professionals, researchers, and analysts use a logical process to define a problem, an issue, a fact, or a phenomenon that requires an investigation and a solution. For example, suppose a National Hockey League team wants a new arena. In order to convince government officials that a new venue will positively impact the local economy, team management summarizes their attendance and in-venue and regional spending figures over a five-year period, projects population growth within the critical radius areas where fans live and work, and gathers information about the impact of other new venues in comparable cities. The team has, thus, used a systematic design to address a problem and then analyzed and interpreted data to arrive at an answer. In other words, the team came to an informed decision.

Obviously, problems often arise in connection with sport. For example, a team's outdated venue becomes unable to meet the growing needs of fans, such as convenient parking, comprehensive guest services, comfortable seating, and luxury accommodations. In this case, a logical procedure to determine a direction for solving such a venue issue might be to conduct a *needs assessment* and determine whether renovation would be sufficient or if new construction is needed. Other problems require a deeper exploration in order to gather necessary information. For instance, when a team renovates or constructs a new venue, it would be helpful to know whether building the new facility will result in a financial gain or loss for a team. A logical procedure to inform managerial decisions regarding the new venue would be a *scientific approach* to information gathering. In the next sections, we will first discuss needs assessment and then the scientific method.

INFORMATION GATHERING VIA NEEDS ASSESSMENT

Problems in sport organizations are often identified by means of an executive decision, such as when a team owner or general manager notices a problem, or through collective expertise, such as when department personnel identify an issue. A **needs assessment** is then conducted, either by internal personnel who have a stake in the outcome, by external consultants who bring objectivity to the process, or by a committee comprising internal and external partners. Problems that require resolution are identified as information is gathered.

Needs assessments are based on goals and targets, and they are valuable in identifying the resources that a sport organization possesses and determining what new resources it might acquire to improve its position. For the outcome of a needs assessment to be useful and meaningful, the objectives of the assessment should be specifically defined, so that the researchers will collect evidence directly related to the stated goals. Evidence collected through the assessment should relate directly to the well-defined purpose. Such an inquiry often has a practical basis, rather than a scientific (literature) basis. The inquiry should be conducted and the results reported free of bias. Finally, the conclusions should be based on the resulting data. As with scientific research, the interpretation of the results should be stated within the parameters of the findings.

In the case of information needed to assist in a decision to renovate a venue or build a new one, needs may become apparent in a number of ways. Suppose that the team's owner proposes to renovate its outdated venue. A needs assessment might reveal an inconsistency between what the team *wants* to do about the venue renovation and what it is *able* to do about it, because, for example, obsolete structural specifications may prohibit extensive renovation. Another way management can assess needs is by forming an internal committee to monitor the current venue and determine what, exactly, it lacks in terms of its current usefulness. The committee might develop a checklist of the best amenities associated with newer venues and use this list to appraise the team's current venue. This exploratory approach is a credible means of assessing need, but it can reduce the decision about the venue to subjective preferences that may be based on maintaining the status quo rather than achieving progress.

Management can also assess venue needs by forming a group of experts and empowering them as a renovation task force. The task force will appraise the current venue, examine other teams' venues, consider construction and operations costs and other variables, and determine specific needs. The group approach encourages democratic appraisal and decision making, but it can also complicate matters, because of the variety of individuals with expert opinions involved in the process.

An additional approach to a team's needs assessment is for the team to analyze its needs based on predictions—how venue and team conditions might improve with certain changes, whether they are through renovation or new construction. As result of this approach to assessment, the team might decide that renovation would be more expensive than new construction and would not provide all the necessary new features. In this analytical approach, an unbiased expert or group with no preset views on the venue's future evaluates the data. The analytical method of needs assessment is closest in purpose to a scientific research study.

INFORMATION GATHERING VIA THE SCIENTIFIC APPROACH

The scientific method of research and analysis is based on a concept, opinion, or guiding principle that explains something. For instance, a new venue might increase fan attendance by enabling fans to have a better game experience. This guiding principle leads the analyst to propose a **theory**—a prediction for a set of facts—such as, "Fans will attend games more often in a suitable new venue, fence-line businesses will benefit, and taxpayers will approve governmental support for the new venue." The scientific approach to research and analysis uncovers facts—empirical information—to support or not support the theory. Thus, if an investigator's theory proves to be accurate at the completion of the study, data will maintain, for example, that a new venue will increase fan attendance, that local businesses will benefit greatly, and that taxpayers do believe that local government should support the team's plan for a new venue.

Essential to the scientific method are the hypothesis and the variables under study.

Hypothesis (Theory or Predicted Outcome)

The theory, or predicted outcome, is stated as a **hypothesis** that expresses a relationship or lack of relationship between variables. It is the result investigators expect to find, what they think will happen. Hypotheses should be specific (i.e., neither broad nor narrow), testable, and (except in the case of qualitative or naturalistic design) value free. For example, a hypothesis might state, "There will be a relationship between a new stadium and fan attendance." Often, a hypothesis is stated in a negative format, or null form. This type of hypothesis is referred to as a *null hypothesis,* and an example would be, "There will be no relationship between a new stadium and fan attendance."

Variables

Variables are features or characteristics that can take on different values and can be measured, such as concessions sales and attendance. Investigators do, however, attempt to manipulate or control some variables. Variables that the investigator controls are termed **independent variables,** sometimes called **classification variables** in descriptive research. Variables that the investigator cannot control, such as outcomes, are termed **dependent variables,** sometimes called **criterion variables** in descriptive research. Variables are most often identified as either independent or dependent, although, strictly speaking, these are terms associated with experimental design rather than with descriptive designs. In the venue example introduced above, the new stadium is the independent (classification) variable and fan attendance is the dependent (criterion) variable.

Another type of variable is the extraneous variable, mentioned in Chapter 2. An extraneous variable is an unplanned variable that emerges during the study, such as the discovery, during a study of perceptions regarding a new venue, that a new playground would be more beneficial to the community than a new stadium. The new information may be valuable and might even prompt an additional study, but a new playground was not part of the problem statement.

Researchers attempt to eliminate the effects of extraneous variables by carefully planning their methodologies, yet it is nearly impossible to eradicate all outside influences. When researchers determine that something other than the independent/classification variables has influenced an outcome, they should explain the extraneous effects so that readers may determine the value of the findings in consideration of outside or uncontrolled influences. Interestingly, extraneous variables can often be a positive influence, leading researchers to further investigation, with the new variable as a research topic.

A **categorical variable** is a variable that changes, that cannot be manipulated, and that can take on only a fixed number of values. Examples are gender, age, and race. If researchers are assessing citizens' opinions regarding a new venue, they cannot control the age or gender of the subjects who respond. However, a researcher could *restrict* the values of a categorical variable as part of the study design. For example, in the assessment of opinions about a new venue, the hypothesis might specifically state that only males aged 18–34 are to be surveyed, perhaps because males of this age range are known to be the most frequent patrons of the current venue.

A **discrete variable** is a numerical variable that is also limited in the values it can take on; its value must be a whole number. Discrete variables often take their values from a count of something. For example, if 15,500 passersby stopped to look at an artist's representation of the new stadium on a downtown billboard, the count would be a discrete value (a whole number). It is not possible to count, say, half a person.

A **continuous variable** is a numerical variable that may take on several values within its range. If researchers measured the time that each passerby spent viewing the downtown billboard, one viewer might have spent 1.6 seconds, another might have looked at it for 60 seconds, and another might have viewed it for 105.9 seconds.

Another type of variable depends on a definition formulated by the researchers. For instance, the investigator observing passersby looking at the downtown billboard could create a variable for the passersby's level of interest. She might define the variable as follows: people who viewed the billboard for fewer than 30 seconds are *slightly interested* in the new venue, people who view the billboard for 30 to 60 seconds are *very interested* in the new venue, and people who spend more than one minute looking at the billboard are *totally engaged* in the idea of a new venue. Here, the time measurement is converted to a descriptive measurement, according to the definition set by the researcher. This is called an *operational definition*. The operational definition gives meaning to a variable by spelling out what the investigator must do to measure it.

Theories enable researchers and analysts to make predictions from a set of facts. Variables make it possible for them to discern what to observe and what to ignore, and help them classify and summarize observable facts. Theories can become new facts through empirical research.

Populations and Samples

Statistics are only as good as the design of the study in which the data were collected. One important aspect of design is the sampling procedures—how the study's participants were recruited. To select an appropriate sample, the analyst must first identify the target population. A **population** includes all individuals that are of interest or relevant to the particular problem or issue at hand. If the population is small and sufficient resources are available, it may be possible to collect data from the entire population. In that case, the sample would be the population. However, it is usually not feasible to collect data from the entire target population (e.g., all residents of a large community), so analysts will use a sample. A **sample** is a smaller group of individuals selected from the target population.

For example, suppose a high school athletic director (AD) has noticed that attendance at select sporting events has decreased over the past two years. Obviously, to study this phenomenon, the AD should select a sample from the population of residents in the community that the high school serves. If the decrease in attendance can be attributed to specific characteristics of that population (e.g., gender, ethnicity, income, sport fandom), then the sample should comprise individuals possessing these particular characteristics, and the interventions (e.g., marketing, promotions) should target that population.

The objective of a sampling procedure is to obtain a sample from the target population that is representative of that population. Inappropriate sampling may introduce bias into the study and thereby cast doubt on its results. For example, if the population in a study includes both men and women, but the sample includes only men, then the results of the study would be biased, because the sample does not accurately represent the population. Appropriate sampling will permit **inference,** the process by which the results obtained from the sample are generalized or applied to the target population. Many different techniques exist for sampling. We will discuss random sampling, systematic sampling, stratified random sampling, and cluster random sampling.

Random sampling

In a best-case scenario, all participants within a population will have an equal opportunity to be selected for a study. A random selection process helps to ensure the representativeness of the sample from the target population. For example, the general manager of a sport team may wish to interview season ticket holders regarding their experiences at events they attended. Because of various constraints, only 20 individuals can be interviewed. A number could be assigned to each season ticket holder, and a random number table or software program, such as Research Randomizer (www.randomizer.org), might be used to select the numbers for a sample of 20 individuals from the entire population of season ticket holders.

Systematic sampling

If the target population is finite and the contact information for each individual is available to the analyst through a directory or generated list, then a systematic sampling procedure may be used to recruit individuals for the study. Depending on the sizes of the population and the sample needed, the researcher could select every nth person from the list and contact them for inclusion in the sample. In the season ticket example, of 1,000 season ticket holders, every 50th person on the list could be recruited to obtain a sample of 20 season ticket holders.

Stratified random sampling

In some situations, the analyst may require that a sample possess important characteristics that are present in the target population or are believed to be particularly relevant to the issue being studied. A stratified random sampling process would be appropriate in such a situation. For example, in the season ticket example, the general manager might want to ensure that the sample has the same percentage of men (60%) and women (40%) as the target population. To meet this requirement, 12 men and 8 women would be randomly selected from the population of season ticket holders. Any number of variables could be selected for stratifying the sample, depending on the variables that the analyst believes to be relevant to the problem under investigation. For example, additional strata variables for the season ticket study could include age, ethnicity, income, education, or number of years as a season ticket holder.

Cluster random sampling

In market research, an analyst may wish to compare naturally occurring groups in the target population. For example, a marketing manager might wish to survey the opinions of health club members in a particular region. If the list of members in the region is small, then all of the members might be included in the survey. However, depending on the size of the region, this could be a very extensive list. In that case, the analyst may decide to select, randomly, a certain number of health clubs from the region and survey their members. Each health club would be considered a *cluster*, in this sampling method. For each club, all of the members might be surveyed, or a random or stratified random selection of members might be used.

Random assignment and other considerations

Depending on the type of study being done, the researcher may need to assign participants to different experimental groups or conditions. **Random assignment**, which is performed after the sample has been recruited for the study, ensures that there is no systematic bias affecting one or more groups or conditions. Bias could occur if participants were allowed to choose their own groups or conditions. For example, less-skilled athletes who wish to improve their performance might self-select into a performance-enhancing condition (i.e., experimental group), whereas higher-skilled athletes might be satisfied with their level of performance and choose a non-intervention condition (i.e., control group). If this were to occur, significant changes in measured performance might simply reflect the greater room for improvement in the less-skilled athletes, rather than a true treatment effect. To avoid bias, the researchers could use a similar process to that discussed above for random sampling to assign participants to groups or conditions in a random manner. That is, a number could be assigned to each participant, and a random numbers table or software program may be used to make assignments.

Random sampling or random assignment may not always be possible. Restricted access to the target population (e.g., professional athletes, injured athletes) or other constraints (e.g., inability to change the work environment at a particular location) may require an analyst to use **convenience sampling** of an intact group of individuals in a particular situation. That is, instead of striving for a representative sample, the researcher simply works with the subjects who are available. In such situations, the researcher could collect data on important key variables in the sample at the outset of the study and test whether the experimental groups differ on these variables. If the groups do not differ at the outset, then it is reasonable to conclude that the groups are similar enough for the study to go on. At the end of the study, the investigator can reasonably attribute the results to the intervention rather than to any preexisting differences between the groups.

Finally, an analyst should always make sure that the sample has the potential to respond to the experimental treatments or conditions. For example, in a study of marketing strategies developed to improve attendance by increasing team identification and affiliation, use of a sample of season ticket holders would probably not show any significant improvement in team identification and affiliation. The reason is that season ticket holders already possess high levels of these qualities and are not likely to improve further.

VALIDITY AND RELIABILITY

Several concepts related to measurement are important in research and analysis. **Measurement** refers to the process of collecting data through the use of instruments, tests, questionnaires, or other types of measures. Before collecting any data, the analyst should examine the *validity* and *reliability* of the measure to be used.

Validity

A measure is considered valid when it measures what it is supposed to measure. For example, a bathroom scale is supposed to measure a person's body weight. If a person's known body weight is 150 lbs, then a valid scale should measure the person's body weight as 150 lbs. If the scale measures 140 lbs, then the measure is not valid. A measure is either valid or not valid; there is no in-between.

For a measure to be considered valid, some form of evidence must support its validity. Unfortunately, in the research literature the term **validity** serves to refer to the various forms of evidence, as well as for the concept itself, which can be confusing. The different forms of evidence for validity are termed *face validity*, *content validity*, *criterion validity*, and *construct validity*.

Face validity

This evidence of validity simply indicates that a measure seems to be or "looks" like it is measuring what it is supposed to be measuring. **Face validity** is a qualitative assessment of the measure. A determination of face validity can be made by individuals with a wide variety of expertise, since all that it requires is an assessment of whether the measure "looks" like it is measuring what it is supposed to measure. For example, if you are attempting to assess sport fandom, then questions about whether the subject considers him- or herself to be a sport fan and how much the person enjoys sports would be logical questions to include on a questionnaire (the measure). The questionnaire would have face validity, even if you are not an expert on fan self-perceptions. As you might surmise, this is the lowest level of evidence that may be used to support the validity of a measure.

Content validity

Content validity refers to whether the measure adequately covers the breadth of a particular topic or area of study; it is used primarily in education. Usually, experts in the area of study review a measure for its content validity. Important factors to measure for sport fandom would likely include self-perception as a sport fan, other-referenced perception of self as a sport fan, enjoyment of sports, and importance of sport. If questions that relate to these factors appear in a measure (e.g., questionnaire) of sport fandom, this would provide evidence that the measure has content validity.

Criterion validity

Criterion validity exists when a measure is validated against another measure, which is known to be valid (i.e., a criterion measure). For example, a measure of business aptitude or entrepreneurial skills could be validated with a sample of business owners, where the criterion measure would be the success of their businesses (e.g., revenue generation, years of operation). Criterion validity is a more rigorous and objective form of validity than face validity and content validity. There are two types of criterion validity: *concurrent validity* and *predictive validity*.

Concurrent validity exists when the measure being examined has been correlated with a known valid criterion measure of the same variable. You might ask, Why come up with a new measure if the criterion measure is already available? Researchers may desire a new measure because the criterion measure is too expensive, is too time consuming to use, or cannot be used in the field (e.g., outside of a laboratory). The two measures (the known measure and the measure under study) are administered at the same time, and a statistical technique such as correlation might be computed to determine the relationship between the two measures. If the correlation is significant, then the measure being examined possesses concurrent validity. (See Chapter 15 for more information on correlation.)

Predictive validity refers to how well the new measure predicts the results of the criterion measure, when the criterion measure is developed or administered at a later time. For example, a sport agency might wish to develop a test (i.e., measure) of knowledge, skills, and aptitude for prospective employees that will be useful in predicting their job performance. If a significant correlation exists between the test results and performance measures taken later (e.g., supervisor ratings), then the measure has predictive validity.

Construct validity

A **construct** is an idea, concept, or theoretical formulation that is typically unobservable. A theory or working hypothesis of the construct describes the various characteristics associated with it, as well as the relationships it should have with other variables. The definition of **construct validity** is very similar to the general definition of validity, which is simply applied to a construct. That is, a measure is considered to have construct validity when it is able to measure the *construct* it is intended to measure. There are two forms of evidence for construct validity: *convergent validity* and *discriminant validity*.

Convergent validity refers to the relationship of the construct to other variables to which it should, theoretically, be related. For example, service quality is a theoretical variable that is unobservable. However, it should be related to other variables that *can* be observed, such as repeat business. Pearson correlations are used to determine the strength of these relationships. Significant correlations provide evidence of convergent validity.

Discriminant validity exists when a construct is *not* related to other variables to which it should not, theoretically, be related. For example, a measure of service quality should not, theoretically, be related to customers' educational background. Once again, Pearson correlations are used to determine the strength of these relationships. A lack of significant correlations provides evidence of discriminant validity.

Reliability

A measure is considered reliable if it consistently provides the same output or answers. A valid measure is always reliable, but a reliable measure is not always valid. For example, suppose a person is weighed on a scale three times within one minute. If the person's known weight is 150 lbs, but the scale consistently measures the person at 140 lbs, then the measure would be considered reliable but not valid. If the scale indicates different body weights for the same person within the same measurement time period, then the scale is not reliable and not valid.

When a measure is being evaluated, various forms of **reliability** may be provided to support the measure's use and, perhaps, its validity. These forms of evidence of reliability include *test–retest reliability* (also termed stability), *parallel-forms reliability, internal consistency,* and *inter-tester reliability* (also termed objectivity).

Test–retest reliability (stability)

Test–retest reliability exists when the same measure is used in separate trials in a specified time period, such as the next day, a week later, or perhaps a month later, and then these trials are correlated with each other. For example, if sport fandom is being measured, the results of the five-point Likert fandom survey should be similar between its first administration and a second administration one month later. The time period is crucial, as the correlation between the two trials is typically stronger for shorter time intervals than for longer ones. Perceptions of fandom should be very similar if customers are surveyed on consecutive days or consecutive weeks, because it is unlikely that, in such a short period of time, their perceptions will change or an intervening event will occur to change their responses. However, if the same customers were measured several months or years later, then intervening negative sport spectator experiences could affect their responses, or the individuals could develop different interests, resulting in lower sport fandom ratings. An intra-class correlation (ICC) is used to compute test–retest reliability (see Chapter 15).

Parallel-forms reliability

Parallel-forms reliability exists when two different measures of the same construct (e.g., behavior, aptitude) are created and then correlated with each other. Typically, a large bank of test items or survey questions is generated. These items are then split to create two equal or similar measures. Since these measures are supposedly tapping into the same construct, the two measures should be highly correlated. Researchers typically use this form of reliability when alternate forms are needed (e.g., standardized tests) or when the analyst feels that use of the same measure as pre-test and post-test may affect the results of the study. For example, if participants (e.g., customers) deduce that the purpose of a study is to improve customer relations, they may bias their responses on the measure of the dependent variable (e.g., customer satisfaction). An alternate or parallel form could help reduce this bias.

Internal consistency

If a measure has several items (or questions) that are designed to tap into the same construct, then those items or questions should be highly correlated with each other, showing **internal consistency** or reliability. For example, the Sport Fandom Questionnaire has five items/questions, with each item rated on a Likert scale from 1 (strongly disagree) to 8 (strongly agree). The five ratings are summed to provide a total score that indicates a person's level of sport fandom. Since these five items tap into the same construct, sport fandom, they should all be highly correlated with each other. A variety of methods are available to indicate the internal consistency of a measure; the most commonly reported is the coefficient alpha, also known as Cronbach's alpha coefficient (see Chapter 15). A measure is considered to have good internal consistency when the alpha coefficient value is 0.70 or higher.

Inter-tester or inter-rater reliability (objectivity)

In certain research designs, several raters or observers score participants on the dependent variable (e.g., ratings assigned to the skill performance of athletes, behavior patterns in a particular setting). The analyst may wish to provide evidence that the measurement procedure is objective. A high **inter-tester** or **inter-rater reliability** indicates that the raters are scoring the same participants in a similar manner. If the measurement ratings are on a continuous scale, such as with Olympic scoring of gymnasts, then intra-correlation may be used, with values above 0.80 indicating high inter-rater reliability (see Chapter 15). In situations where the responses or behaviors of participants are being categorized, then a common but crude reliability estimate is the *percent absolute agreement* (or inter-observer agreement, IOA), the percentage of participant responses or behaviors that were categorized the same. A more accurate measure of agreement, known as kappa, may also be reported. An IOA or kappa value above 0.75 (or 75%) is typically considered to demonstrate high agreement.

COMMON MISTAKES IN INFORMATION GATHERING

The research process is exceptionally methodical, and studies require precision in planning and implementation. Still, mistakes often arise because of oversight or because processes can break down during data collection. Researchers might encounter the following mistakes in their design and processes.

■ **Lack of theoretical base:** Research studies should be based on a prevailing theory. Theories form the foundation of a study and enable researchers to predict the generalizations associated with their study. Basic theories that sport management and sport-related researchers have examined include: match-up hypothesis, used to examine the effects of product endorsements and the fit of athletes with products; meaning transfer, used to examine the factors involved in why sport figures' endorsements influence consumer purchases; social developmental theory, used to examine the notion that sport builds self-esteem, contributes to moral development, and teaches participants various essentials of good character, such as teamwork, grace in losing and winning, and composure; relationship theories, used to examine administrator relationships to groups; and transactional leadership theories, used to examine the relationship of supervision to employee performance.

■ **Lack of specificity:** The research problem should be specific. Specificity enables researchers to identify a problem precisely and, thus, design a process to address it.

■ **Lack of a logical problem statement:** The problem under investigation should be stated in such a way that solutions can be proposed.

■ **Lack of previous knowledge:** Studies typically flow from what is already known about the problem. The review of literature indicates the state of existing knowledge.

■ **Lack of assumptions:** A set of assumptions should guide the study. Assumptions indicate that the researcher understands the environment in which the study will be conducted.

IN PRACTICE

Using Research and Analysis for Solving Problems and Making Decisions

Richard Irwin, *Vice Provost for Academic Innovation & Support Services; Director, Bureau of Sport & Leisure Commerce, University of Memphis*

There is a common notion that the dawn of the Information Age was the driving force that motivated commercial interest in facts and figures. However, effective sport managers made data-based decisions long before "big data" became trendy. Large sport organizations have always had internal departments to collect, analyze, interpret, and explain data, while midsize and smaller companies have long hired outside specialists from research houses to perform the essential function of information management. I am a founding partner of one of those outside research firms, Strategic Marketing Services (SMS).

Sport organizations contract with companies like SMS when their own research departments are overextended with current projects, when they need additional staffing for special projects, or because they do not have the resources to conduct their own inquiries. Thus, our firm, and other similar enterprises, are vital to sport organizations' bottom lines, as we conduct research and analyses on their behalf regarding such transactions as product improvement, enhanced fan experiences, increased employee satisfaction, public perceptions of their company, and myriad other business decisions that are informed by research and analysis.

Any successful sport manager will tell you about the important role that research and statistics play in their company's decisions. Whether data are collected internally or externally, all upper-level managers need to understand what they are being told, and for this reason anyone aspiring to be a sport manager must be familiar with data collection and analysis and be able to critique the information presented to them.

For instance, SMS conducted research for a well-established Major League Baseball team with a world-wide fan base. The franchise opened a new stadium early in the 21st century, and ticket sales went through the roof. However, within two seasons, ticket plan holders were defecting in droves as the team struggled on the field. We were hired to conduct in-game research with all attending fans and to hold focus discussions specifically with non-renewing season ticket holders in order to uncover issues contributing to problems and opportunities. Our key finding was that plan holders had discovered alternative ways to find better ticket deals, as the team was cannibalizing its own season ticket sales with sponsor-supported deep discounts available at the sponsors' locations. In essence, the sponsorship staff and the ticket sales staff were not communicating and did not coordinate promotions and season ticket sales.

A secondary finding was that partial ticketing plans were likewise eating away at full-season plans. Too many of the team's stronger games were packaged in partial plans, thus allowing plan holders to "cherry pick" plans and purchase a significantly smaller ticket package. Subsequently, the next year's partial game packages were modified and released later in the season in order to protect season ticket sales. In other words, unbeknownst to the team, many of the same fans remained loyal in their attendance, but they were purchasing tickets in smaller quantities and purchasing them through alternative channels. Primary data from the fan base informed the team of this issue and compelled the staff to enhance their internal communication and strategic timing.

When firms such as SMS present their findings to sport managers, those managers who understand research conceptually are able subsequently to judge the value, ask probing questions, and make more informed decisions. When managers understand what they are being told and can judge the quality of information from its initial planning stages to the final analysis, they are in a better position to make qualified decisions. Managers who find themselves overly reliant on their research and development staff may be unable to comprehend research and analytics and, thus, may be unable to take advantage of the essential information presented.

Sport executives, like most individuals in important positions, rely somewhat on their own instincts and experiences in decision making. Their biases and preferences are valuable to an extent, but they can be reinforced, amended, or often superseded as the managers gain access to data, appreciate the methods by which data were collected, understand the processes by which they were interpreted, and are ultimately able to grasp their meanings. It is absolutely essential that successful 21st-century sport managers working at any organizational level understand and appreciate research and analysis.

- **Poor sampling:** To obtain meaningful results from a research study, investigators should be careful to recruit or select subjects or artifacts that are directly related to the issue being studied.

- **Inappropriate analysis and interpretation:** Data exist in many forms (e.g., means, frequencies, and other forms of central tendency; qualitative data), and the proper test must be used for each type (see Part III). In addition, researchers' interpretations should not "go beyond" the data by stating conclusions that the data do not fully support.

TALKING POINTS

Information Gathering

- Decisions are best made based on information.
- Information is available in the form of common knowledge, personal intuition, authoritative opinion, and the results of unbiased inquiry.
- The most reliable form of inquiry is a needs assessment or scientific inquiry.
- Needs assessments yield practical, factual information, whereas research studies yield empirical data. Both forms of inquiry are valuable to sport managers in decision making.
- A sample should consist of suitable individuals from the target population; samples are selected through a variety of techniques, including random, systematic, stratified, and cluster random.
- Reliable and, more importantly, valid measures should be used to collect data.

4

Descriptive Research Design and Methods

EXECUTIVE SUMMARY Descriptive research is a very common design in sport management studies. It is by far the methodology of preference in sport marketing, because the descriptive technique is tailor-made to yield answers for the types of questions that emerge in marketing. It provides invaluable information for those who make marketing decisions. Descriptive research may be performed in several formats, but questionnaire-based data is used most frequently.

DESCRIPTIVE RESEARCH: A STRAIGHTFORWARD ACCOUNT OF AN ISSUE

When a sport manager merely needs to know something about current conditions, with no additional need or desire to know causes and effects and no need to make predictions, **descriptive research** is the most appropriate method to find answers. Descriptive research is well named—it simply describes characteristics and conditions of populations and phenomena. Descriptive methodology or design is best used for studying social situations and other aspects of human behavior. Thus, it is often used to reveal the needs, interests, and opinions of fans who attend games or of a sport organization's readers, viewers, listeners, participants, clients, sponsors, advertisers, donors, and other supporters. Descriptive design is a means of studying facts that other research designs cannot address. The information collected through a descriptive design yields practical information, and it can be used to justify or improve services and situations. It sometimes provides the factual foundation for other forms of inquiry, such as historical or experimental analyses.

Like most research methods and designs, descriptive research examines variables in order to answer questions. The variable that the investigators know and can control is termed the classification variable. The variable that the investigators are attempting to find out is termed the criterion variable. For example, suppose that an analyst wants to find out the differences between amounts donated to small and large women's and men's college basketball programs, as well as differences in the motivations of the donors. The classification (independent) variables are the small and large colleges, the teams, and the donors, who may be female or male. The criterion (dependent) variables are the amounts donated and the donors' motivations.

USING DESCRIPTIVE DESIGN

Many mechanisms can go awry in a descriptive study. The design requires careful planning and control, since it deals primarily with humans, who may change their minds or who may not be candid in their responses. Descriptive research is not well suited to generating statements about cause and effect. However, the descriptive technique is the leader in generating functional sport management data. To prepare a strong study, researchers should follow these guidelines:

- Determine whether a descriptive design is the most appropriate way to find the required information.
- As with any design, ensure that the appropriate people are selected to conduct the study. It is particularly critical in descriptive research to employ people who have sufficient background and experience to answer the specific question with expertise.
- Make certain that the classification variables are well defined operationally and used appropriately. Operational definitions enable researchers to delineate a concept for purposes of analysis. For example, a researcher studying college basketball boosters might want to isolate those who donate large amounts from those who donate smaller amounts, for analysis purposes. He might operationally define major donors as those who give over $100,000 annually.
- Take caution to be sure that the procedures are designed and controlled adequately in order to eliminate any factors that could interfere with the results.

Ideally, the conclusions drawn upon completion of the study will be solid and meaningful enough to serve as the basis of decisions or be generalized for use in other, similar circumstances.

COLLECTING DATA IN DESCRIPTIVE INQUIRY

Analysts want to gather reliable data that will allow them to answer questions and arrive at conclusions. To gather useful data, the researchers may employ mass-distributed questionnaires, personal or group interviews, or analysis of existing (secondary) data (e.g., information collected through previous scholarly studies, census data, and accessible reports).

Questionnaire: The Go-To Data Collection Technique

Sport management's most common use of the descriptive method is likely survey research. Sport organizations, particularly marketing departments, use questionnaires to discover fan preferences for game amenities, fan likes and dislikes, and, in particular, **demographics** (fans' personal characteristics, such as age, gender, education level, household income) and **psychographics** (information about fans' behavior and preferences, such as where they dine prior to a game, how much they are willing to pay for premium food compared to standard concessions, how much merchandise they will buy in the off season).

When deciding on a specific questionnaire to use, it is always best to select an instrument that has already been tested for validity and reliability. Instruments used in published, refereed research articles have often been adjudicated for psychometric properties (i.e., the instrument has been tested and retested over time to confirm that it addresses what it is supposed to address). Some adjudicated instruments are in the public domain, meaning they can be obtained at no cost. Instruments are also available for purchase through research houses, publishers, and scholarly and professional societies. Regardless of whether an instrument is obtained through a research house or academic department, or whether it was specially designed for a specific study, researchers should report the properties of any instrument they use, so readers may judge its qualities. Here are a few examples of valid and reliable instruments that sport management researchers have used:

- Hersey/Blanchard Leadership Style Questionnaire, Job Descriptive Index (www.bgsu.edu/arts-and-sciences/psychology/services/job-descriptive-index.html)
- Leadership Scale for Sports (http://ess220.files.wordpress.com/2008/02/leadership_scale_for_sports-_lss_.pdf)
- Sport Motivation Scale (www.er.uqam.ca/nobel/r26710/LRCS/echelles/EMS28_en.pdf)

Questionnaires can take a number of different forms, and investigators select one based on their information goals. All consist of a prepared series of questions that guide subjects to provide answers. The two most common types of instruments used in sport management research are closed-ended and open-ended questionnaires. Pictorial questionnaires are another, less frequently used option.

Closed-ended questionnaires

In **closed-ended questionnaires,** respondents choose an answer from a prepared list. Closed-ended instruments are more time consuming to prepare than open-ended instruments, but they are easier to administer and easier for respondents to answer. Because the respondents choose their answers from a list, closed-ended instruments may not obtain respondents' true meanings or reveal their true motives. Closed-ended selections are stated in general terms to accommodate a large sample of respondents, and they may not reveal individual participants' innermost attitudes or beliefs.

Example: If a college marketing director wants to find out why students prefer to watch their team on television and not in the arena, inquiry may start with a simple question, such as:

I prefer watching college basketball on television because:

(a) The student seating is in the worst part of the arena.
(b) I like to hear the announcer commentary and analysis.
(c) I like the instant replays on television.
(d) It is more fun to watch at home with friends.

Open-ended questionnaires

Respondents answer **open-ended questionnaires** in their own words, without prompting. Compared to closed-ended questions, developing open-ended questions can be less time consuming for the preparer, but it is very time consuming for respondents to provide their answers. Also, open-ended data are difficult to analyze and summarize. The advantage of open-ended questionnaires is that the data can reveal respondents' true attitudes, because the respondents answer in their own words rather than selecting the closest response from a listing. For instance, if the college marketing director mentioned above wants to determine what would bring students back to the arena for basketball games, an inquiry might start with the simple question, "What would convince you to attend basketball games in the arena?" Subjects would likely respond with numerous specific answers.

Pictorial questionnaires

A **pictorial questionnaire** presents drawings, photos, or graphics from which respondents choose. This methodology requires laborious preparation. However, it might encourage better and deeper responses, because subjects may react to photos with more enthusiasm. For example, the college marketing director could show photographs of the arena floor taken from the seating sections of three arenas in the athletic conference and ask, "Which of these views do you think presents the best accommodations for students?"

Note that the pictorial method is particularly useful when detailed representations would be inconvenient to deliver verbally. Pictorials are also practical when the investigator is interviewing young children, who may have limited reading skills.

Note on question design: Precision counts

Participants respond to questions as they understand them, and they will answer according to their own interpretation. Thus, the researcher must write questions carefully in order to obtain results that are related to the problem. Poorly written questions yield inaccurate information.

Imagine that an arena management company wants to convince a local Chamber of Commerce that basketball games at the site infuse significant amounts of money into the local economy. The management company asks 15,000 fans at each of 20 basketball games during the season, "How much money did you spend on food in our city as a result of attending this basketball game?" Data indicate that each fan spends no less than $18, and the management company rushes to tell the chamber and its restaurant owner members that at least $270,000 is added to their collective bottom line every time there is a home basketball game, for a total of at least $5,400,000 across a 20-game season. However, the question merely addressed food purchases; there were no questions about food purchases specifically in local restaurants. The fans might have assumed that they were being asked about how much they spent at arena concessions, or they might have responded based on the amount they spent at local fast-food franchises, as well as at the arena.

Investigators must ask exactly what they want to know. If the arena management company wished to show the economic impact of games on city commerce, the questions should have asked fans to indicate exactly where they spent money on food (e.g., local restaurants, the arena, fast-food chains, grocery stores) once they arrived in the city, because these data would be more complete and accurate. Unless a question is asked with precision and without bias, the answers will not be specific and useful. When responses can be interpreted in various ways, the conclusions that are based on them will be incomplete and often wrong.

Researchers may have a sure understanding of what, exactly, they want to ask, but their questions must be presented in such a way that they are well defined for others. For this reason, researchers should write in clear language, avoid academic or business jargon, and use an everyday, conversational style. Many researchers give their survey questions a tryout with a small sample of respondents long before they formally test the questions for validity and reliability.

Questionnaire dissemination

Getting the questionnaire to the subjects and, more importantly, having them respond are perhaps the most problematic issues with questionnaire research. In the past, direct mail contact with potential respondents was the most reliable method for distribution and return. However, it is time consuming to prepare a mailing and difficult to motivate respondents to reply, and direct mail surveys can be expensive, depending on the costs of printing and postage. *Return rate* is the percentage of surveys that the researchers receive back from respondents, compared to the number mailed. Many analysts believe that a return rate of 35% to 50% is acceptable if a finite population has been sampled, but many others believe that a return rate of 85% to 100% is necessary, no matter what the population is. When a questionnaire is used to collect data, the researchers should set the acceptable return rate in advance. If the final return rate falls below the target, additional attempts should be made to elicit responses. If the rate remains low after multiple attempts, the analysts must explain why they feel the final rate is adequate, when the research is completed.

Electronic surveys are now more widely used. Sites such as Survey Monkey (www.surveymonkey.com) are convenient for investigators and for respondents, because they are expedient and cost effective. Online survey platforms such as Qualtrics (www.qualtrics.com) have been well received for scholarly use. As with printed and mailed surveys, response rate is a critical issue in online data collection. It is risky to rely on respondents to take the time to log on and complete a questionnaire, just as it is risky to ask people to fill out and return a printed questionnaire.

Sport teams have an advantage in that the subject pool is the fan base, and many teams give out questionnaires to fans on-site or ask fans to respond via the official website. Teams often offer fans the opportunity to win free tickets or merchandise as incentives to boost return rates. Exhibit 4.1 outlines the types of questions pro teams have asked of fans in recent years. Note that all of the questionnaires ask for demographic and psychographic data, in addition to questions related to their specific goals. Also note that the teams' questionnaires range in length from one to four pages. Many researchers have found that participants are more likely to respond to a brief questionnaire, usually one to two pages in length, that they can complete quickly, compared to longer forms.

Interviewing

The most time-consuming information-gathering technique is the interview; however, this technique has the advantage of enabling analysts to investi-

		EXHIBIT 4.1
Summary of typical information collected via sport team questionnaires.		

TEAM QUESTIONNAIRE	INFORMATION COLLECTED
Atlanta Braves 3 pages	Game experiences, attendance history, TV and radio game viewing/listening history, merchandise purchases, staff courtesy, stadium operations (security, cleanliness, access)
Cleveland Indians 4 pages	Parking, will-call experiences, ballpark interior and exterior appearance, ticket purchase convenience, concessions, guest services
LPGA Marathon Classic 3 pages	Media preferences, golf playing experience, attendance history, merchandise purchases, economic impact information over three days
Orlando Magic 1 page	Personnel courtesy, arena operations (security, cleanliness, access), and other questions about services
Pittsburgh Pirates 4 pages	Game attendance, fans' information sources, transportation used to attend game, activities before game, stadium operations (security, cleanliness, access), open-ended message to management
Thistledown Race Club 4 pages	Favorite summer weekend entertainment, knowledge of track promotions, ratings of services
Toledo Mud Hens 4 pages	Past/future attendance history and why, ranking of services, ranking of typical problems (e.g., prices, concession lines, restroom lines), overall satisfaction

gate a topic in great depth. Interviews are usually conducted in private settings, where one or more respondents may address a single issue or many issues in a single session. There are three common formats for conducting interviews that yield sport management data: structured, unstructured, and group interviews.

Structured interviews

Structured interviews employ a rigid technique in which many respondents are asked the same questions in the same order. The questions are usually closed-ended, since the rigidity of the format disallows impromptu responses. Data are collected under exact conditions (i.e., respondents are questioned in the same or similar settings), usually by the same person using the same voice inflections and, as closely as possible, the same mannerisms. For example, a college marketing director who wants to know why students would rather watch a game on television than in the arena might begin an interview with a student by reading a script that explains each step in the interview process. She then might ask a series of questions such as:

I am going to ask you several questions about watching our basketball games on television and then about the student seating in our basketball arena. Please respond as candidly as you like to each question.

- What is it that makes television viewing better for you?
- What would make you attend a game in person?
- Have you attended a game in the arena?
- When you attend a game in the arena, what do you miss about a televised game?
- When you attend, do you like the location of the student section?
- Is the view of the game from the student section adequate for you?
- What is the best thing about the view from the student section?
- What is bad about the view?

Interviewers using a structured format of questioning usually do not ask follow-up questions, because the structured method requires that subjects be asked the same questions in the same order, and there is no room for spontaneity. In addition, respondents are usually discouraged from digressing from the topic in their responses.

Unstructured interviews

Unstructured interviews use a flexible technique, where the same initial questions are asked of respondents, but the questions may be asked in any order, the interviewer may ask follow-up questions, and the respondents can then expand on their responses. For example, the college marketing director investigating students' preferences for watching basketball on television rather than in the school's arena could begin an interview either by using a script or through extemporaneous conversation. She can steer the conversation toward a specific subject and ask follow-up questions to gain deeper information. After she asks, "What is it that makes television viewing better for you?" she can continue that line of questioning according to the participant's response. If, for instance, a student indicates that viewing a game on television is better because of the instant replay and commentator analysis, the interviewer can delve deeper into the student's preferences and ask how instant replay via mobile devices might affect viewing and attendance decisions.

Group interviews and focus groups

Researchers use group interviews to determine trends among a set of similar respondents or to compare trends among divergent respondents. Interviewers must take care to prevent one respondent from dominating the interview or intimidating others in the group. Often, an icebreaker is necessary to stimulate the discussion. The group technique can yield a wide range of information and provide investigators with varied viewpoints.

Suppose the college marketing director finds a group of students who like to attend games in the arena and assembles them in the student section. The

IN PRACTICE

Data-based Decisions

Kathryn Bobel, *Group Sales Representative, Charlotte Knights Baseball Club*

It is critical to know how to gather and consider information without bias and subsequently use that information for improving the game experience for our fans, as well as serving the needs of our business partners. Here are three situations that occurred while I was working as Director of Group Sales for the Hickory Crawdads baseball team, where information makes or breaks a decision that affects our team's bottom line.

1 We were in the process of looking at minor renovations to the ballpark and were attempting to see if we made these renovations, how many more people (and revenue) we could potentially bring out to the ballpark because of them. For example, if we added an outdoor suite on the concourse, made it available at $500 with 15 tickets, and sold it during a minimum of 33 events (every home game on Thursday, Friday, and Saturday), that would be an additional $16,500 in revenue for the year. Over ten years, that would be $165,000. So, that gave us a starting point to see if our monetary investment on the front end was worth it.

2 We had an owner of a hair salon who wanted to come on as a sponsor. Their main goal was to drive traffic to their salon. So, we thought, all right, who goes to salons? Women, especially those women with some disposable income. Then we asked ourselves, "At our ballpark, where can we find women with disposable in-come?" We thought that mothers who book birthday parties at the stadium for their children would fit that mold. So, we decided that the sponsor would provide $15 gift cards to birthday mothers. The day after the birthday party, we sent out a letter thanking each mother for having her child's birthday there, and included the gift card. Our hope was, obviously, that the recipients would walk into the salon, spend their $15 gift card and ideally even more. At the end of the season, we analyzed how many were redeemed, and, based upon the redemption rate, we amended the sponsorship agreement for the next season to best fit the company's needs.

3 Each year when we set goals in the group sales office, we looked at what our trends had been from year to year. For example, if we increased our Little League team's attendance to 5% this year, 7% for next year, and 8% for the following year, we would look to increase that to 10% or 11% in the fourth year. Then, once we decided upon the percentage, we equated that to a number of teams, and then to a monetary amount. If we wanted to raise X amount more revenue, we would know how many groups that would require and how to accommodate the groups in every one of our group target areas: picnics, suites, birthday parties, Little League teams, and other groups that enjoy an afternoon or a night out at the ballgame.

first question could be, "What is the best thing about the student seating in the arena?" More often than not, one person will start the conversation, and others will follow. If no one starts the conversation, trigger questions might be, "Is it the view?" "Are the seats comfortable?" "Who likes the location?" "What do you like about the view?" "Who thinks the seats are comfortable?" "Who agrees?"

Which format to use?

Interviews are valuable when in-depth information is needed about prevailing issues. The type of interview method that will work best depends on the audience. For instance, the following interview formats are likely the best methods in these or similar situations:

- If a researcher is attempting to test a premise that city youth sports programs work as a deterrent to crime, a structured format may be best. The structure can help the researcher control for irrelevant information that will not add significantly to the results.

- If a researcher is attempting to discover issues associated with athletic directors' changing position from one athletics conference to another, an unstructured format may be best. There may be multiple adjustment and operating issues, and the researcher would not want to be restricted to asking the same questions with no fitting follow-up.

- If a researcher is attempting to discover information about minority players' experiences in major league sports, a focus group format may be best. The researcher will want to hear responses from a wide spectrum of individuals, who may interact with each other while the researcher guides their conversation.

Other Formats for Collecting Descriptive Data

Other forms of data collection can yield sound answers to questions that are descriptive in nature. Sport organizations commonly use the following formats.

Case study

The case study format is an intense investigation of factors that contribute to some circumstance. The method is narrow in focus, in order to delve deeply into a single issue or describe a specific set of circumstances. For example, the college marketing director can follow a large group of select students over a single college basketball season in order to document the student fan experience. Such information may be useful in developing ways to attract more students to games. (See Chapter 9 for more information on case studies.)

Correlational study

Researchers use the **correlational study** format, sometimes referred to as a causal study, to examine the extent to which two variables are related. For example, in the case study described above, if the college marketing director found that students did not enjoy their experience because the student seating is uncomfortable and badly situated in the arena, then the director can perform a correlational study to determine whether a relationship exists between student attendance and inferior seating. This information about the student seating section can then form part of the renovation proposal, helping to show that a renovation would likely increase student attendance.

Longitudinal study

In a **longitudinal study,** the investigators examine the same participants at different ages. For example, the college marketing director might study the attendance patterns of a group of student basketball fans in their first year on campus and subsequently study the same students when they are sophomores, juniors, and seniors.

Cross-sectional study

A cross-sectional study examines different participant groups at a single point in time. For example, the college marketing director could work with counterparts from schools in the same conference to study student groups (e.g., females, males, commuters, resident students) to describe their experiences in the student seating sections at their first game.

Mixed design

A study with a **mixed design** uses both longitudinal and cross-sectional methods to investigate an issue. In the college marketing director's study of student attendance and seating, the data collection might involve a large population of students from all the conference schools over multiple years (e.g., first-year students, sophomores, juniors, seniors).

TALKING POINTS

Descriptive Study Components

- The critical variables should be operationally defined and used within the limits of the study.
- Instruments should be tested for validity and reliability.
- The sampling procedure should target people who have expertise on the subject.
- The data should be analyzed in such a way as to support or reject the hypothesis.
- The study's conclusions should relate directly to the study's results.
- The study's conclusions should be generalizable.

5

Historical and Philosophical Research Methods and Design

EXECUTIVE SUMMARY **Historical research** examines existing information in such a way as to address questions or test hypotheses and draw conclusions about past experiences, incidents, and trends. Researchers address historical issues by analyzing news accounts or interviewing eyewitnesses to an event and presenting the facts without bias. The aim of **philosophical research** is to address facts and values and examine the meaning of and make assumptions about phenomena from a conceptual perspective.

HISTORICAL RESEARCH: TO UNCOVER MYTHS AND FACTS

Some questions are more easily resolved than others. Who scored the most goals in a single professional hockey season? What World Cup coach holds the record for overall soccer wins? Which college gymnasts have accumulated the most points over their four-year careers? Answers to questions such as these are readily available through official records, media kits, and archived hard-copy or digital sources. Still, uncertainties might arise when we attempt to answer seemingly straightforward questions. What might have happened if the second-highest scorer in hockey history had been able to play a full schedule during a strike season? Should we count professional, amateur, and junior wins for the World Cup coach? What if the high point scorer in gymnastics completed some of his college career at a less competitive conference before transferring to a top-ranked school? Even solutions to questions that seem simple can require a deeper inquiry.

Other questions require a comprehensive exploration in order to gain insights into solutions or explanations. Did Major Abner Doubleday really invent the game of baseball in Cooperstown, New York, and did Philadelphia socialite Mary Outerbridge introduce tennis to North America? Why did Dr. James Naismith decide to invent an indoor game based on running, jumping, throwing, and catching and not incorporate the remaining basic skills kicking and striking? Finding indisputable solutions to complicated questions might require years of study, and answers can sometimes lead to more questions. Historical inquiries evaluate past "facts," circumstances, and trends to explain their meaning and provide a plausible account of them.

Historical inquiry has uncovered information and given meaning to facts in science, religion, education, law, medicine, and other aspects of society. Sport, in particular, values its past, and history has an impact on nearly every aspect of sport management. The following examples of inquiry in sport might best be addressed through historical methods:

- A franchise player's professional journey
- The evolution of sports broadcasting
- The development of sports equipment
- The roots of recreational sports
- The development and professionalization of campus intramurals
- A team's history for the last 50 years

Using Historical Research Design

Historical researchers may first hypothesize a position and predict an outcome, or they might start with a straightforward question that leads to an interpretation of facts. They then examine and criticize multiple source materials that enable them to deduce answers to questions or provide support for their position. Source selection is critical, and the types of sources that the investigator uses will affect not only the researcher's answers and interpretations but also the potential for acceptance by the greater community of scholars and readers.

Primary sources are documents and other forms of information that provide a firsthand account of an incident. Government documents, relics, eyewitness accounts, photographs, minutes of meetings, and other records of this type are examples of primary sources that can yield significant information. *Secondary sources,* such as periodicals, newspapers, almanacs, and hard-copy and digital encyclopedias, also yield good information. However, secondary sources are

IN PRACTICE

Historical Research: The Bob Feller Documentary

Curtis Danburg, *Senior Director of Communications, The Cleveland Indians Baseball Organization*

Pitcher Bob Feller is a sports icon. His on-the-mound triumphs are universally known, but Feller's life story transcends baseball. His story is truly an All-American tale of a hero on and off the field, and the Indians, along with the regional cable network that carries our games, wanted to chronicle Feller's remarkable life in a feature program. We decided to write and produce a comprehensive documentary about Feller and set about gathering information that would do justice to this national hero.

Because the Cleveland Indians and Major League Baseball are meticulous record keepers, the primary sources of information about Feller's Hall of Fame career were easily accessed. Still, we matched the official records with secondary sources, such as accounts in daily newspapers, magazines, and baseball almanacs, not only to verify information but also to gain insight into any firsthand accounts of Feller's activities. We examined still photographs and film, much of which we ended up using in the documentary.

Gathering information about Feller's off-the-field life required us to dig deeper into his pre- and post-baseball activities. Through a process of assessing eyewitness accounts from relatives and friends, examining government documents, and reviewing other types of official accounts, we found that Feller's personal life story is as legendary as his career—the kind of story that Hollywood might make into a feature film.

Our research on his pre-baseball years enabled us to portray Feller accurately as a farm kid from Iowa who played catch with his dad every day after chores and played high school ball during the school year and American Legion ball during summers. While still in high school, he signed with the Tribe for a dollar and a signing bonus of an autographed ball. Following his rookie season, he returned home to Van Meter, Iowa, to ride the school bus with his sister Margarite to finish his senior year of high school.

At the height of his baseball career, when the United States entered World War II, Feller enlisted in the Navy the day after the attack on Pearl Harbor, to become the first professional athlete from any sport to volunteer for service in the armed forces. A hearing deficiency kept him from his dream of being a Navy fighter pilot, so he was assigned to be a fitness instructor and also pitched some exhibition games for morale tours. Eventually, though, the Navy caved in to his many requests to serve in combat, and he was assigned as a gunner on the *USS Alabama,* where he kept his arm in pitching form by throwing on the battleship's deck. He achieved the rank of Chief Petty Officer and is the only member of the National Baseball Hall of Fame with that classification.

Near the end of his career and in the years following, Feller was an advocate for his profession as a member and, in fact, first president of the Major League Baseball Players Association. He had a creative business mind, having formed his own company, Ro-Fel, Inc., to manage his image and interests, and he continued to serve baseball, the City of Cleveland, and many charities, as well as his adopted hometowns of Shaker Heights and Gates Mills.

Historical research does not appear only in scholarly journals or encyclopedias. Through the exhaustive historical research that the Indians organization and our media partner conducted on one of our most notable historical figures, we were able to show the personal side of one of the 20th century's famous figures, and recount a story that gave Bob Feller his deserved stature both on and off the baseball field.

more easily criticized than primary sources, because they rely on the original correspondents' interpretations of information or events.

Collecting Data in Historical Inquiry

Historical researchers understand that the history they write will necessarily be incomplete, because full knowledge of something that happened in the past is difficult to establish. Still, research can lead to a better understanding of the past. In addition, historical information can be put to use in important decisions.

Imagine that a minor league baseball team is about to celebrate its 50th year, and a local sports reporter has been assigned to write the franchise's history for the team's golden anniversary media guide. At the same time, a professor from the local college elects to write an account of the team's impact on the community, and she hypothesizes that the presence of the team has had a significant influence on the region's economic vitality. The two analysts would likely examine the same types of sources.

The reporter and the professor might start by checking city archives for primary sources, such as records and statements related to stadium construction, including land deeds, contractors' bids, architectural proposals, blueprints, payment invoices, worker contracts, and other sources that predate the actual presence of the team. Then, the analysts might interview workers who helped build the stadium, review minutes of meetings held between the city and the contractors, and collect photographs from groundbreaking to completion. After the team's move into the stadium, the analysts would have access to additional primary sources, such as the team's records and financial statements, to find fans who attended opening day and families that may have held season tickets throughout all 50 years of the team's history. They would also have access to physical relics, such as tickets, uniforms, equipment, and scorecards. Secondary sources would also be readily available in the form of media accounts, team media guides from past years, and any archival materials stored in the team's collections.

The value of historical inquiry is related directly to the value of the sources of information, and problems often arise when archive conditions are substandard. Sources, even those catalogued in a well-organized archival collection, can be inaccurate. Some historical aspects cannot be measured accurately because individuals investigate history over different time periods and may apply modern values to historical data. Thus, historical inquiry is subject to *external criticism*—examination of the research and analytical data for its authenticity and validity, as well as *internal criticism*—examination of the study's content and meaning.

PHILOSOPHICAL RESEARCH: SUBJECTING BELIEFS TO CRITICISM

 nlike historical models of research, which uncover information, philosophical research investigates thought—what is being thought and what should be thought about a problem. Philosophical research identifies basic assumptions in the area where a problem might exist and offers principles that give a rational explanation for behavior or response to the problem. A philosophical investigation of the minor league team's golden anniversary celebration might address the logic behind the community's support or affection for the team, and the investigator might conclude by stating and defending a position regarding why the team holds such high status in the region. For example, a philosophical explanation of community support for the team's golden anniversary might be that the team's presence provides the greatest good to the greatest number, a rationale associated with a distinct school of thought called Utilitarianism.

Philosophical inquiry usually addresses opposing points of view in pursuit of answers. Hence, a researcher engaged in philosophical inquiry should state what, exactly, the problem entails, what he is going to report about it, and how contrasting views are going to be considered. He might follow this introduction with a report of the findings from his research, and end with a decision that is based on the philosophical inquiry.

TALKING POINTS

Historical Research Components

- The inquiry should test a hypothesis or theory or address a premise.
- The information collected should withstand external criticism.
- The information collected should withstand internal criticism.
- The inquiry should contain more primary than secondary sources, when possible.
- The information collected should directly answer or address the hypothesis, theory, or premise.
- The inquiry's conclusions should flow from the information that was collected.

Philosophical Research Components

- The hypothesis should be presented as a position statement.
- Positions may be defended by citations of literature rather than data.
- The information posited should directly defend the stated position.
- Opposing points of view should be presented and then supported or refuted.

6

Qualitative or Naturalistic Inquiry

EXECUTIVE SUMMARY Qualitative inquiry is useful in social and market research, and investigators often use this method of inquiry to gather information about certain focused issues. The object of qualitative or naturalistic inquiry is to address problems of a certain nature—usually, to gain thorough and detailed insight into behavioral issues. Usually, qualitative samples are smaller than those used in other types of inquiry, and the method often serves as a precursor or follow-up to other types of inquiries, in order to extract meanings behind behavior and opinions. Qualitative or naturalistic inquiry is not bias free. Summarizing data from naturalistic inquiry can be complicated, because the investigator has to find common themes among the data.

QUALITATIVE RESEARCH: TO UNCOVER EXISTING REALITIES

Whereas the designs described in earlier chapters enable an investigator to collect data without biases in order to reach impartial conclusions, in some research situations it is more beneficial for the analyst to consider biases in data collection. In other words, there can be an advantage to weaving opinions into the data gathering.

| EXHIBIT 6.1 | Summary of distinctions between qualitative and quantitative research. |

COMPONENT	QUALITATIVE	QUANTITATIVE
HYPOTHESIS	Inductive	Deductive
SAMPLE	Purposeful	Random
SETTING	Natural	Controlled
DATA GATHERING	Subjective	Objective
DESIGN	Flexible	Uniform
DATA ANALYSIS	Interpretative	Statistical

In **qualitative research** or **naturalistic inquiry,** investigators assume that there are multiple realities. Since those realities are socially related, the data are collected in a natural setting, and the investigators' personal values play a role in the investigation. Whereas investigators in quantitative research design studies attempt to remove as many biases as possible that would interfere with an impartial conclusion (i.e., they pursue objective, **value-free inquiry**), investigators in qualitative research believe that biases *cannot* be removed, and, thus, their own personal values often drive their inquiry (i.e., they pursue subjective, **value-bound inquiry**). Qualitative researchers are apt to use **inductive methods,** whereby they make specific observations and uncover facts that lead to broader realities; qualitative researchers employ **deductive methods**, testing a general theory by searching for specific facts. Exhibit 6.1 outlines the major distinctions between quantitative, value-free and qualitative, value-bound research.

Examples of studies that might be addressed through qualitative methods include:

- Interviews with college coaches of individual sports to obtain their perceptions of access to resources as compared to team sport coaches,
- An assessment of challenges affecting new sport managers in their office environments, and
- An explanation of athletes' issues associated with retirement from professional sport.

USING QUALITATIVE RESEARCH DESIGN

Q ualitative researchers and analysts form questions based on conditions and circumstances that emerge in specific settings. Quantitative researchers and analysts may or may not be in attendance during the data-gathering phase, but the qualitative investigator is often present when data are gathered. For this reason, proponents of qualitative design believe that they can delve more deeply into participants' meanings. Thus, investigators negotiate meanings to make their interpretations clearer and better represent realities. Unlike quantitative findings, which are usually reported in statistical form, qualitative results are reported in narrative form, constructing new realities that can be confirmed as credible and dependable.

For example, suppose a general manager of a private country club is pressuring the board of directors to open the club to the public in order to increase dwindling membership. Several realities may emerge as the board analyzes the issue. The board might speculate that moving from private to public will prompt many current members to resign their memberships. Club members may state their beliefs and rationales as to why inviting public players will not appreciably increase profit nor attract new members. The course superintendent may suggest that increased use by the public will diminish the beauty of the links. To address these and other issues, the board members empower the manager to gather information on the proposal.

COLLECTING DATA IN QUALITATIVE RESEARCH

Qualitative investigators use purposeful or **purposive sampling** when they want to study a specific group to learn about explicit realities in their surroundings. The researchers might collect data by interviewing, analyzing documents, or observing participants interacting in their natural surroundings. The country club's general manager might interview long-standing and newer members on-site to discover why they chose to join a private club, how they feel about a public club, and what they consider to be the benefits of each. The manager may or may not start each interview with the same set of questions, because naturalistic inquiry presumes that each participant's reality is different. As a result, initial and follow-up questions may be formulated on the spot, and they may be more formal for some participants and more informal for others. Club documents, such as member applications, annual surveys, and board minutes, might be inspected. In addition, the manager may ask a cross-section of members to write an *auto-ethnography,* a unique type of self-study that is common in anthropological studies. An auto-ethnography is an autobiography that provides insight into cultures and social concerns by examining the personal experiences of individuals. Through auto-ethnographies, the manager can learn how membership in the country club impacts its members. With qualitative techniques such as these, the manager might find that members prefer a private club setting because its atmosphere is more relaxing than public clubs; tee times and court reservations are more convenient; the pool areas, dining room, and lounges are less crowded; and the surroundings are better for business interaction. The manager's final step would be to reconnect with the

IN PRACTICE

Questioning in Person

Simone Eli, *Sports Reporter/Anchor, KPRC Local 2, Houston, Texas*

As you have probably observed in interviews conducted by others, some questions and questioning techniques work better than others. Sometimes, the difference of one word in a particular question can make or break your research, story, or project as an interviewer. With more than seven years in broadcast journalism, I've developed ways to gather information effectively from my interviewees for feature stories, and these same techniques can be applied in research studies.

Every part of an interview is important, from the moment you begin recording to the moment you shake the interviewee's hand and thank her for her time. I will walk through fundamental ways to better your questioning and ultimately better your findings, answers, and research.

PREPARATION

It is very important to prepare yourself prior to conducting an interview. As a researcher, your responsibility is to have the necessary details worked out. Knowledge is power. You must know about the interviewee, the background, and the subject matter. I would suggest creating a list of questions you plan to ask your interview subject. However, note that these are *not* the only questions you will ask throughout the interview; this is a "skeleton list" of questions that will help guide you through questioning and keep the dialog focused.

THE BEGINNING

The beginning of an interview is critical. Make certain your interview subject is comfortable with the setting in which the discussion is taking place and clearly understands why he or she is involved in the research process. When you turn on your recording device, whether it is a camera or sound recorder, the first question to ask your subject is to state his or her first and last name, and to spell it out for the recording device. This simple question saves time and possible confusion for the researcher. Having the subject's name not only makes certain the researcher has the correct spelling, but it also lets the researcher know whose voice and interview are on the recording.

TYPES OF QUESTIONS

Throughout the interview, the researcher will use the "skeleton list" of questions as a *guide.* The first question of the interview should always be a simple, easy question, which allows the interviewee the opportunity to warm up for the interview process, as well as to feel relaxed for the remaining questions.

Example: My research question is: "What are the challenges male coaches face in coaching collegiate women's basketball?" My interview subject is a 50-year-old male who is a former college women's basketball coach.

To help get the interview started, I would begin with a question such as: "Why did you originally become a head coach?" This question allows the interviewee to reflect on his past, with an easy question that could be answered with a funny, inspiring, or memorable story—relaxing the interview subject.

Throughout the interview process, it is key to make sure you, as the researcher, are asking questions that will create the best results and responses. These types of questions are called *open-ended* questions. An open-ended question keeps the interview subject from being able to answer the question with a one- or two-word response, such as "yes" or "no." Those types of responses will be useless in your research. Questions that begin with the words "did" or "was" often allow the interviewee to reply with minimal words. These types of questions are called *closed-ended* questions.

Example: While talking to the former head coach about his experiences as a collegiate coach, I might ask: "Did you experience challenges as a male coaching a women's game?" However, that question can simply be answered with a "yes" or "no." To achieve the response I want, I could ask the same question, but better: "What challenges did you face, being a male coaching a women's game?" This question nearly *forces* my interview subject to answer the question with details concerning challenges he did or did not face throughout his career.

FOLLOW-UP QUESTIONS

As mentioned, the "skeleton list" is created only as a guide. It is crucial to ask questions following the original question; these are, of course, called *follow-up* questions. The only way to ask a good follow-up question is to *listen* to the responses of your interviewee. Often, the interviewer can get caught up in asking questions and forget to listen to the responses. Listening will allow you to ask appropriate, important follow-up questions, which ultimately creates a better product.

Example:

Interviewer: [ORIGINAL QUESTION] How did you experience challenges being a male coaching a women's game?

Interviewee: [ORIGINAL ANSWER] It was difficult for me to connect with the women on a personal level. As a coach, I was able to instruct the athletes on the court, but struggled speaking with the women off the court about their personal lives.

Interviewer: [FOLLOW-UP QUESTION] How were you able to address the challenge to speak with the women on a personal level?

This follow-up question was not on my original skeleton list, but it is an expansion of an original question that was on the list.

FINISHING YOUR INTERVIEW

The end of the interview is as important as the preceding parts. Close an interview with two simple actions. First, when you're finished with your questions, ask the interviewee: "Would you like to add anything?" This simple question can make your interview even better. For me as a journalist, this question has created great information and material for my stories, on numerous occasions. And don't be afraid to ask a follow-up to "Would you like to add anything?"

Finally, always thank your interview subjects for their time; shake their hand and make sure they're aware of how appreciative you are.

subject–participants, consult with them on data interpretations, and clarify that the results as presented represent their realities.

To analyze qualitative data, the researcher arranges the data by categories or codes (some of which might be predetermined, e.g., responses arranged by gender or age), views that may appear (e.g., positive or negative responses to an issue), or other themes that emerge, which might be expected or unexpected. Usually, the researcher then blends like themes together, depending on the question or mission. The researcher interprets the responses and presents the results in narrative form, organizing the information for readers according to the categories that the researchers identified. For instance, in his report to the board, the country club's manager might decide to group members' information into the categories of Exclusivity (e.g., relaxing atmosphere), Access (e.g., course, court, pool, dining room, lounge availability), and Contact (business interaction).

Qualitative data must pass the test of trustworthiness (the investigator's belief that the data are dependable and the interpretations reflect the participants' intended meanings). Although investigators are permitted to introduce their own biases into the design and analysis, the data must be meaningful, and the interpretations must be on target. Since the investigation begins with a bias—for example, that opening a golf course to the public will increase membership—data collected from research participants should be reported without preconceived notions.

TALKING POINTS

Qualitative Research Components

- The study should be grounded in the notion that there are multiple realities that are socially constructed.
- The study is value-bound; it is not a value-free inquiry.
- The study should be conducted in the natural setting or context.
- Purposive sampling should be used to increase the likelihood that multiple realities will be uncovered.
- Qualitative methods (interviewing, document analysis, participant observation) should be used to collect data.
- Inductive data analysis techniques should be used.
- The study questions or design can be changed during the conduct of the inquiry.
- Constructed realities (i.e., the findings) are presented to the subject–participants in order to "negotiate" meanings and interpretations and represent their realities as clearly as possible.
- The data should be trustworthy.
- The results are reported in a narrative form.

Delphi Study

EXECUTIVE SUMMARY A Delphi study is a means of forecasting or a method of gaining group consensus. The technique is useful when researchers and analysts need opinions from several experts to solve a problem or find an answer to a question. Delphi studies can be conducted in a brief time period if consensus is reached early; however, experts often participate in multiple rounds to arrive at solutions. Thus, the method can sometimes be time consuming and expensive.

DELPHI TECHNIQUE:
REACHING CONSENSUS AMONG EXPERTS

Delphi was the ancient Greek shrine where citizens came to receive predictions of future events from a high priestess. Today's **Delphi studies** use a technique of data gathering in which the researcher acquires a series of expert opinions for the purpose of forecasting or problem solving. Several variations of Delphi-based procedures exist, with differing procedures for data gathering, but each adaptation involves a group of individuals who have expertise related to a particular issue under consideration. The group is surveyed for a specified number of rounds or until a conclusion is reached by consensus or a satisfactory answer is determined. Data collected via a Delphi method may be quantitative (based on statistical analyses), or it may be qualitative, with outcomes reported in narrative form. Delphi studies can be conducted in a matter of weeks, or they may take several months to conclude, depending on the composition of the group, the problems and issues to be addressed, and the locations of the participants. Following are examples of expert groups that might be engaged to solve a problem in a sport organization through a Delphi process:

- University president, athletics director, booster club president, key coaches, and key alumnae/i deliberate on a proposal to change conferences.
- Mayor, city manager, city parks department, and citizen groups study the issues in renovating a community park center.
- Country club manager, golf course superintendent, architect, and players investigate benefits and detriments of adjacent land acquisition.
- Fitness center administrator, investors, selected staff, and member representatives explore the most efficient method of meeting members' needs in their small and busy venue.

In addition, consider the case of a city sports commissioner who proposes to write and submit a bid to host the senior games. The commissioner would need to assemble a group of experts to weigh the benefits and detriments of hosting such an event and determine the steps to a submitting a successful bid.

USING DELPHI TECHNIQUE

The first and likely most important step in a Delphi study is to select the participants. Although sampling is crucial in any research, each participant in a Delphi study must be carefully selected to provide a specific expertise or astute knowledge to contribute to the process. The group must be large enough to offer diverse opinions yet small enough to be manageable. A group size of no less than three and no more than six is generally considered to be ideal. However, a study involving complex issues may require a larger group, because it may require a broad range of expertise. A group considering whether or not to bid on an event as complex as the senior games might be large, because of the many factors in play. The group might include the following members:

- The city sports commission general manager, who knows the intricacies of staging large sport events
- The sports commission officer in charge of bid writing
- The city manager, who knows the municipal budget and projections for finances and can represent the mayor's office

- The city parks and recreation director of buildings and grounds, who knows the current condition and availability of appropriate activity venues

- The local school superintendent, because school district facilities might be used for various functions and because some school activities may need to be postponed during the games

- A local college athletics director, because college facilities might be used for various functions during the games

- A representative from the bureau of travel and tourism, who knows local and regional details regarding transportation, lodging, meals, and other concerns relevant to visitors

- Local and state law enforcement and security teams, because athlete and fan safety is vital

Various combinations of industry professionals and others may be appropriate. For instance, including a representative from the governor's office might be advantageous, because state resources may need to be accessed. A citizen-at-large might be a good addition, and a representative from a city that previously hosted the games might be helpful. Although numerous individuals may offer needed expertise, the group should not be so large that agreement will be unattainable.

Once the participants have been selected, the Delphi technique takes place through a roundtable approach that enables each participant to contribute opinions to the conversation and interact with the others, with the goal of reaching a consensus. This process may take several rounds, and the participants must commit to participating in all rounds. A Delphi study usually requires no fewer than three rounds, although it can take longer to reach a consensus, depending on the problem and the group.

COLLECTING DATA IN DELPHI TECHNIQUE

Although a Delphi group might be in the same room at times, it does not have to be assembled in the same place in order to operate. Delphi techniques have been conducted by mail, email, phone, and video conference. Data collection can start with each expert generating a list of concerns, opinions, or issues, or the group leader might provide a list of topics for consideration. The Delphi group tasked with exploring the senior games might operate in the following manner:

- Round 1: The sports commission general manager (GM) starts the inquiry by listing budget and venue concerns and disseminating the list to the rest of the experts.

- Round 2: The experts add to the list by pointing out their own issues in bidding, preparing, and staging the games and return their list to the GM.

- Round 3: The GM summarizes the list and sends out the new list, asking the group to rank the issues in order of importance. The group members return their rankings for summarization.
- Subsequent rounds proceed in a similar manner. The rankings are summarized, ordered, and re-distributed, with any disagreements identified, until

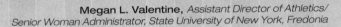

IN PRACTICE

Using Information to Reach Consensus

Megan L. Valentine, *Assistant Director of Athletics/ Senior Woman Administrator, State University of New York, Fredonia*

I am constantly involved in professional situations that require specialists and professionals to reach consensus on important decisions. Countless issues arise when one is involved in committee work with a group of experts who need to contribute to the decision process, and each expert also brings a unique and important bias to the table.

I chaired a committee that was heavily involved in the process to purchase equipment for Fredonia's new $1.5 million campus fitness center. After deliberations, we settled on two vendors who were able to provide the equipment we needed, and many debates and decisions followed—about the types of equipment to purchase, how much equipment we were going to purchase from each vendor, and what complementary equipment might be provided with the purchase of certain pieces. In addition, because Fredonia is a state institution, we had to decide on these purchases according to state contractual obligations that define the number of bids to seek and limits on pricing (purchases over $2,500 require three quotes), and we had to deal with other decisions that made committee consensus difficult to reach.

Once the equipment decisions were made, other groups were assembled to address procedural-type decisions. Hours of operation for our fitness center may change each semester, based on previous usage data. So, consensus had to be reached in order to set

the center's open hours by using information derived from total usage. Thereafter, the staffing budget had to be adjusted to accommodate the new hours. Other sensitive issues quickly emerged regarding usage and access.

The new fitness center was funded primarily from increases in student fees, with the understanding that access would be limited solely to students. Faculty and staff could use the old center or purchase a $150 annual or $50 semester membership to the new center. Since the previous center was open to everyone on campus at no charge, the new fee structure prompted meetings with other groups, including me, our Director of Athletics and Recreation, the Fitness Center Director, the Vice President for Student Affairs, our university President, and the presidents of the two very visible unions on our campus. Our challenge was to reach consensus on open hours for the old and the new venues, appropriate staffing, risk management protocols, and the strategies to fund two centers while accommodating the needs and desires of students, faculty, administrators, staff, and unions.

All of this being said, everything from equipment selection and layout to hours, access, and other operational concerns are discussed and negotiated on a fairly regular basis. Expert opinions are valuable for successful deliberations, and consensus is essential to solve issues when numerous cohorts have a stake in the outcome.

a consensus is reached about the bid and the games. The group leader may have to decide when there is sufficient agreement among the participants to reach consensus.

A round might last days or weeks, or it might last considerably longer. If the Delphi group deciding whether to bid for and stage the senior games agrees that circumstances are favorable for submitting a bid, and the bid is selected, a local organizing committee will likely be formed to operate the games. The Delphi method would then have been a successful first step in the process of determining the feasibility of holding the games in the city.

TALKING POINTS

Delphi Technique Components

- The Delphi group should comprise experts who each can make a unique contribution to the group.
- The experts should agree to participate in every round.
- The experts are supposed to be subjective in their opinions but able to decide objectively on the best solution to the problem.
- If rounds are lasting unusually long, the group leader may declare consensus, if terms are favorable.

Experimental Research

TESTING THE EFFECTS OF A VARIABLE

EXECUTIVE SUMMARY Experimental design involves testing participants under stringently controlled conditions in order to judge the effects of changes in a variable. In **experimental research**, investigators make predictions (generate a hypothesis) about how participants might react to the introduction of a variable, determine a procedure to test the predictions, conduct the experiment, and determine whether the variable affected the outcome.

EXPERIMENTAL RESEARCH: THEORY, PREDICTION, CONTROL, AND EVALUATION

S ometimes investigators need to plan a study in such a way that they can have full control over the procedure. That is, to test an explicit prediction, the investigator must control conditions and introduce variables at will in order to arrive at a conclusion. The method that enables investigators to exert the most control is experimental in nature. Many variations of experimental methods are appropriate for use in sport management inquiry. In each variation, a treatment is introduced under the total control of the investigator, and that treatment is evaluated to determine its effect on the outcome. In other words, the researcher or analyst performs some function to affect the outcome.

Experimental inquiry examines the effects of one variable on another. The independent variable is the treatment—what the investigators are doing or controlling—and the dependent variable is the element that might or might not be affected by the treatment (commonly stated as what the researcher is "testing to"). For example, suppose that a baseball team's stadium store manager wants to determine the effects of mobile marketing on player jersey sales to find out what type of message works best. The manager discounts the team star's jersey by 10% and sends two different messages about the discount via Twitter to two different groups of fans in the ballpark during a game. At checkout, fans are required to show the tweet to receive the discount. The independent variables are the two mobile messages. The dependent variables are the total number of jersey sales sold by each message. Results will indicate which message was more effective in persuading fans to purchase a jersey.

The following are other examples of sport-related studies that might be best addressed in experimental design:

- A venue operations manager tests several large samples of artificial turf and subjects them to different climate conditions before deciding on the most suitable brand.

- A director of communications makes available three editions of a yearbook on the team's website—one containing still advertisements, one with video advertisements, and one with no advertisements—and records the number and duration of views to determine which edition fans spend the most time viewing.

- An equipment manufacturer designs bowling balls of three different compositions and tests the balls' trajectory by using bowlers with differing abilities.

USING EXPERIMENTAL DESIGN

In true experimental design, the study participants are randomly selected (i.e., each member of the group under study has an equal chance of being selected to participate). In many studies, some participants are randomly assigned to an experimental group to receive the treatment (the independent variable), and some are assigned to a control group and receive no treatment. In the bowling ball study, for example, some participants may receive three balls with the same composition. In other studies, the participants may be randomly assigned to receive one of two or more different treatments, as in the mobile message study. In both cases, the researchers will compare the results from each group, looking for differences.

Depending on what the investigators wish to find out and what resources are available to find the information, various experimental methods can be used. In **quasi-experimental design,** investigators study a problem without having 100% control of the procedure. For instance, a venue manager studying satisfaction among suite holders who have been given differing amenities might not be able to use a random sample in that type of inquiry. In **field** or **action research,** there may be no control or randomization, but investigators study a real situation with specific treatments. The baseball team store manager in the mobile marketing example is conducting action research to discover whether mobile messages make a difference in sales and is gathering evidence to support that premise.

Another experimental research design is the **one-group method of pre- and post-testing.** In this design, the same group is tested before and after a treatment in order to judge the effects of the treatment. For example, a footwear brand might test a group of runners who are wearing a previous design of the brand's running shoe and test the group again, after a reasonable recovery time, with a newly designed shoe. The brand manufacturer and the brand's marketing agency will be interested in promoting any positive, significant difference between the two trials. The manufacturer and agency might also elect to use other experimental methods in their shoe testing, such as the *equivalent-group method*. In this method, one of the groups would act as a control group and continue to use the "old" shoes in the second trial. Alternatively, the experimenters might use a rotation group method by testing the new shoes with the same groups at different times.

COLLECTING DATA IN EXPERIMENTAL RESEARCH

An examination of sport management literature indicates that experimentation was rarely used in early research. However, the experimental method is becoming more common in sport management academic and industrial inquiry, because the controlled nature of the methodology yields exceptionally dependable results and conclusions.

For example, suppose an entrepreneur invents a device to help tennis players increase their racket head speed while serving. The device is a series of weights that clamp onto the top of the racket beam, enabling players to develop a quicker swing and, thus, generate a faster serve. In anticipation of the advertising and marketing rollout, the inventor must prove that players who use the device actually can increase the speed of their serve. An experiment is conducted to measure the effectiveness of the weights.

The inventor gathers experienced players (participants) of each gender and tests their service speeds in miles per hour, using the same radar technology as used at grand slam and other major tennis tournaments. Players then practice their serve for five weeks, with technicians applying the weights to their racket beams. The players are then retested after the five weeks of treatment, and their service speeds are recorded and compared to the previous measurements. This research method is a *pre–post test* experiment (see Exhibit 8.1), with the

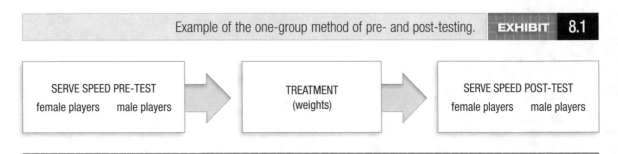

Example of the one-group method of pre- and post-testing. **EXHIBIT 8.1**

independent variable being the weights (because the analyst can control the weights attached to the racket) and the dependent variable being the service speed (because the analyst cannot control this outcome).

Numerous experimental designs measure the effects of various treatments on various outcomes. Experimental designs can become complicated and involve several independent and dependent variables. The hallmark in each design is control. Experiments must be controlled so that investigators can conclude without question that any change or outcome in a dependent variable is the result of changes in an independent variable.

TALKING POINTS

Experimental Method Components

- Experimental design is characterized by great procedural control.
- Various experimental designs can be used as appropriate means of answering research questions.
- At least one hypothesis is tested in experimental research.
- There are numerous threats to experimental research, which should be addressed in an experimental study's planning.
- In experimental design, one or more variables are introduced to test their impact on other variables.
- Data from experimental studies are analyzed to test the hypotheses under study.
- The results from an experiment are presented in a way that directly relates to the researchers' hypothesis.

Case Studies

EXAMINING A SOLITARY ISSUE IN DETAIL

EXECUTIVE SUMMARY A **case study** examines one aspect of a specific problem or question in depth. The researchers gather extensive information based on observations or reliable reports related to a single phenomenon. In other words, case studies marshal a large amount of evidence and data to explain one issue. The results of a case study may not be generalizable (i.e., applicable to a larger population) and, thus, may not generate theory (i.e., provide an overarching concept that guides future research).

CASE STUDY: DESCRIBING AND ANALYZING CIRCUMSTANCES AND CONDITIONS

Many times, researchers and analysts wish to explain a specific situation or particular series of conditions within a strictly defined focus, in order to understand events or trends that may or may not be based on a prediction or theory. Case study methodology is a popular design to use in social inquiries or to describe a single topic in detail. Case studies can take several forms, but the following two methods are prominent in scholarly literature.

Descriptive case studies present an overview of a condition in great detail, in order to report "insider"-type information. Descriptive case studies can be non-theoretical (i.e., not based on established theory and not conducted to generate new theory). In other cases, a descriptive case study examines two existing theories to determine similarities or differences between them. **Evaluative case studies** assess existing information and generate judgments about the information. Case studies can also be interpretive, if researchers attempt to generate new ideas or explain facts based on a theory. **Interpretative case studies** might describe a single individual circumstance or a set of trends, or they might go further and evaluate and explain how something happened. Examples of case study issues that might be found in sport include the following:

- Study of a successful high school athletics program with a rich history of championships in many sports over a number of years
- Study of a national sporting goods franchise that began business as a small shop in a mid-size city
- Study of an athlete from a mid-major university who is attempting to launch a successful pro career

Another type of case study that has gained popularity in scholarly or focus journals takes the form of a "short story." *Story-type case studies* describe a situation that may or may not be based on existing data—it may be contrived, or it may have a fact-based premise. Cases presented in story form are often accompanied by questions and are commonly used as teaching tools for students in the classroom or in industry professional development programs.

USING THE CASE STUDY METHOD

Although the case study method may appear to be simpler in technique than other designs, it is, nonetheless, very structured, and a case study can easily become a long-term commitment. Case study researchers and analysts collect data from many sources and often use the same techniques as do investigators who are studying issues via other methods (e.g., descriptive, historical, philosophical, qualitative, Delphi).

To develop a good case study, researchers and analysts consult existing studies on their selected topic, conduct interviews, make in-person observations, and interpret documents. Thereafter, the process of sorting, organizing, and categorizing data can be very time consuming. The case study process is often similar to a media reporter's job of decoding the who, what, why, when, where, and how of events, but the analysis and results are subjected to a more intense academic scrutiny and criticism.

COLLECTING DATA IN CASE STUDY DESIGN

Participants in a case study are not randomly selected; instead, they are specially selected because of certain characteristics, such as a specific

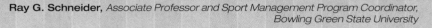

IN PRACTICE
A Case Study in Promoting College Football Players

Ray G. Schneider, *Associate Professor and Sport Management Program Coordinator,
Bowling Green State University*

It is rare for a football player from a mid-major conference to receive pre-season attention as a Heisman Trophy candidate. Rarer still is the anomaly of three mid-major players hyped as Heisman hopefuls. It would be exceptional if all three mid-major players happened to be from the same athletics conference. Yet these three variables intersected when the Mid-American Conference (MAC) had three Heisman hopefuls in 2006. Since I attended a MAC school, taught at a MAC school, and knew one of the Heisman hopefuls, I was interested in how the three MAC athletics departments (viz., Bowling Green State University [BGSU], Miami University, and Northern Illinois University [NIU]) would publicize their candidates amid the surge of Heisman promotional materials for candidates from highly visible major college football programs. I was especially interested in the effects that the promotions might have on the Heisman vote and the immediate effects on player recruitment. The "Flutie Factor," the effect that player visibility has on institutional admissions data, was also of interest. I determined that the best approach to study the MAC promotions, as well as the major schools' publicity strategies, was a case study of the Heisman promotional campaigns.

I needed to gather case study data from multiple sources, starting the with the schools' sports communication directors. I contacted and interviewed the three directors, who were open and cooperative about discussing their plans for their Heisman candidates: Josh Harris from BGSU, Ben Roethlisberger from Miami, and Michael Turner from NIU. I found that each campaign featured a strong online presence: BGSU's *Lethal Weapon 5* site, named for Harris's jersey num-

ber; Miami's *Where Have You Ben?* site, a play on Roethlisberger's first name, which is easier to remember and spell than his last name; and NIU's creative *Turner the Burner* site, which opened with a dash of flame flashing across the screen, illustrative of Turner's speed. Each site was updated several times per week, with the players' game stats, interviews, and other pertinent information of interest to Heisman voters, as well as fans and followers of the players and teams. I maintained contact with the directors and collected data via unstructured interviews with them throughout the football season and post-season.

Through the interviews and my observations of the websites, I was able to gain a great deal of insight into the campaigns. BGSU, in addition to posting information about Harris's accomplishments, staged retail promotions featuring *Lethal Weapon 5* T-shirts and number 5 jerseys and advertised on regional billboards. The communications department was also able to build up Harris's performance success in the national media (e.g., ESPN, CNN/SI, CBS SportsLine). Miami had *Where Have You Ben* yard signs posted around Ohio's Miami Valley and arranged for many national feature stories on ESPN (e.g., "A Day in the Life of Ben"; "How Do You Spell Roethlisberger?"). Miami's media releases were directly targeted to Heisman voters. Northern Illinois went the distance for Turner. The sports communication office placed unique premiums in the home stadium press box—hot sauce, notepads, T-shirts, rubber stamps, and other items, all with a "Turner the Burner" label, were available for the media's use. Only action photos of Turner were released to the media, and he was featured on the front page of *USA Today's* sports section.

As the football season was ending and Heisman candidates emerged from among the major football conferences (Pittsburgh's Larry Fitzgerald, Mississippi's Eli Manning, Michigan's Chris Perry, and Oklahoma's Jason White), I extended the case study to examine what those candidates' sports communication staffs were promoting on their behalf. Each of the major-level sport information departments used promotional strategies similar to those of the mid-majors (i.e., online presence, stats dissemination, and so forth). The media regularly reported on the major players' performances, even without athletics department intervention, since they were from visible football programs and most of them were faring well in their seasons. Fitzgerald caught at least one touchdown pass in each game he played that season. Manning, from a famous football family, had his career stats compared to his father and older brother. Michigan made sure that the word "Perry" appeared in 90% of the headlines on their website and provided a link to Michigan's Heisman history. Oklahoma posted numerous White quotes and photos with his stats. In essence, the major programs' promotional strategies were nearly indistinguishable from those of the mid-major schools.

In the end, Roethlisberger was the only mid-major player to receive any significant Heisman recognition, finishing in ninth place. White was the Heisman Trophy winner, with Fitzgerald second, Manning third, and Perry fourth. However, two of the mid-major players enjoyed a championship post-season. Harris was MVP of the Motor City Bowl as he led BGSU to a win over the Big 10's Northwestern, while Roethlisberger led Miami past Big East opponent Louisville.

The players' performances and team success appear to have had an influence on recruiting, according to Rivals.com, as each of the mid-major schools signed star players for the 2007 season. However, the greatest effect appears to have benefitted institutional admissions. Although figures were unavailable from Miami, BGSU's first-year applications increased 11% from 2005, and NIU applications increased by an impressive 30%. NIU's Office of Enrollment Management attributes the increase directly to the visibility that Turner brought to the school. Finally, each of the players was signed by a professional team—Harris by the Ravens, Roethlisberger by the Steelers, and Turner by the Chargers.

What began as a curiosity about mid-major football player promotions morphed into a bona fide research project that shed light on the ways football programs of different sizes and reputations promote their top players. The case study method was the only viable approach to use in collecting the type of information needed. The case study methodology permitted the freedom to collect data via multiple sources in order to examine one aspect of a phenomenon and make decisions and draw conclusions on my specific questions: what did the mid-major schools do to promote their players, how did the promotions relate to those of the major conference schools, and what were the effects of those campaigns on recruitment?

education level and academic major, or because they meet specific criteria, such as having been employed in the same job at the same place for a certain number of years. Participants are carefully screened and selected because the researchers and analysts are not testing them in order to generate theory; rather, they are assessing the participants in order to describe or evaluate their circumstances or awareness.

Imagine that an investigator wishes to study the job requirements, job specifications, and typical workday for an aquatics director in a public facility and wants to show how the skills and abilities needed to manage such a venue have changed over a generation (20 years). The researcher finds a qualified director who has worked in the same public venue for 25 years and who is willing to be the participant. The next step might be to examine the original job description and specifications that were in effect when the director applied for the position. It might be useful to compare the original job description and specifications to others from the same era. An examination of Red Cross lifesaving and other aquatics documents from that period might add some relevant data to the study. Suppose those data indicate that 20 years ago, current valid Red Cross certifications in lifesaving, first aid, and cardiopulmonary resuscitation (CPR) were required, and managerial supervisory experiences were preferred. An assessment of current job descriptions/specifications from similar venues would be useful for comparison purposes.

Next, the investigator might interview the director. The investigator must decide whether the interview should be conducted in the natural setting (at the aquatics center) or at an off-site location, and later may also have to decide how many interviews should be conducted. Suppose the investigator and the director decide to hold interviews as necessary at the natural setting. During the interview, the director reports that, although certifications were and are essential and non-negotiable, most of his time is spent in everyday supervisory and managerial roles, as well as special event management. Also, over the last 20 years, the certifications have evolved from lifesaving, first aid, and CPR to include, in addition, qualifications in water aerobics and knowledge of bloodborne pathogens.

As another part of the case study, the investigator wants to observe the director at work. There are numerous ways to conduct such an observation. The investigator can be a spectator and watch the director at work, or the investigator could assume the role of participant–observer, both spectating and asking questions or making comments when the occasion arises. Sometimes, an investigator secretly places a collaborator in the setting to report information and observations.

The case study in our example could take one of three forms: a *descriptive case design* would be used to report details about the director's current duties, an *evaluative design* would be used to delve into contemporary conditions and express opinions about the director's duties, and an *interpretive design* would be used to interpret the data, in order to shape a new theory of aquatics administration or apply the resulting data to an existing theory.

Case studies enable outsiders to look into unique environments and make decisions about specific issues and circumstances. This methodology enables researchers and analysts to collect a great deal of information about one particular case.

TALKING POINTS

Case Study Components

- The case should present an overview of the topic through a review of literature and should list the objectives of the inquiry.
- The procedures should be described fully, with a complete explanation of information sources.
- The case study should address a specific question or series of questions.
- Data should have been collected from multiple sources and should have been sorted, organized, and categorized.
- Questions or goals should be answered or addressed, or any lack of inferences should be justified.
- Results or conclusions should be presented as unbiased observations.
- Decisions should have been made about the who, what, why, when, where, and how, in relation to the topic and goals or objectives.

10

Feasibility and Profitability Studies

DETERMINING THE POSSIBLE

EXECUTIVE SUMMARY Sport managers need data in order to make decisions about new product proposals or ideas. A **profitability study** will provide information about the marketability of a product, facility, event, or service. A **feasibility study** will indicate whether it is even possible to manufacture a product, build a facility, host an event, or provide a service.

FEASIBILITY AND PROFITABILITY: CAN IT BE DONE, AND CAN IT MAKE MONEY?

Information is always needed when a manager is making decisions based on financial projections, especially for new, redesigned, or reintroduced products, facilities, events, or services. In other words, researchers and analysts frequently want to determine whether a project will make a profit that is substantial enough to justify proceeding. A profitability study is conducted to inform such decisions. Investigators must also determine whether it is even possible to produce the new item or service or improve on an existing concept. A feasibility study is conducted to obtain data on viability.

When making bottom-line decisions about products, facilities, events, or services, the manager must analyze the steps in production, construction, technology, delivery, and marketing. Information can come from commercial sources, interviews, or group consensus, and, at the end, all of this information may lead to a single decision (e.g., to launch or not to launch, proceed or not proceed, build or remodel), based on myriad data from a multitude of sources. Following are examples of issues that might be best addressed via a feasibility study:

- Should a collegiate athletics department submit a bid to host a post-season event in their venue?
- Should a city-owned stadium undergoing renovation opt to build suites and other types of premium seating in order to generate long-term commercial contracts?
- Should a local sporting goods retailer open additional locations in neighboring cities?
- Should a high school with successful sports teams change league affiliation in order to increase visibility and publicity?

Brown et al. (2010) suggest several other examples of sport-related feasibility studies. For instance, a feasibility study would be useful in determining whether a city should use funds to construct a recreation center, a pool, or a new stadium or arena. A feasibility study might also help a city determine the benefits and detriments of attracting a professional sport team to their area, whether or not to submit a bid to host a major sporting event, or whether the city should use funds to build a new soccer pitch in the community. Results from feasibility studies can also assist college and university athletics departments in determining the benefits of renovating current facilities or building new venues. Entrepreneurs may use feasibility study results to shape their decisions regarding business start-ups such as opening a new health club.*

USING FEASIBILITY AND PROFITABILITY STUDIES

When a company wants to introduce a new product or improve an existing product—whether it be a golf club, an event, or a facility—or when an entrepreneur has an idea about manufacturing and marketing a product or service, the first step is to determine whether a market exists for the venture. To assess the marketplace, the decision maker conducts a **market analysis** to determine present and potential consumer markets and to determine whether the public really wants such a product, facility, event, or service. The market analysis addresses distribution channels, general trade practices, and market comparables, and it can provide information about past and present demands that might predict consumption.

A feasibility study is conducted to determine whether it is possible to produce the product, facility, event, or service. A **technical analysis** will identify all the technology needed, such as equipment, materials and methods, time lines and schedules, essential facilities, and labor needs.

A **financial analysis** then indicates whether a profit is likely to exist for a product, facility, event, or service by determining costs of the project, such as manufacturing, construction, management, advertising, and sales costs, as well as revenue projections. The financial aspects might be based on a break-even analysis or balance sheet that compares expenditures and revenues or on other appropriate estimations of costs for operations. The financial analysis may show potential for investments and may analyze the channels of approval needed for the project, such as legal and governmental requirements (licenses, permits).

COLLECTING DATA FOR FEASIBILITY AND PROFITABILITY DECISIONS

Suppose a clothing brand wants to establish a presence in the regional marketplace by merchandising polo shirts for all the individual teams in a high-profile minor league baseball conference. The shirt will have a team's logo on the front upper right side and the conference logo on the front upper left side. Feasibility and profitability analyses would indicate whether there is a market for the shirts and whether they can be produced.

The company needs to decide on the quality points of the shirt (fabric, stitching, collar band, buttons) and other factors that influence price and consumer preference. An analysis would be conducted. One part of the analysis would show how the conference and the individual teams issue rights for new merchandising. Rights fees would be paid to each individual team in order to place their logos on the shirts, as well as to the conference for the right to use its logo. Next, the analysis would consider the best outlets for sales (e.g., team stores, locally owned stores, franchises), investigate each outlet's income from sports-related shirts, and determine how many shirts the outlets purchase per order, their payment schedules, shipping costs, promotional costs, and any shelving charges (i.e., costs to place the shirts in a visible place in stores).

A technical analysis would then be conducted to determine whether the shirts could be manufactured. The shirts would require the services of a designer, a digital expert to prepare the logos, garment experts, and other manufacturing experts, as well as fabric and buttons.

Knowing the market and the technical requirements, the company can run a financial analysis based on costs for design, materials, fees, freight, salaries, taxes, inventory, manufacturing, and marketing. This analysis would include revenue predictions, a break-even calculation to show the point at which sales will cover all production and marketing costs, and, thus, projected profit or loss. If revenues are projected to be greater than costs, resulting in a profit, then the company analyst might make the recommendation to produce the shirts for sale.

There is no template for reporting the results of a feasibility or profitability study. Essential data are reported in text form, often with sections for procedures, decisions, and conclusions, and in spreadsheet form for cost analyses, break-even analyses, and other financial information that factors into a final decision.

TALKING POINTS

Feasibility and Profitability

- Determine profits based on current market conditions.
- Account for all fees, royalties, period/product fixed costs, and sunk costs (fixed, unavoidable costs).
- Use accurate profit margin forecasts.
- Pre-production, production, and distribution costs cannot exceed retailers' demand.

*Brown, M. T., Rascher, D. A., Nagel, M. S., & McEvoy, C. D. (2010). *Financial management in the sport industry*. Scottsdale, AZ: Holcomb Hathaway, p. 280.

CHAPTER 11

Grants and Contracts

FUNDED INVESTIGATIONS

EXECUTIVE SUMMARY External funding in the form of grants or contracts is essential for many special programs or projects. Grants and contracts help investigators complete projects that may go unfinished without external support. Sources of funding include corporate research and development departments, governmental agencies, foundations, and other organizations that support science, the arts, and industry.

INQUIRY FUNDED BY AN EXTERNAL SOURCE

Investigations conducted to uncover facts or add to the knowledge base (i.e., what we know or believe about a certain topic) may be self-funded, or essential resources may be provided to investigators by their employers. However, an outside source or funding agency often provides the means to conduct or support an investigation of relevance to its profitability, in the case of a company, or its mission, in the case of an agency or foundation. The grant or contract process is competitive, and only the most promising projects receive funding.

The external funding process is mutually beneficial to the investigator and the funding agency. External funding enables individual investigators to complete projects that they may not be able to afford

		EXHIBIT 11.1

Examples of differences in the funding orientation of grants and contracts.

RESEARCH GRANT	SERVICE GRANT	CONTRACT
A researcher receives funding to study the long-term effects of performance-enhancing drugs on college athletes.	A team of experts receives funding to implement a drug-free campus program.	A state education department sponsors experts to present a series of workshops to high school athletes regarding the detriments of drug use.
A city recreation director receives funding to assess community interest in establishing a skate park.	A city recreation department receives state and federal funding to build a skate park.	A city hires an expert to select a site for a skate park and to design the venue around the site's natural terrain.
A researcher receives funding to determine which of a series of sports gear advertisements are best received by a focus group.	A market analyst receives funding to select appropriate consumer markets and manage a rollout of sports gear advertisements.	A sports gear manufacturer hires an assessment team to monitor consumers' responses to sports gear ads.

with institutional or individual resources, and it enables companies and agencies to expedite and complete projects for which they may lack the proper personnel. Many cutting-edge projects have benefitted from external funding.

Research grants are awarded to investigators in order to add to the knowledge base of a topical area. The results of the research are submitted to the funding agency and may be published or presented through a scholarly forum, such as an academic society or professional association (see Chapter 1 for a list of those in sport management). **Service grants** are awarded in order to accomplish a practical objective for the agency or an institution or to make a contribution to society as a whole.

A **contract** is awarded when an agency, usually a company or governmental agency, funds a project that will enhance operations or a community. Agencies and foundations with interests in social issues have traditionally been the best funding sources for sport-related studies, particularly when sport issues relate to mainstream issues (e.g., racism, sexism, ageism). Although commercial enterprises and brands usually support their own research and development departments, they nonetheless extend contracts to outside agencies, such as universities, for special short-term studies (e.g., youth marketing, product testing, image ascertainment).

Exhibit 11.1 outlines differences in orientation among the types of funding.

FUNDING SOURCES

Although they sometimes outsource their research projects, many large sport corporations, particularly shoe, clothing, and equipment manufacturers, support their own research and development departments to improve their product lines. When a corporation does outsource a project, the resulting data are usually private and belong to the company for its use in promotion or further study.

Funding for sport projects can originate from other sources, as well. Governmental agencies, such as the federal and various state departments of education, fund some types of sport inquiry in order to share the results with the public for general knowledge. As stated earlier, social science foundations, such as the American Philosophical Society, also provide resources for projects that are congruent with their mission. Results of research studies that are funded by agencies may belong to those agencies, but the investigators may have the freedom to disseminate the results, depending on the funding agreement that was offered and accepted. Professional organizations and societies, such as the North American Society for Sport Management and SHAPE America, also support inquiry, and results from studies funded by these groups are nearly always published in the organizations' associated journals or presented at their conferences or conventions. Other funding sources can be found in federal registers, which are catalogs listing federal assistance programs. These sources include national endowments and foundations for humanities, arts, and sciences and national, state, and local departments of education, as mentioned earlier.

BASIC STEPS IN APPLYING FOR EXTERNAL FUNDING

The application process for grants and contracts is decidedly structured. Application forms are usually several pages in length and contain explicit instructions for completing each section. Although each application and process is unique, the basic information required is likely to include a title page, an abstract, a summary of the purpose and significance of the project, a review of literature, an outline of procedures, a budget, a time line, and an evaluation and procedure. Some agencies request a plan for disseminating results, and some agencies prohibit sharing of results.

Title Page

Unless a specific format is required, the title page usually gives the name of the project, the names of the applicants and the funding agency, the inclusive dates of the project, the total amount of the budget requested, and signatures of the applicants.

Abstract

Just as in a research article, the abstract provides a brief summary of the project, with some reference to the major points (problem, method, and hypotheses or projected outcome).

Purpose

The purpose statement outlines the objectives or explicitly details what, exactly, is to be accomplished. In this section, the funding agency can discern the information to be uncovered and how the investigator can help in discovery. The purpose section may end with a statement of the problem.

Significance of the Study

The significance is usually explained in one detailed paragraph. It states why the investigation is important, who or what it will affect, who or what it will help, and what will be known as a result of the investigation.

Review of Relevant Literature

The literature review, similar to that of a research article, communicates what has already been discovered by previous investigators. The agency will define whether an exhaustive review is needed or only recent findings are important.

Procedures (Methodology)

In the procedures section, ideas are converted into actions. The procedure communicates how the investigator will explain or address the issue or attempt to solve the problem. This section is often a step-by-step explanation of the project activities to be undertaken, as well as the participants and analyses (treatment of the data) involved.

Budget

Many agencies will fund a project only to a certain level—a dollar amount or a percentage of total project costs. The financial resources needed to complete the project should be described in intricate detail. The budget request should outline personnel salaries and benefits; costs of equipment, supplies, and other materials; travel needs; and costs that will be incurred in data collection, facilities rental, and any other project activities that will require funds. Budgets sometimes must outline how costs will be shared, by listing those items and activities that will be funded primarily by the external funding source and those that the investigator will fund. Costs might also be categorized as direct costs (those directly associated with the project, such as computers and software) or indirect costs (such as insurance and maintenance).

Time Line

Investigators usually indicate how long it will take to fulfill the purpose of the project. On the other hand, many agencies will define the time line and cut funding after a certain period. Once the project is started, it is often possible to negotiate the time line and extend the project activities.

Evaluation

This is the section where the investigators state how they will determine if the project purposes were met and if the project as conducted was successful. Many agencies will also require a final report of activities and an accounting of funds used in the project once the project is completed.

Dissemination

Many agencies require that the results of the investigation be shared, because their financial support is a function of their commitment to inquiry. A good dissemination plan is essential. If a professional or scholarly society is the funding source, then the results are often first disseminated through the society's publication channels before they are shared through other sources.

TALKING POINTS

Grants and Contracts

- Countless dollars are available through external agencies.
- For a proposal to be taken seriously, the grant proposal document must follow the funding agency's directions to the letter.
- Grant adjudicators must be able to locate and understand the information in the proposal, as there are few second chances with a funding agency.

PART THREE

USING STATISTICS TO ANALYZE AND INTERPRET INFORMATION

12

Introduction to the Research Scenarios and the Data Analysis Software

EXECUTIVE SUMMARY Most sport organizations use some form of data collection as a normal business practice, and managers frequently make decisions based on the resulting data. When making any business decision, a manager should give careful consideration to the evaluation of statistics and the tests that indicate whether significant differences or relationships are present in the data.

To help connect the various statistical measurements and tests to their practical applications in the sport industry, we will use two hypothetical scenarios that present real-world problems or questions. For Research Scenario I, we provide the statistical calculations, analysis, and interpretation. Research Scenario II is in the form of a practice problem for which you will first apply the statistical tests and then provide the analysis and interpretation. This chapter introduces these scenarios, as well as the software that will be used in analyzing the data from these scenarios. Additional examples are provided in each subsequent chapter to help explain statistical terms and analyses.

INTRODUCTION TO RESEARCH SCENARIO I

A lthough attendance at a Minor League Baseball (MiLB) team has been on par with previous years, the marketing and sales team believes there is potential to increase game attendance (and revenue).

You are the analyst for the baseball team, and the managers of these departments have contacted you to conduct a study prior to the start of the upcoming season (Time 1). Because of time urgency and financial considerations, a large-scale study is not feasible. You, together with the marketing and sales team, have decided that a smaller study with 150 participants is more appropriate, and you have selected the participants by using a stratified sampling technique (the population under study has been divided into subgroups, i.e., men and women) to ensure equal sample sizes of men and women living within 25 miles of the baseball stadium.

A review of sport management research literature (see Chapter 2) identifies that attendance at sport events is positively related to whether a person considers himself or herself as a sport fan (i.e., sport fandom). The research also shows that sport fandom can be measured with the Sport Fandom Questionnaire (Wann, 2002), which includes five items, with each item rated on a Likert scale from 1 (strongly disagree) to 8 (strongly agree). You and the marketing and sales team have created a brief survey to collect demographic information, sport fandom scores, the number of tickets purchased for last year's season, and the primary reason why the respondent purchased a baseball ticket (or tickets) last year (see Exhibit 12.1). You

Survey used by the MiLB team in Research Scenario I to collect demographics, sport fandom scores, and ticket purchase information.	EXHIBIT 12.1

Sport Fan Survey

Gender: _____ Male _____ Female *(please check one)*

Age: _____ *(in years)*

For questions 1–5, use the scale below and write the most appropriate answer in the space next to each item.

Strongly Disagree   Strongly Agree
　　1　　　2　　　3　　　4　　　5　　　6　　　7　　　8

_____ 1. I consider myself to be a sport fan.

_____ 2. My friends see me as a sport fan.

_____ 3. I believe that following sports is the most enjoyable form of entertainment.

_____ 4. My life would be less enjoyable if I were not allowed to follow sports.

_____ 5. Being a sport fan is very important to me.

6. *Last season*, how many tickets did you purchase to see this baseball team? _____

7. Please select one of the following as the most important reason for purchasing a ticket to see this baseball team *last season*.

_____ event cost   _____ distance from home   _____ venue appearance/environment

_____ team win/loss record   _____ team(s) who are playing   _____ opportunity to attend with friends

Questions 1–5 from Wann, D. L. (2002). Preliminary validation of a measure for assessing identification as a sport fan: The sport fandom questionnaire. *International Journal of Sport Management, 3,* 103–115. Used with permission.

and the marketing and sales team intend to use the survey data to create a market profile of the community and to plan a marketing strategy to increase the number of tickets purchased for the current baseball season.

Upon the conclusion of the current baseball season, the research team contacts the 150 participants again to complete a second survey (Time 2). This survey includes the Sport Fandom Questionnaire and a question about how many tickets the respondent purchased during the current baseball season. You and the marketing and sales team plan to use the data from the second survey to evaluate whether the marketing strategy used in the current season was effective and to improve the strategy for the upcoming season. For the purposes of this scenario, we assume that all participants provided data at Time 1 and Time 2. In an actual situation, some participants may not wish to participate in a second survey, or it may not be possible to locate all of the previous participants, resulting in fewer participants at Time 2.

INTRODUCTION TO RESEARCH SCENARIO II: PRACTICE PROBLEM

Health clubs and parks and recreation facilities will often collect demographic information about members or visitors and survey them about the facility and/or available services (e.g., http://wvhealthclub.com/survey, http://parks.ky.gov/survey/). In this scenario, the owner of a health club has received some communications from a few club members that they wish the hours of operation were expanded and that they may not renew their membership if they are not able to use the health club as often as they would like. The owner wants to know if this concern is affecting other members' satisfaction with the club and has hired you to study the problem. In addition to this question of club hours, the owner has noticed that men seem to use the facility more often than women and wants to know if this is truly the case. A review of the research on health club member satisfaction suggests that you and the club owner should also examine club member income and marital status.

You survey a total of 60 members from the list of all current members and decide to use a stratified sampling technique to ensure equal numbers of men and women (30 each), as this is an important variable the owner wants to examine. You create a brief survey to collect demographic information, perceptions about the hours of operation, weekly facility usage, and expectations of health club membership (see Exhibit 12.2). One month after the changes in the health club's hours of operation, you survey the same members again. You and the owner plan to use this information to determine whether changes in the hours of operation for the health club have had a desirable effect on member perceptions and facility use.

Note: As was the case with Research Scenario I, this scenario assumes that all participants provide data at both Time 1 and Time 2, although this likely would not occur in an actual research project. Any analyses involving two time points, however, will include only those participants with data on both time points.

	EXHIBIT 12.2
Survey used in Research Scenario II to collect demographic information, perceptions about hours of operation, weekly facility usage, and expectations of the health club membership.	

Health Club Survey

Gender: _____ Male _____ Female *(please check one)*

Marital Status: _____ Single _____ Married

Annual Income: _____ under $35,000 _____ $35,000–$70,000 _____ above $70,000

How would you rate the hours of operation for this health club?

Poor			Average			Excellent
1	2	3	4	5	6	7

On average, how frequently do you come to use the facility? _____ times per week

How does our health club stack up to your expectations?

_____ Exceeds expectations _____ Meets expectations _____ Below expectations

OVERVIEW OF THE STATISTICAL TESTS AND THEIR PRACTICAL USES

In subsequent chapters, you will see how to use statistical measures and tests to analyze data and interpret results. We will use each statistical measure or test to examine a data analysis problem from the above scenarios. Exhibit 12.3 lists the statistical measures and tests and the data analysis problems based on the two scenarios that we will use to demonstrate the measures and tests.

	EXHIBIT 12.3
Statistical measures and tests, their practical uses, and data analysis problems from the two research scenarios.	

STATISTICAL MEASURE OR TEST	CHAPTER	SAMPLE PRACTICAL USE	DATA ANALYSIS PROBLEM SCENARIO I	DATA ANALYSIS PROBLEM SCENARIO II
Mean	14	Average values for demographics (e.g., age) and other variables, such as tickets purchased	What is the mean number of baseball tickets purchased in a season?	What is the mean number of weekly visits to the health club facility for men? For women?
Median	14	Middle values for variables, especially demographics that may have outliers (e.g., income) or single Likert-based questions	What is the median of the rating of participants on whether "my friends see me as a sport fan"?	What is the median of visits per week for men in the health club? For women?

(continued)

EXHIBIT 12.3 Continued.

STATISTICAL MEASURE OR TEST	CHAPTER	SAMPLE PRACTICAL USE	DATA ANALYSIS PROBLEM SCENARIO I	DATA ANALYSIS PROBLEM SCENARIO II
Mode	14	Most frequent age, sport fandom score, health club visits, or response selected	How many baseball tickets did fans most often purchase in a season?	What number of visits per week to the health club facility appears most frequently?
Standard Deviation	14	Spread or dispersion in demographics (e.g., age) or other variables (e.g., sport fandom scores, health club usage)	Is there small or large variability in sport fandom scores for men and women?	Is the variability in weekly health club usage for men and women large or small?
Range	14	Difference between highest and lowest number of tickets purchased, concession sales, visits, demographics	How many years separate the youngest and oldest fans who purchased baseball tickets this year?	How many visits separate the most active health club members from the least active?
Simple Correlation	15	Relationship between sport fandom and spectator enjoyment or between satisfaction with hours and health club usage	Is there a correlation between sport fandom and the number of baseball tickets the participant purchased last year?	Is there a correlation between satisfaction with health club hours and the number of visits per week?
Intra-class Correlation	15	Test–retest scenarios, sport fandom over a period of time, club usage over time	Is the measure of sport fandom stable over a six-month period?	Are club members satisfied with club hours on a weekly basis?
Multiple Regression	16	Employee satisfaction, spectator enjoyment, future sport consumptive behavior, club visits	What variables are important in predicting sport consumptive behavior?	What variables are important in predicting health club facility usage?
Independent t-test	17	Comparisons between experienced and inexperienced employees, season ticket holders and non–season ticket holders, athletes and non-athletes, exercisers and non-exercisers, younger and older, men and women, etc.	Do men and women differ on sport fandom?	Do men and women differ in perceptions of club facility hours?
Dependent t-test	17	Effectiveness of a marketing campaign based on revenue, effectiveness of a marketing campaign based on client satisfaction, effectiveness of a change in leadership style based on employee satisfaction, effectiveness of a change in leadership style based on productivity, effectiveness of a change in hours	Were the new marketing strategies effective based on the difference between last year's ticket sales and this year's ticket sales?	Were the changes in club hours effective in increasing weekly visits based on the difference between ExWeekT1 and ExWeekT2?

(continued)

Continued.   **EXHIBIT** **12.3**

STATISTICAL MEASURE OR TEST	CHAPTER	SAMPLE PRACTICAL USE	DATA ANALYSIS PROBLEM SCENARIO I	DATA ANALYSIS PROBLEM SCENARIO II
One-way ANOVA	18	Experience of employees compared to productivity; experience of employees compared to job satisfaction; comparison of multi-level groups based on age, education, exerciser status, venue size, departments in a sport organization, or differences in income	Does the number of tickets purchased vary between different age groups? (young = 18–29 yrs, middle = 30–49 yrs, older = 50+ yrs)	Does the perception of club hours vary between different levels of income for members? (low income = <$35,000, middle income = $35,000 to $70,000, high income = >$70,000)
One-way ANOVA with Repeated Measures	18	Feelings about a sport team among fans measured during different times in the season; changes in workplace productivity, such as ticket sales, sponsorship sales, new memberships over time; changes in employee satisfaction over time	Did the new marketing strategies create a significant difference between last year's ticket sales and this year's ticket sales?	N/A
Factorial ANOVA	18	Effects of the length of employment and gender on productivity (e.g., average calls or sales made) or job satisfaction; comparison of multi-level groups as in one-way ANOVA	Does the number of tickets purchased differ by age group or gender? Specifically, are gender differences larger or smaller in certain age groups? (young = 18–29 yrs, middle = 30–49 yrs, older = 50+ yrs)	Do perceptions about the hours of operation differ by gender or income level? Are potential gender differences larger or smaller in certain income groups?
Chi-square Test of Goodness of Fit	19	Compare recommendations and non-recommendations of a service to a friend; compare frequency of men and women in upper management against expected frequency based on the percentage of men and women in the sport organization; compare number of products sold to expected frequency of products sold established from prior sales figures or by corporate headquarters	What is the predominant reason for attending a game out of the six possible reasons: event cost, distance from home, teams playing, home team's record, venue appearance, and opportunity to be with friends?	N/A
Chi-square Test of Independence	19	Compare responses of men and women to whether they recommended a service to a friend; compare frequency of men and women in upper management across several different sport organizations within a league; compare responses of men and women to how well the health club meets expectations	Based on the survey of 75 men and 75 women on their primary reason for attending a game, is their predominant reason related to gender?	Based on the survey of 30 men and 30 women on how well the health club meets expectations, is the predominant response related to gender?

MICROSOFT EXCEL: A PRACTICAL DATA ANALYSIS PROGRAM

T his book focuses on the use of Microsoft Excel in data analysis. Although more complex statistical software packages are available, such as IBM's SPSS Statistics, which could perform some of the statistical tests covered in this book, Excel has several advantages over these other programs, as well as other spreadsheet software. First, Excel is ubiquitous in the sport industry. Analysts and other personnel in the industry are familiar with Excel, and, thus, data may easily be transferred from person to person or organization to organization. Also, Excel is much less expensive than other statistical software programs, contributing to its popularity and widespread use. In fact, statistical programs such as SPSS Statistics cost several thousand dollars for a single-user license across multiple years, with increased cost for concurrent users across multiple years. Last, data stored in an Excel spreadsheet may be transferred to other statistical software programs for more advanced analysis, if needed, and its data and charts can easily be added to word processing documents and presentations.

Data Entry

Excel allows for the data to be entered in multiple ways. There is no one best way to enter the data, and, regardless of the method chosen, the data will probably have to be reorganized for some statistical tests. We recommend that you use the following method of data entry, because it keeps each participant's data on a single row and, thus, the data can most easily be transferred for use in other statistical programs, if necessary. In the typical Excel spreadsheet (Exhibit 12.4), the rows correspond to each participant's data. Descriptive column headings convey the type of data that was collected, and these headings should appear in the first row of the spreadsheet. You can "freeze" the column headings by using the *Freeze Panes* function within the *View* tab, which keeps the column headings in view while you scroll down the spreadsheet. Regardless of the data entry method, you must enter the data carefully to avoid mistakes or omissions.

For Research Scenario I, the data that were collected before the start of the current season (Time 1) and immediately after the current season (Time 2) included:

- Gender (column A), with M = male and F = female
- Age (column B)
- The five individual item scores that make up the sport fandom total score at Time 1 (columns C through G)
- Sport fandom total scores collected at Time 1 (column H); scores range from 5 to 40, with a higher score indicating that the person considers herself or himself to be more of a sport fan
- Sport fandom total scores collected at Time 2 (column I)
- Sport consumptive behaviors for last season, i.e., number of baseball tickets purchased for last year's season (column J)

- sport consumptive behaviors for the current season, i.e., number of base-ball tickets purchased for the current season (column K)
- primary reason for purchasing tickets last year (column L), with partici-pant responses coded in the following manner: event cost (EC), distance from home (DH), teams playing (TP), home team's record (TR), venue appearance (VA), and opportunity to be with friends (OF)

Note: Any codes may be used for data entry, but each code, including the use of up-percase and lowercase letters, should be consistently used. Use of consistent codes is necessary for the Sort and Filter functions to work effectively and accurately.

Appendix A contains the remaining data collected from the MiLB survey. An electronic version of this data may be available from your instructor.

For Research Scenario II, the rows will also correspond to each participant's data, and descriptive column headings will be used to convey the type of data that was collected. The following types of data were collected in Research Scenario II:

- Gender (column A), with M = male and F = female
- Marital status (column B), with S = single and M = married
- Income (column C), with L = low (<$35,000), M = middle ($35,000–$75,000), and H = high (>$75,000)
- Perceptions about the hours of operation *before* expanding the hours (column E, heading: ExWeekT1), with scores ranging from 1 to 7 (1 = poor; 4 = average; 7 = excellent)

Partial view of the spreadsheet of the data collected by the MiLB team in Research Scenario I.   **EXHIBIT 12.4**

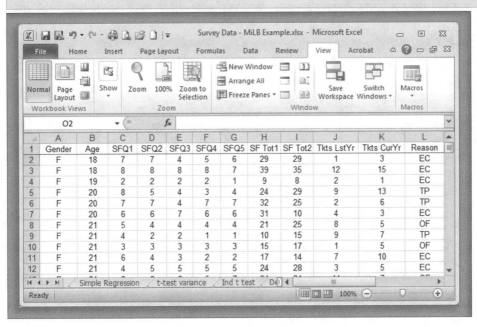

- Perceptions about the hours of operation *after* expanding the hours (column F, heading: ExWeekT2)
- Expectations about health club membership (column G), with EE = exceeds expectations; ME = meets expectations; BE = below expectations

Appendix B contains the remaining data collected from the health club survey. An electronic version of this data may be available from your instructor.

Installing the Data Analysis ToolPak included with Excel for Windows

Before analyzing the data with the statistical tests covered in this book, you will need to check whether the Data Analysis ToolPak has been installed in your Excel program, if you are working in the Windows environment. (If you are using a Mac, you will use StatPlus, as discussed below.) Click the *Data* tab, and "Data Analysis" should appear on the far right at the top of the spreadsheet (see Exhibit 12.5).

If "Data Analysis" does not appear, you will need to install the Analysis ToolPak. For the 2007 Excel PC version, click on the Excel logo at the top of the screen and select *Excel Options*. For 2010 and 2013 Excel PC versions, click on the *File* tab and select *Options*. For 2007 to 2013 versions, within Excel Options, select *Add-Ins*. At the bottom of the Add-Ins screen, make sure the Manage pull-down menu shows Excel Add-Ins, and then Click *Go* (see Exhibit 12.6). When the Add-Ins box appears, place a check mark next to Analysis ToolPak and then click *OK*.

EXHIBIT 12.5   Location of the Data Analysis tab.

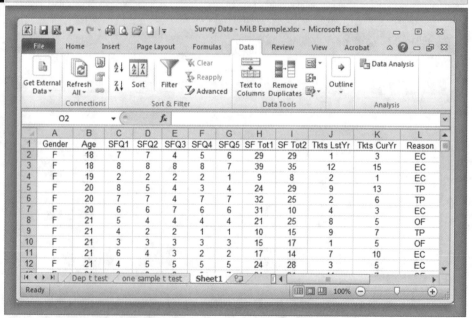

Location for loading the Data Analysis ToolPak.   **EXHIBIT 12.6**

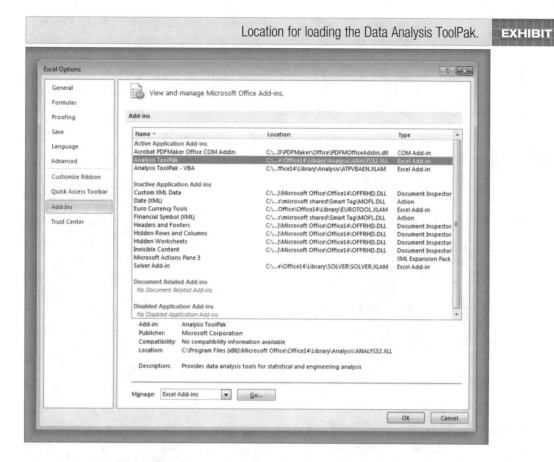

Installing StatPlus for Excel for the Mac

The Data Analysis ToolPak is not available for Mac versions of Excel. Instead, you will need to install a separate program, StatPlus, which is available free for the statistical tests covered in this book (i.e., descriptive, correlation/regression, independent and dependent *t*-tests, and one-way and two-way ANOVA). For additional tests, a free 30-day trial of the full version of StatPlus is typically available. StatPlus uses an Excel interface and is compatible with Excel 2004, 2008, and 2011. Use the following link: www.analystsoft.com/en/products/statplusmacle/. Click on the *Download* button and follow the instructions.

Using the Data Analysis ToolPak and StatPlus

We will use the Data Analysis ToolPak and StatPlus to perform a variety of statistical tests. Recall that researchers and managers use statistical measures and tests to analyze data, and then, based on the results of these tests, the researcher or manager determines whether relationships between variables are significant or whether groups significantly differ from each other on the variable(s) of interest. We will describe the steps in using Excel's Data Analysis ToolPak to perform the tests, while noting any differences in the process for StatPlus (Mac).

The output from ToolPak and from StatPlus may be slightly different, even when the data are exactly the same. See Exhibit 12.7 for example statistics output tables from both programs.

EXHIBIT 12.7   Descriptive statistics output for ToolPak versus StatPlus.

SF Tot1	
Mean	23.5867
Standard Error	0.7570
Median	24.0000
Mode	21.0000
Standard Deviation	9.2709
Sample Variance	85.9488
Kurtosis	-0.7819
Skewness	-0.0944
Range	35.0000
Minimum	5.0000
Maximum	40.0000
Sum	3538.0000
Count	150.0000
Confidence Level(95.0%)	1.4958

(a) ToolPak output

Alpha value (for confidence interval)	0.05		
Variable #1 (SF Tot1)			
Count	150	Skewness	-0.0935
Mean	23.58667	Skewness Standard Error	0.19671
Mean LCL	22.0909	Kurtosis	2.20422
Mean UCL	25.08243	Kurtosis Standard Error	0.38569
Variance	85.94881	Alternative Skewness (Fisher's)	-0.09444
Standard Deviation	9.27086	Alternative Kurtosis (Fisher's)	-0.78187
Mean Standard Error	0.75696	Coefficient of Variation	0.39306
Minimum	5.	Mean Deviation	7.65102
Maximum	40.	Second Moment	85.37582
Range	35.	Third Moment	-73.7567
Sum	3,538.	Fourth Moment	16,066.61716
Sum Standard Error	113.54436	Median	24.
Total Sum Squares	96,256.	Median Error	0.07746
Adjusted Sum Squares	12,806.37333	Percentile 25% (Q1)	17.
Geometric Mean	21.35912	Percentile 75% (Q2)	31.
Harmonic Mean	18.61639	IQR	14.
Mode	21.	MAD	7.

(b) StatPlus output

As the example tables show, the ToolPak output and the StatPlus output provide the same descriptive statistics, although they may be organized differently, and the StatPlus output may include additional advanced statistics that are beyond the scope of this book. The Confidence Level (95%) might not be readily apparent in the StatPlus output, but this information is provided in the form of Mean LCL (Lower Confidence Level) and Mean UCL (Upper Confidence Level). If the Confidence Level reported in ToolPak (i.e., 1.4958) is subtracted and then also added to the mean (i.e., 23.5867), then the same values will be obtained for the Mean LCL (23.5867 − 1.4958 = 22.0909) and Mean UCL (23.5866 + 1.4958 = 25.0824). In Chapter 14 we discuss Confidence Levels of the Mean.

TALKING POINTS

Research Scenarios and Data Analysis Software

- Data collection and analysis are essential for making any business decision.
- Surveys are often used for collecting data.
- Statistical techniques may be used to analyze data and interpret the results, and we will use a Minor League Baseball scenario and a health club scenario to explain and practice this process.
- We will use Microsoft Excel for data analysis. For Windows users, the Data Analysis ToolPak add-in should be used. Mac users will need to download a free software program, StatPlus, in order to analyze the data.

13

Issues in Analyzing Data

EXECUTIVE SUMMARY Statistics are used in many facets of life, including sport management, but for one reason or another, people become apprehensive when they hear the word *statistics*. For example, some people may immediately envision complicated formulas. While it is true that certain statistical formulas can be quite involved, sport managers do not necessarily have to memorize these formulas in order to make use of statistics. As long as they know the uses for the tests and how to analyze and interpret the results, sport managers should be able to use the information statistics provide in their jobs. Statistics are simply ways of interpreting a collection of observations or data obtained through appropriate sampling techniques and valid measures, and this information can help sport managers make informed decisions.

SUBJECTIVE VERSUS OBJECTIVE DECISION MAKING

Perhaps one of the most popular examples of the use of statistics in sport is described in Michael Lewis's book *Moneyball: The Art of Winning an Unfair Game* (2004). In essence, the book and subsequent movie describe how the Oakland Athletics' front office, especially general manager Billy Beane, was able to overcome the team's financial limitations by making use of baseball statistics, or sabermetrics. Sabermetrics was pioneered and advocated by baseball writer, historian, and statistician Bill James, along with others, and it offers an alternative to the prevailing notion held by most baseball front offices that a team needs high-priced talent in order to compete. Player evaluations and roster decisions traditionally have relied heavily on the subjective opinions of scouts and other front office personnel. However, the book describes how the As' front office, despite a small budget, was able to assemble a winning team by using baseball statistics to select affordable yet productive younger and older players.

This example is particularly important, because it also highlights potential problems or issues that can arise from subjective decision making. Although statistics are prevalent in sports, and the use of research and data analysis in decision making is becoming more valued, many sport professionals still primarily base their decision making on past experience, guesswork, simply copying what others have been doing, and other mostly subjective factors. While these strategies are not necessarily bad, they should be used only at the initial developmental stages of an event or campaign and then should be followed by statistical data analysis. Failure to do so increases the probability of wasting time and resources, as well as potentially facing negative public relations or legal issues should something go wrong.

Event organizers have used impact studies to provide statistics on the proposed and actual economic, social, and environmental impact of small or large sport events. For example, an economic impact study reported that the 2014 Rock 'n' Roll Marathon's impact exceeded $8 million for the city of Raleigh (www.newsobserver.com/2014/07/08/3992618/rock-n-roll-marathon-study-says.html), and the 2013 Super Bowl Visitor Study and Economic Impact project reported a total net economic impact of $480 million for New Orleans (http://media.nola.com/business_impact/other/Super%20Bowl%20XLVII%20 Economic%20Impact%20Study%20UNO.PDF). Facility planners may use statistics to describe a community's demographics, such as its median income, in a feasibility study to make decisions on a proposed facility, such as a multi-sport complex, and to estimate the impact of the facility on the community (www. woodridgeparks.org/pdf/ARC_FeasibilityStudy.pdf). A good sport marketing manager may collect data from focus groups and surveys and then use statistics to develop and refine the marketing strategies for a campaign. A concessions manager may use descriptive statistics when ordering food, beverage, and other items to replenish inventory, minimize waste, and ensure customer satisfaction by having the right type and right amount of items available for purchase. The manager may use daily, weekly, or monthly attendance for the current year, as well as historical attendance (e.g., past five years) for the same time period, in order to make informed buying decisions.

In these examples, many types of statistics can aid the sport professional. These include descriptive statistics (statistics that describe the characteristics of a data set, e.g., mean values), as well as statistical tests that compare sets of data (e.g., *t*-tests, analysis of variance) or analyze how sets of data are related to each other (e.g., correlation, regression). These specific statistics and statistical tests are discussed in subsequent chapters.

TYPES OF DATA

Recall the types of data that were collected for the research scenarios described in Chapter 12. Data for gender fall into categories (male or female). Number of tickets bought in a season is a number, with zero being a possibility. These examples illustrate the fact that data come in different forms. Statisticians recognize four different measurement scales for the different types of data: nominal, ordinal, interval, and ratio. Understanding the measurement scales will allow you to select the appropriate statistical test to analyze the data.

Nominal Scale

In a **nominal scale,** the data fall into mutually exclusive categories. For example, a demographic question, such as gender or ethnicity, will typically require a participant to select a category from the available options (e.g., male or female). Other questions may require a participant to answer yes or no to a question, such as, "Do you intend to purchase a seat license for next season?" or "Would you recommend this park or facility?" There is no numerical value associated with the category; there is simply the name for the category.

Ordinal Scale

In an **ordinal scale,** the data are organized into rank-ordered categories. The data allow the analyst to order participants according to the category they selected. An example of a rank-ordered scale would be a demographic question asking a participant to select her level of education (e.g., 1 = less than high school; 2 = high school diploma or equivalent; 3 = some college; 4 = undergraduate degree; 5 = graduate degree). Another common example occurs in survey research, where a question includes response options on a Likert scale, such as 1 = strongly disagree; 2 = somewhat disagree; 3 = neutral; 4 = somewhat agree; 5 = strongly agree. If a single question using a Likert scale is to be analyzed, then it should be considered an ordinal scale. (If multiple Likert scale questions are used to formulate a scale score or total score, the scale or total score will be measured on an interval scale.) In each of these examples, a higher number implies more of the attribute being measured, whether it is education or agreement or some other quality. There is an order to the data, but the unit of measurement between the categories is not necessarily the same. In other words, the difference between 2 and 3 (e.g., somewhat disagree to neutral) is not necessarily the same as from 4 to 5 (e.g., somewhat agree to strongly agree), because the categories are not necessarily evenly spaced.

Interval Scale

In an **interval scale,** there is order to the data, and the distances between the units of measurement are the same. However, there is no absolute zero point on the scale, even though the scale may contain a 0 point. For example, in a Fahrenheit temperature scale, the difference between 20 degrees and 40 degrees is the same as the difference between 60 degrees and 80 degrees. However, we cannot state that 40 degrees is twice as hot as 20 degrees, because 0 degrees does not reflect the absolute zero point on the scale, or an absence of heat, because the temperature may go below 0 degrees. Another example relevant to sport would be a judge's ratings of athletic performance. Because a score of zero would not reflect a total absence of skill, a rating of 8 would not mean that the performance was twice as good as a performance that received a rating of 4.

A measurement scale may be considered interval if multiple Likert-based questions or items are used to measure a particular attribute. As described in previous sections, the Sport Fandom Questionnaire includes five items, with each item rated on a Likert scale from 1 (strongly disagree) to 8 (strongly agree). The total Sport Fandom score may be analyzed as data from an interval scale, because the scale does not have a zero end-point and the lowest score on the scale does not indicate that the person is not a sport fan at all.

Ratio Scale

In a **ratio scale,** there is order to the data, the distances between the units of measurement are the same, and there is an absolute zero point on the scale. Common examples of measures using ratio scales include age, distance, time, and weight. For example, an object that weighs 10 lbs is twice as heavy as something that weighs 5 lbs, and the difference between 5 lbs and 10 lbs is the same as the difference between 45 lbs and 50 lbs. Another example, related to sport, is the number of tickets purchased or dollars spent by a sport consumer. A purchase of $100 in merchandise is twice as much as $50, and this difference of $50 is the same as the difference between $325 and $375. There is also an absolute zero in this example, since there could be a person who did not buy any tickets or merchandise, and this person, therefore, spent $0.

Statistical Tests for Different Types of Data

There are two categories of statistical tests that we can use to analyze data collected on the four measurement scales: parametric tests and nonparametric tests. **Parametric tests** may be used for data measured on interval and ratio scales, and these tests are the most typical ones reported in scholarly journals, as well as in professional reports. The parametric tests to be covered in this book include *t*-tests, correlation, regression, and analysis of variance (ANOVA). Certain assumptions are associated with using parametric tests; these include:

- *Normality:* The sample data were drawn from a population that is normally distributed (see Chapter 14).
- *Homogeneity of variance:* The sample group variances are equal.
- *Independence:* The observations are independent of each other, so that scores in one group are not associated with scores in another group.

When the data distribution is skewed, or non-normal, this introduces bias or noise in the sample means and variances. (See Chapter 14 for a discussion of means and variances.) In other words, the sample means would not be good estimates of the data, and the variances within each group would not be equal, making comparisons between the groups invalid. Using non-random sampling techniques (e.g., intact groups, no random assignment) may result in group data that are skewed or that differ in variability (i.e., some groups have scores tightly bunched around the mean, while other groups have scores that are spread out). In general, if the largest group variance is less than twice as big as the smallest group variance, then violations of the assumption of equal sample variances will not have a substantial effect on the analysis. If the independence assumption is not met, then statistical tests accounting for repeated measures (e.g., dependent *t* test, ANOVA with repeated measures) may be used. Sound sampling techniques, such as random sampling and random assignment, will help improve the likelihood that the assumptions listed above are not violated. That being said, parametric tests are fairly robust against violations of normality and equal variances.

If the assumptions for using parametric tests cannot be met, then **nonparametric tests** may be used, because there are no assumptions about the distribution of data for nonparametric tests. For data that are measured on nominal or ordinal scales, we use nonparametric tests. This book will discuss one nonparametric test: the chi-square test. A chi-square test does not analyze means but tests the discrepancy between the observed and expected frequency data (see Chapter 19). Many other nonparametric tests are available, and each is analogous to a parametric test (in parenthesis), such as the Mann–Whitney *U* test (independent *t* test), Wilcoxon signed-ranks test (dependent *t*-test), Kruskal–Wallis ANOVA by ranks (one-way ANOVA), Friedman two-way ANOVA by ranks (ANOVA with repeated measures), and Spearman rank-difference correlation (Pearson correlation coefficient).

ERRORS IN PROBABILITIES

Statistical tests make use of probability. **Probability** refers to the likelihood that an event will occur. In statistics, the researcher is testing whether the null hypothesis (e.g., no difference between sample groups or no relationship between variables) should be rejected or not rejected. This conclusion is based on sample data collected from the target population. Because analysts use sample populations in their data analysis, errors may occur when they infer the results from the sample to the larger population.

Type I and Type II Errors

One type of error is called a Type I error. A **Type I error** refers to rejecting the null hypothesis when the null hypothesis should not have been rejected. This would be equivalent to a false positive. Stated another way, the investigator concludes that a significant difference or relationship exists when the difference or relationship does not really exist in the population. For example, in the case of the health club research scenario, an analyst might conclude from a biased study that extended business hours would increase revenue; however, when actually implemented, an increase in business hours does not result in greater revenue. The second type of error that can occur is called a Type II error. A **Type II error** refers to not rejecting the null hypothesis when the null hypothesis should have been rejected. Stated differently, the researcher concludes that there is no significant difference or relationship when the difference or relationship really does exist in the population. For example, an analyst may accept that a new sport promotion did not have any effect on customers when, in actuality, it did.

Levels of Probability for Committing Errors

There is a level of probability to control for committing each type of error. The levels of probability are referred to as alpha and beta.

Alpha

Alpha (α) is the level of probability used to control for committing a Type I error. The alpha level is a level set by analysts, and they make the determination before any data is collected, or *a priori*. The most conventional alpha levels used in research are 0.05 and 0.01. If the alpha level is set at 0.05, this means that the analyst is willing to accept a 5 percent probability that the results observed with the sample are attributable to chance. In this case, the analyst can be 95% confident that the results observed with the sample also exist in the population. If alpha is set at 0.01, then the analyst can be 99% confident that the results observed with the sample also exist in the population.

The stringency of the alpha level chosen depends on the type of research being performed and the need to be more confident when making inferences from the sample to the population. For example, survey research in sport management typically uses a less stringent alpha level ($\alpha = .05$) compared to clinical research on drug effects, which often uses more stringent alpha levels (e.g., $\alpha = .001$) due to the more serious ramifications associated with a Type I error in this setting. Despite the need or desire to be as confident as possible in our findings, there is always a chance for error, so an analyst can never really be 100 percent confident.

p value. A concept used in conjunction with alpha level is *p* value. When conducting a statistical test (e.g., *t* test, ANOVA), a test statistic is calculated and a p value is reported for that test statistic. The **p value** is the probability that a test statistic of a size indicating a finding of significance would emerge from the data, assuming the null hypothesis is true. The p value is compared against the alpha level and used to establish the level of significance. If the p value is less than the alpha level (e.g., $p = .02 < \alpha = .05$), then the test statistic is considered significant. In other words, the analyst would reject the null hypothesis and conclude that the difference or relationship is statistically significant at the established alpha level. If the p value is greater than the alpha level (e.g., $p = .14 > \alpha = .05$), then the analyst would not reject the null hypothesis, and the finding of that statistical test would not be considered significant.

For example, a sport marketing team might use a focus group to provide ratings for two different price promotions to be used in the upcoming season. In one promotion, ticket prices will be priced $2 less than in the other promotion. A statistical test could be performed to examine whether the ratings were higher for one item over the other. If the p value for the statistical test was less than the alpha level, then the marketing team could conclude that the item with the higher rating (i.e., the lower-priced ticket) was significantly different from the other item. If the p value was greater than the alpha level, then the conclusion would be that the ratings for the two items did not differ. The marketing team could then use the information as a basis to decide whether they should discount the tickets even more or offer some other ticket purchase promotion.

Beta

Beta (β) is the level of probability used to control for committing a Type II error. Most researchers consider a Type II error as less grievous than a Type I error, so the beta may be set at a level higher than the alpha. Once again, the beta level is an *a priori* decision made by the analyst. The most common beta level used in research is 20%, but lower percentages may be used to increase the power of the study, as discussed below. To clarify, if the beta level is set at 0.20, then this means that the analyst is willing to accept that the likelihood of committing a Type II error is 20%. Or, to restate, the analyst is willing to accept a 20% chance of not rejecting the null hypothesis when it should have been rejected.

Power. An important concept associated with the beta level is power, which may be calculated as $1 - \beta$. Analysts want their statistical tests to have **power**, because this concept refers to the probability that their tests will detect real or statistically significant differences that exist in the population. If beta is set at 0.20, then the power is $1 - 0.20$, or 0.80. A power of 0.80 means there is an 80% chance of detecting a real difference that exists in the population based on the sample data that were collected.

You may ask, "Why not use a stringent alpha and beta so that an analyst can be as confident as possible, with the most power?" As you may recall, a level of probability is associated with each type of error, and these probabilities are based on the sample size used in the study. Remember, you are inferring results obtained with a small sample to a larger population. As the sample size increases, the sample typically provides a better representation of the population, thus reducing the probability of committing Type I and II errors when inferring results from the sample to the population. In other words, larger sample sizes are needed if the analyst wants more power or wishes to use a more stringent alpha, but this will often result in a greater cost for the study. The researcher must carefully consider the design of the study that will best be able to answer the research questions given the resources that are available.

STATISTICAL SIGNIFICANCE VERSUS PRACTICAL SIGNIFICANCE (MEANINGFULNESS)

Suppose you ask a friend which team won the game last night, and you find out that your favorite team won. Would you stop with that question? Probably not. You would probably want to know the score, as well. Why? Because the score helps you interpret the results (e.g., was it a close game or a blowout?). Knowing just the outcome of the game is analogous to statistical significance, and knowing the score is similar to a measure of practical significance.

Statistical tests report findings of **statistical significance.** In statistics, the investigator is testing whether the null hypothesis (e.g., no difference between sample groups or no relationship between variables) should be rejected or not rejected. The researcher uses statistical tests to analyze the data, and the results of these tests allow the analyst to conclude whether relationships between variables are significant or whether groups significantly differ from each other on the variable(s) of interest.

Another method to assist in interpreting statistical findings is to use measures of **practical significance,** or *meaningfulness.* A variety of measures of practical significance may be calculated for the various statistical tests, and these will be discussed along with each statistical test (see Chapters 15 through 19). Since sample size plays a role in determining statistical significance, a small sample size will reduce the power of a study and can contribute to a lack of significant findings, even though the findings may be meaningful. Conversely, a very large sample size may result in too much power, with potentially trivial differences being found statistically significant. For example, the relationship between customer satisfaction and service quality may be strong, but it may not be considered statistically significant ($p > .05$) if we have data from only five people. Statistical analyses rely on probability, and we have to have a very strong relationship if we are to conclude that the result we are finding with so few people also exists in a much larger population. The statistics yielded by very large samples are considered more stable, and we may be more confident that the relationship between customer satisfaction and service quality exists in the population, even if this relationship is weak. In each case, a measure of practical significance can help the analyst interpret the results and determine whether some non-significant findings deserve further consideration in a future study or if some significant findings are not really that meaningful.

TALKING POINTS

Analyzing Data

- Subjective decisions are appropriate at the initial developmental stages of an event or campaign but should be followed by objective decisions based on statistical data analysis.

- Data may be measured with four different measurement scales: nominal, ordinal, interval, and ratio.

- Use of parametric tests assumes that the data are normally distributed, have homogeneity of variance, and are independent, whereas use of nonparametric tests does not require any assumptions about the data distributions.

- Statistical tests make use of probability, and analysts should give careful consideration to alpha and beta to control for the Type I and II error rates.

- Both the statistical significance and the practical significance of results should be evaluated when stating conclusions.

Descriptive Statistics

EXECUTIVE SUMMARY **Descriptive statistics** describe the characteristics of a data set. These statistics include measures of central tendency (the mean, median, and mode) and measures of variability (the standard deviation, variance, and range). The formulas for these statistics are not complicated, and Excel can easily provide them.

WHAT IS CENTRAL TENDENCY?

Sport managers and analysts use measures of central tendency because they provide important information for making good decisions. A **measure of central tendency** is a single score that represents all the scores or values in a set of data. Why is this important? These measures allow the analyst to describe a collection of scores or values quickly and to evaluate how any one particular score or value compares with the middle (or central) scores in a set of data. There are three measures of central tendency: the *mean, median,* and *mode.*

Mean

The **mean,** or arithmetic average, is one measure of central tendency, and its symbol is M. The mean is simply the sum of all scores or values in a data set divided by the total number of scores or values in the set. For example, a sport marketing director may wish to know the average number of calls made by members of the sales team last week to evaluate how each member of the team compares with the team as a whole. This will help to identify employees who are performing well and those who are not.

The mean is one of the most frequently used and most sensitive measures of central tendency. However, the mean should be used only when the data were measured with an interval or ratio scale (see Chapter 13). Also, the mean is susceptible to extreme values, or **outliers.** For example, if a researcher collects information on the ages of season ticket holders, the presence of a few individuals who are much older than the rest may result in a mean age that is not representative of most season ticket holders. This is especially true when there is a limited number of observations (scores) in the data set. Let's suppose that we collected data on 10 season ticket holders, and their ages were: 30, 34, 38, 42, 42, 43, 45, 46, 79, and 84. The sum is 483, and dividing this by 10 results in a mean of 48.30 years. The mean age is higher than the ages of eight season ticket holders and is not an accurate representation of this sample. In situations like this, the median might be a more appropriate measure of central tendency.

Median

The **median** is the middle point in a set of data, where 50 percent of the scores fall above it and 50 percent fall below it. If the middle point falls between two scores, then we report the value that is halfway between these two scores. In the example of the ages of season ticket holders, 10 observations formed the data set. The median is 42.5 years, because it is the middle point between the fifth value (42 years) and sixth value (43 years). The median is most appropriate for use with ordinal-scaled data (see Chapter 13) or when extreme scores or values (outliers, e.g., age 84) are present in a set of data. As stated above, the influence of outliers on the mean is more pronounced when the data set contains fewer scores (e.g., 10 scores vs. 100 scores).

Mode

The final measure of central tendency is the **mode.** The mode is defined as the most frequently occurring score in a set of data. The mode may be used for nominal-scaled data (see Chapter 13), as well as for interval-, ratio-, and ordinal-scaled data. A set of data may contain more than one mode. For example, if two scores are tied as most frequent, then the data set has two modes, and it is called a bi-modal distribution; if three scores are tied as most frequent, it is called a tri-modal distribution, and so on. In the example of season ticket holder ages, the mode is 42 years, because that age was reported twice and all other ages were reported only once. The mode is only a rough estimate, and it is not typically reported or commonly used. One example of when it may be reported is for yes-or-no questions, such as "Would you recommend to your family or friends to purchase tickets to see a baseball game at this stadium?" If 70 out of 100 people answered yes while 30 answered no, then the mode (70) would be meaningful to report.

WHAT IS VARIABILITY?

As noted, sport analysts use measures of central tendency in many ways. However, the usefulness of these measures of central tendency can depend on the variability of the scores in a set of data. **Variability** measures how far apart (or widely dispersed) scores are in a data set. For example, if scores on an opinion survey can range from 0 to 100, variability tells us whether most of the scores are clustered together (e.g., between 60 and 80)—meaning there is low variability in the data set—or whether the scores are spread across the entire scale, meaning the data set has high variability. Why is this important? In both cases, the mean (i.e., $M = 70$) is the same, but if the scores are very widely dispersed, then the mean might not be representative of the data set.

Three of the most common measures of variability are *standard deviation, variance,* and *range.*

Standard Deviation

Among the three measures of variability, **standard deviation** is the most commonly used and most often reported, in conjunction with the mean. It is most appropriate for use with interval- or ratio-scaled data. The symbol for standard deviation of a sample is *s* or *SD,* and the symbol for standard deviation of the population of interest is σ. The standard deviation is expressed in the original units that were measured. For example, years of age were the original unit for the season ticket holder example discussed earlier. Essentially, standard deviation represents the amount of difference between each of the individual scores and the mean. The formula for standard deviation is

$$\sqrt{\frac{\sum(X - M)^2}{N - 1}}$$

For small sample sizes, *s* may be calculated as follows:

- subtract each score (X) from the mean (M),
- square these differences,
- sum ($\sum$) the squared differences,
- divide by the total number of scores (N) minus one, and
- take the square root of this value.

For example, recall that for the 10 season ticket holders, the ages were: 30, 34, 38, 42, 42, 43, 45, 46, 79, and 84. The mean (M) age was calculated as 48.30 years. The table in Exhibit 14.1 demonstrates the calculation of the standard deviation for this data set.

EXHIBIT 14.1	Example of the calculation of standard deviation. Note that a table such as this one can easily be created in Excel.

X	M	(X – M)	(X – M)²
30	48.3	−18.3	334.89
34	48.3	−14.3	204.49
38	48.3	−10.3	106.09
42	48.3	−6.3	39.69
42	48.3	−6.3	39.69
43	48.3	−5.3	28.09
45	48.3	−3.3	10.89
		Σ	2986.10

The sum of the $(X - M)^2$ values in the right-hand column is 2986.10. Since N refers to the 10 scores (or ages) in the data set, $N - 1 = 9$. We can insert these values into the formula as follows:

$$s = \sqrt{\frac{2986.10}{9}} = \sqrt{331.79} = 18.22$$

The standard deviation for age in this data set is 18.22 years. For large data sets, Excel may be used to calculate the standard deviation (see the research scenario later in this chapter).

The standard deviation can provide important information about the representativeness of the mean, but it is necessary for the analyst to consider the context of the data. For example, a high positive customer satisfaction mean with a small standard deviation may be desirable, because it would indicate that most of the satisfaction ratings are positive and high in value. However, in a different context, such as the mean of season ticket holder ages, a large standard deviation might be desirable, because it would indicate that sport fans of different age demographics are participating and, thus, that the team or club appeals to individuals of a wide variety of ages.

Moreover, standard deviation can help us understand how the data are distributed. A **normal,** or **bell-shaped, curve** has an equal distribution of scores on either side of the measure of central tendency. This distribution is referred to as a **normal distribution.** In a normal distribution, the mean, median, and mode will be equal. When a data set has a normal distribution (see Exhibit 14.2), we know the following:

- approximately 68% of the scores in the data set will fall within one standard deviation above and below the mean (i.e., $M \pm 1s$);

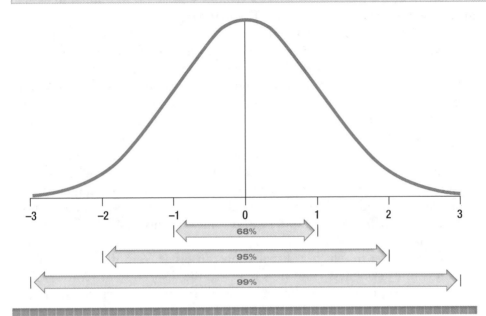

- approximately 95% of the scores will fall within two standard deviations of the mean (i.e., $M \pm 2s$); and

- approximately 99% of the scores will fall within three standard deviations of the mean (i.e., $M \pm 3s$).

For example, if an investigator recorded the ages of 200 survey respondents, and the mean age was 40 years with a standard deviation of 7 years, then the analyst could estimate that the ages of about 95% of the survey respondents (i.e., 190 people) would lie between 26 and 54 years. Depending on the scope of the survey, this information may be useful for a variety of purposes, such as marketing and promotional strategies, ticket pricing, or event management policy. In general, the more observations (scores) included in a data set, the greater the chance that the variable of interest will be normally distributed. The general recommendation is to have a minimum of 30 observations; then, the data will begin to approximate a normal distribution.

Data that are not normally distributed may vary in two ways: kurtosis and skewness. **Kurtosis** refers to the *vertical* characteristics of the data distribution. Excel provides a statistic called excess kurtosis. A normal distribution is called **mesokurtic** (excess kurtosis = 0). Distributions that are more peaked than the normal curve are called **leptokurtic** (excess kurtosis > 0), and ones that are flatter than the normal curve are called **platykurtic** (excess kurtosis < 0). The **standard error of kurtosis** is calculated as $\sqrt{(24 / n)}$, where *n* is the sample size. A data set may not have a mesokurtic distribution if the absolute value of the excess kurtosis is more than twice as large as the standard error of kurtosis.

Suppose, for example, that data from a sample of 100 individuals had an excess kurtosis value of –0.85. The standard error of kurtosis is √ (24 / 100) = 0.49, and twice this number is 0.98. Since the absolute excess kurtosis value of 0.85 is less than 0.98, we would conclude that the data is mesokurtic. If it exceeded this value, then we would need to transform the data so that it would be more normal or symmetric, but this transformation is beyond the scope of this book. For an example of a leptokurtic distribution, suppose a sport survey asked sport spectators to report the number of games they attended in the current season. Depending on the sport and the cost of attendance, most fans would probably report attending just two or three professional sporting events, while a few, such as season ticket holders, would report attending many more events. In this scenario, the cluster of small values would result in a more peaked curve than in a normal or more spread-out distribution. Exhibit 14.3 graphically illustrates the concepts of kurtosis in a distribution.

Another way in which a distribution can differ from the normal distribution is in its skewness. **Skewness** refers to the dispersion of scores around the mean, when one side, or "tail," of the distribution is more drawn out, or skewed, than the other side (Exhibit 14.4). Excel provides a skewness statistic. A perfectly symmetrical distribution will have a skewness value of 0. If the skewed tail is in the direction of positive values, then the distribution is considered **positively skewed** (a positive skewness value is reported in Excel). In the example of the number of event tickets purchased by individual sport fans, which we discussed above as an illustration of a leptokurtic distribution, the data would more than likely be positively skewed. This is because season ticket holders would probably report attending many sport events, thus skewing the

EXHIBIT 14.3   Kurtosis in a distribution.

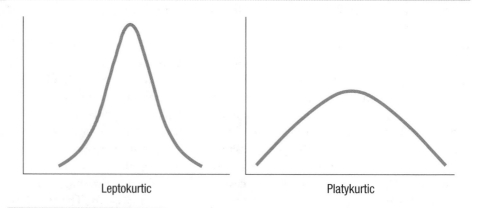

Leptokurtic   Platykurtic

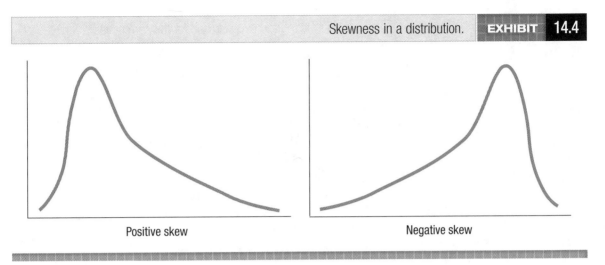

Positive skew   Negative skew

tail of the distribution to the positive side. If the skewed tail is in the direction of negative values, then the distribution is considered **negatively skewed** (a negative skewness value is reported in Excel). The **standard error of skewness** may be calculated as $\sqrt{(6 / n)}$, where n is the sample size. A data set with an absolute skewness value that exceeds twice the standard error of skewness has a distribution that is either positively or negatively skewed.

If the data do not appear normally distributed, then the data set should be checked for outliers. As stated earlier, outliers are extreme values that may be found at one or both ends of the distribution of scores. An outlier may simply be a data entry mistake, which would be easily corrected. If the data are correct, then values that are more than ±3 standard deviations from the mean may be considered as possible outliers (see the discussion of central tendency and variability earlier in this chapter).

A **histogram,** or graphic illustration of the frequency of the data (e.g., bar graph), may be helpful in this regard. For example, a histogram of the frequency of tickets purchased for the current year was created from the MiLB data (see Exhibit 14.5). Notice that the frequency intervals start with 0 tickets purchased and then group the data in intervals of two: 1–2 tickets purchased, 3–4 tickets purchased, 5–6 tickets purchased, and so forth.

For the data used in Exhibit 14.5, the mean was 6.8 with a standard deviation of 5.0. No values in the data set were greater than three standard deviations from the mean (i.e., $6.8 + 5 + 5 + 5 = 21.8$), so we may conclude that this data set does not include any outliers. The normal distribution does provide for outliers, so caution should be used when removing an outlier. If the outlier is not a data-entry mistake and the value could be reasonably obtained from the target population, then the outlier may be kept. The analyst should carefully consider the data to see if a cause can be determined for the extreme value(s).

EXHIBIT 14.5 Histogram of the frequency of MiLB tickets purchased for the current year.

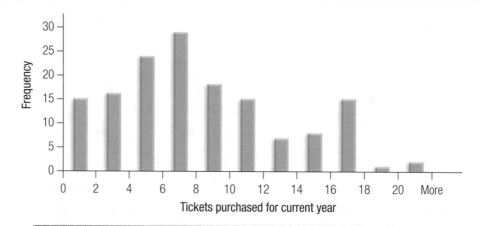

Variance

Another measure of variability is **variance,** a statistic that is related to standard deviation. Variance is another measure of the dispersion of data away from the mean. The variance may be calculated by squaring the standard deviation, and its symbol is s^2. For example, in the survey data of number of tickets purchased, the standard deviation was 6.8, so the variance is 46.24 (i.e., 6.8^2 = 46.24). Since the variance is a value that is not easily interpreted, the variance is rarely, if ever, reported in scholarly articles or professional reports. The standard deviation is typically reported instead.

Range

Range is the final measure of variability. It provides a quick but crude estimate of the variability in a data set and is typically reported in conjunction with the median. We calculate the range by finding the difference between the highest and lowest scores in a set of data. For example, if the youngest and oldest respondents in a survey were 18 and 75 years old, respectively, then the range of age would be 57 years (i.e., 75 − 18 = 57). As we noted in the discussion of standard deviation, the range provides information about the sample that may be used for a variety of marketing and management purposes (examples might be selecting the services to be provided or music to be played at an arena). A small or large range relative to the measure of central tendency gives information about the demographics of the target population. For example, a manager might randomly survey fans who make use of premium seating and suites at a sport venue in order to tailor services to this target population. The manager might focus on more adult-related services (e.g., alcohol sales, more sophisticated food choices) if the age range is relatively small (e.g., 30 to 50 years = 20-year age range). More family-oriented or "kid friendly" services might be considered if the age range is larger (e.g., 5 to 65 years = 60-year range).

MEASURING CENTRAL TENDENCY AND VARIABILITY

You are a member of the front office personnel for a Minor League Base-ball team. Although attendance this season has been on par with previous years, you feel there is potential to increase attendance (and revenue) at these events. Before making any changes, you collect data from 150 participants residing in communities near the stadium (see Chapter 12). You intend to use the data to create a market profile of this community.

Measuring Mean, Median, and Mode

The data for this example are provided in Appendix A and the Excel file available from your instructor. Specifically, for this example, you will focus on the column of sport fandom scores (Column H).

Open the file and highlight a specific cell where you will enter the statistical formula for the mean of the sport fandom scores in this data set. For example, you might select cell H152. Note that in Excel, statistical formulas may be inserted in any cell of the spreadsheet. However, it usually makes the most sense to place the formulas at the end of the associated columns and highlight them in different colors. For example, in this spreadsheet make row 152 the mean and color it orange, make row 153 the median and color it blue, and make row 154 the mode and color it red.

STEP 1

Click on the *Formulas* tab and then select *Insert Function,* found on the left (see Exhibit 14.6).

STEP 2

The Insert Function box should appear (see Exhibit 14.7). From the drop-down menu for selecting the category, select *Statistical.* Highlight AVERAGE in the Select a Function box. Click *OK.*

STEP 3

The Function Arguments box (see Exhibit 14.8) should appear. Place the cursor in the Number1 box. The cells that contain the values for which you wish to calculate the mean might already appear (i.e., H2:H151). However, this may not always be the case, so make sure the correct cells are indicated. If not, then highlight the appropriate values in Column H. To highlight, left-click on cell H2 and hold the mouse button while you scroll down to H151. This should highlight the values from H2 to H151. Notice that the box automatically fills in H1:H151. Click *OK.*

STEP 4

EXHIBIT 14.6   Excel Formulas tab and Insert Function tool for the mean, median, and mode.

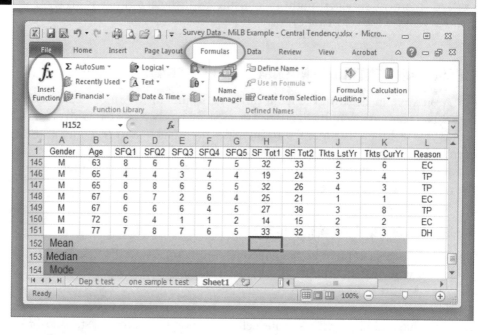

EXHIBIT 14.7   Insert Function box for the mean.

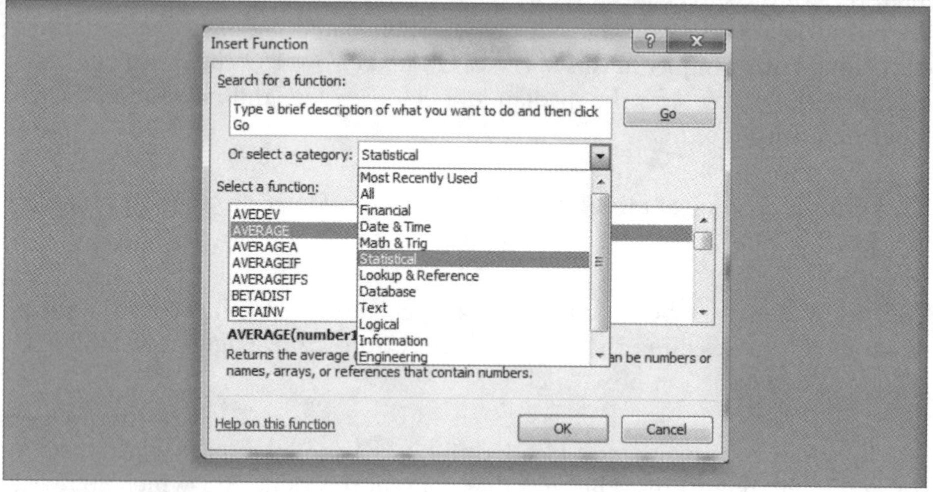

STEP 5   Check to see that the mean appears in cell H152. In this example, the mean sport fandom total score at Time 1 for the 150 community members is 23.59.

Notice that, in Exhibit 14.9, the median for sport fandom total scores at Time 1 appears in cell H153 (i.e., 24.00), and the mode for sport fandom scores appears in cell H154 (i.e., 21). Insert these formulas in the appropri-

Function Arguments box for the mean (average)..   **EXHIBIT** **14.8**

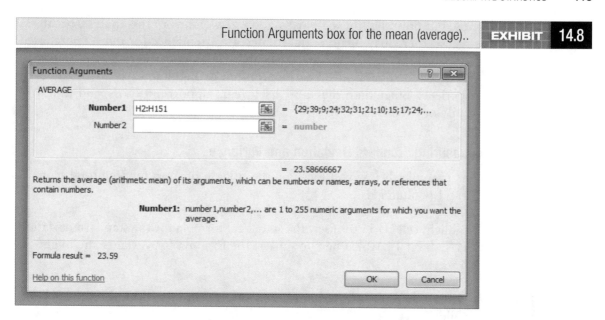

Measures of central tendency in Excel spreadsheet.   **EXHIBIT** **14.9**

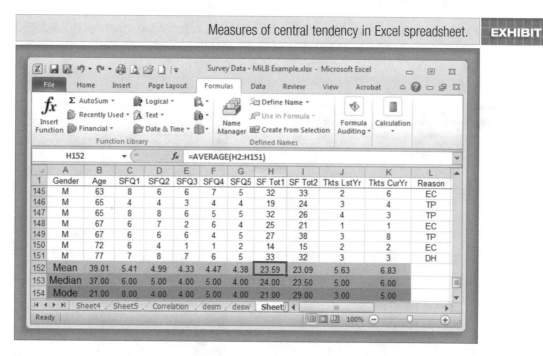

ate cells in the same way you inserted the mean formula in cell H152, except choose MEDIAN or MODE from the Select a Function menu. For completeness, the values for the other columns are also provided in the exhibits.

The mean and median values for sport fandom in this sample of community participants indicate that they do perceive themselves to be sport fans, but only slightly so. This is good news for you, the analyst, because it suggests there may be potential to increase attendance (or tickets purchased) in this community. However, to be successful, any marketing or promotional efforts will probably need to incorporate or highlight aspects of the event experience other than the sport itself (e.g., opportunity to spend time with family or friends).

Measuring Standard Deviation and Variance

The examples below will focus on the column of sport fandom total scores at Time 1 (Column H).

STEP 1   Highlight cell H155 to insert the statistical formula for the standard deviation. (See Exhibit 14.10.) When you insert the formula for variance, highlight cell H156.

STEP 2   Click on the *Formulas* tab and then *Insert Function,* found on the left (see Exhibit 14.10).

STEP 3   From the Select a Category drop-down menu, select *Statistical*. In the Select a Function box, highlight STDEV.S for the standard deviation. When you insert the variance formula, highlight VAR.S. See Exhibit 14.11.

EXHIBIT 14.10   Excel Formulas tab and Insert Function tool for standard deviation and variance.

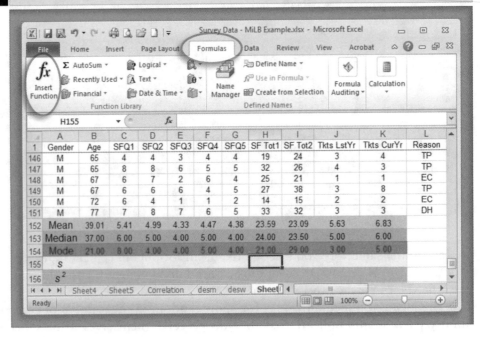

Insert Function box for standard deviation. **EXHIBIT** **14.11**

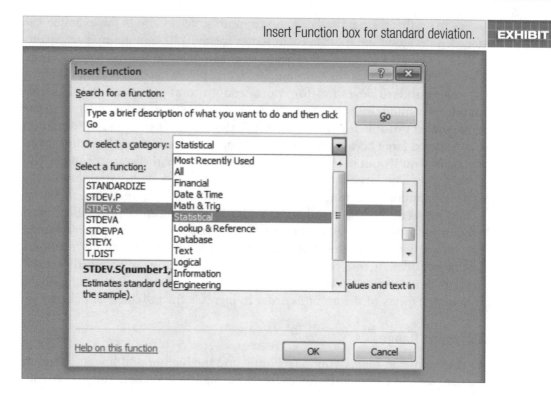

The *Function Arguments* box (see Exhibit 14.12) should appear. Place the cursor **STEP 4** in the Number1 box. Make sure the correct cells are indicated (i.e., H2:H151). If not, then highlight the appropriate values in Column H. Notice that when you highlight the cells, the box automatically fills in H2:H151. Click *OK*.

Function Arguments box for standard deviation. **EXHIBIT** **14.12**

STEP 5   Check to see that the standard deviation appears in cell H155. In this example, the standard deviation for sport fandom scores for the 150 community participants is 9.27. Exhibit 14.13 shows the measures of variability in the Excel spreadsheet. Notice that the variance for sport fandom scores (85.95) appears in cell H156.

The standard deviation for sport fandom total score at Time 1 in this sample of community participants is 9.27. This is a large value, relative to the range that is possible for sport fandom (i.e., 5 to 40). This standard deviation is considered large because if you moved one or two standard deviations from the mean, you would more than likely arrive at either the lower or upper end of the scale. The large standard deviation indicates a high variability in the scores on fandom, meaning that the scores are spread out and you can expect to find scores at the lower and upper ends of the scale rather than tightly clustered around the mean. Since the mean was only slightly above average (i.e., 23), an analyst could infer that a significant portion of community members do not consider themselves to be sport fans. As previously noted, this result suggests that event organizers and marketers will need to include and highlight non-sport aspects of the event in order to increase the purchase of tickets.

Measuring Range

To determine the *range*, you may simply find the highest and lowest values in the data set and subtract the lowest from the highest. Excel can do this for you,

EXHIBIT 14.13   Measures of variability in Excel spreadsheet.

Survey Data - MiLB Example.xlsx - Microsoft Excel

H155 f_x =STDEV.S(H2:H151)

	A	B	C	D	E	F	G	H	I	J	K	L
1	Gender	Age	SFQ1	SFQ2	SFQ3	SFQ4	SFQ5	SF Tot1	SF Tot2	Tkts LstYr	Tkts CurYr	Reason
145	M	63	8	6	6	7	5	32	33	2	6	EC
146	M	65	4	4	3	4	4	19	24	3	4	TP
147	M	65	8	8	6	5	5	32	26	4	3	TP
148	M	67	6	7	2	6	4	25	21	1	1	EC
149	M	67	6	6	6	4	5	27	38	3	8	TP
150	M	72	6	4	1	1	2	14	15	2	2	EC
151	M	77	7	8	7	6	5	33	32	3	3	DH
152	Mean	39.01	5.41	4.99	4.33	4.47	4.38	23.59	23.09	5.63	6.83	
153	Median	37.00	6.00	5.00	4.00	5.00	4.00	24.00	23.50	5.00	6.00	
154	Mode	21.00	8.00	4.00	4.00	5.00	4.00	21.00	29.00	3.00	5.00	
155	s	15.51	1.96	2.07	2.06	2.02	2.03	9.27	8.80	4.26	5.01	
156	s^2	240.62	3.84	4.30	4.25	4.08	4.10	85.95	77.46	18.17	25.05	

Sheet4 / Sheet5 / Correlation / desm / desw / Sheet1

Ready   100%

but the process is slightly more involved. The example below will again focus on the column of sport fandom total scores at Time 1 (Column H).

Highlight cell H157, where you will insert the statistical formula.   **STEP 1**

Click on the *Formulas* tab and then *Insert Function,* on the left (see Exhibit 14.14).   **STEP 2**

The Insert Function box should appear (see Exhibit 14.15). From the Select a Category drop-down menu, select *Statistical.* Highlight MAX in the Select a Function box. Click *OK*.   **STEP 3**

The Function Arguments box should appear. Place the cursor in the Number1 box. Make sure the correct cells are indicated (i.e., H2:H151), and correct them if necessary (see Exhibit 14.16). Click *OK*.   **STEP 4**

Check to see that the score of 40 appears in cell H157.   **STEP 5**

In order to find the range, you now need to subtract the minimum value in the data set from the maximum value. The function for the minimum value is MIN(H2:H151). Be sure cell H157 is highlighted. In Exhibit 14.17 (p.119), look at the circled box, and find the same box on your screen. Position your cursor after the closing parenthesis and type in the rest of the formula. The contents   **STEP 6**

Excel Formulas tab and Insert Function tool for range.	**EXHIBIT**	**14.14**

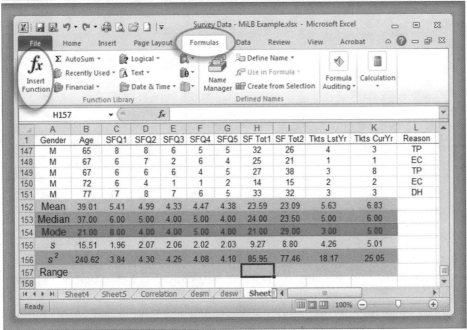

EXHIBIT **14.15** Insert Function box for maximum value in a data set.

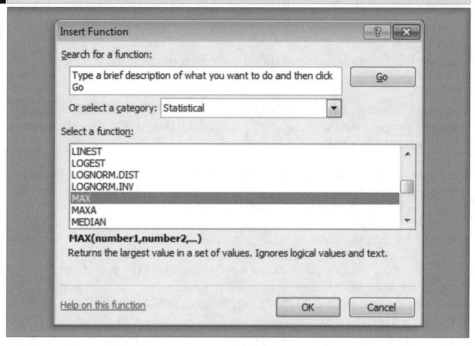

EXHIBIT **14.16** Function Arguments box for maximum value in a data set.

of the box should read = MAX(H2:H151) - MIN(H2:H151). Hit *Enter,* and the range should appear in cell H157. In this example, the maximum value is 40 and the minimum value is 5, so the range is 35.

The range for sport fandom total score at Time 1 in this sample of community members is large (i.e., 35), and it includes the full range of possible scores

	A	B	C	D	E	F	G	H	I	J	K	L
1	Gender	Age	SFQ1	SFQ2	SFQ3	SFQ4	SFQ5	SF Tot1	SF Tot2	Tkts LstYr	Tkts CurYr	Reason
147	M	65	8	8	6	5	5	32	26	4	3	TP
148	M	67	6	7	2	6	4	25	21	1	1	EC
149	M	67	6	6	6	4	5	27	38	3	8	TP
150	M	72	6	4	1	1	2	14	15	2	2	EC
151	M	77	7	8	7	6	5	33	32	3	3	DH
152	Mean	39.01	5.41	4.99	4.33	4.47	4.38	23.59	23.09	5.63	6.83	
153	Median	37.00	6.00	5.00	4.00	5.00	4.00	24.00	23.50	5.00	6.00	
154	Mode	21.00	8.00	4.00	4.00	5.00	4.00	21.00	29.00	3.00	5.00	
155	s	15.51	1.96	2.07	2.06	2.02	2.03	9.27	8.80	4.26	5.01	
156	s^2	240.62	3.84	4.30	4.25	4.08	4.10	85.95	77.46	18.17	25.05	
157	Range	59.00	7.00	7.00	8.00	7.00	7.00	35.00	34.00	20.00	20.00	
158												

Formula bar: H157 fx = MAX(H2:H151) - MIN(H2:H151)

(i.e., 5 to 40). Consistent with our earlier interpretation, there are members of the community that consider themselves to be die-hard sport fans, while others are not sport fans at all, again indicating the potential to increase the team's fan base. Although efforts to increase attendance should rely on more than just one variable, a sport manager might use this information in multiple ways. Campaigns highlighting the success of the baseball team or other sport-related aspects may increase attendance among sport enthusiasts. Efforts that focus on the contribution and role of the baseball team in the community and the non-sport aspects of attending a baseball game may increase attendance among community members who are not sport fans.

Using the Data Analysis ToolPak or StatPlus to Calculate Descriptive Statistics

The use of *Insert Function* to calculate descriptive statistics in an Excel spreadsheet (e.g., mean, standard deviation) is particularly useful if you plan to perform other types of analyses, such as a *t*-test, that may require this information. However, the Data Analysis ToolPak or StatPlus can also provide the measures of central tendency and variability (see Chapter 12 for instructions on installation). If descriptive statistics are all that is required, then this process may be the preferred method, because it can provide all of the information with only a few steps. Below, we describe the process for obtaining the descriptive statistics for the sport fandom total score at Time 1 (Column H) with the Data Analysis ToolPak and StatPlus. Differences in the process for StatPlus will be noted in the steps below. As discussed in Chapter 12, there may also be slight differences in the output.

STEP 1   Click on the *Data* tab and then *Data Analysis,* found on the far right. The *Data Analysis* box should appear (see Exhibit 14.18). For Mac users, in StatPlus, click on *Statistics*, then *Basic Statistics and Tables*.

STEP 2   From the *Analysis Tools* menu, select *Descriptive Statistics* (see Exhibit 14.19). Click *OK*.

STEP 3   The Descriptive Statistics box (see Exhibit 14.20) should appear. Place the cursor in the Input Range box, and then highlight the appropriate values in Column H on the spreadsheet (the values for which you wish to find the descriptive statistics). The input should read $H$2:$H$151. Select *Grouped By Columns*. Under Output options, select *New Worksheet Ply* and type in a title for the new worksheet (i.e., Descriptive). If you wish, you may select *Output Range* or *New Workbook* instead of *New Worksheet Ply,* which will place the output on the current spreadsheet or in a new workbook, respectively. Last, make sure to select the boxes for *Summary Statistics* and *Confidence Level for Mean*. Click *OK*. For StatPlus, place the cursor in the *Variables* box and then highlight the appropriate values. Click *OK*.

EXHIBIT 14.18   Excel Data tab and Data Analysis option.

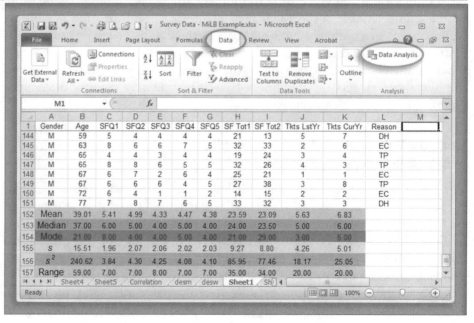

Data Analysis box for descriptive statistics.   **EXHIBIT 14.19**

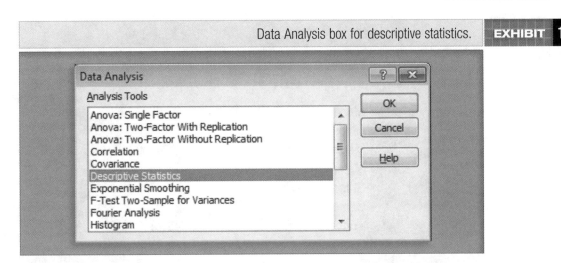

Descriptive statistics box.   **EXHIBIT 14.20**

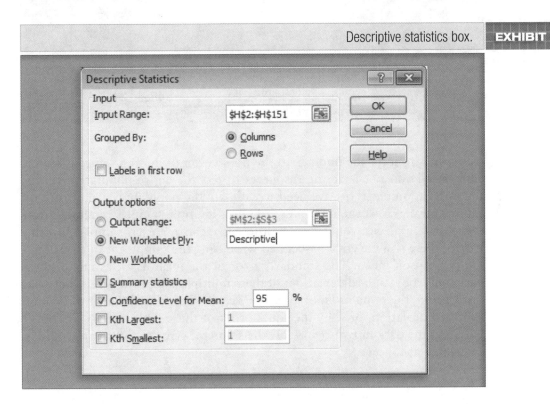

Exhibit 14.21 shows the output for the descriptive statistics that will be calculated. As you can see, all measures of central tendency and variability are provided, as well as some other measures. Of particular relevance are the standard error and the confidence interval (CI).

The standard error given in this output is actually the **standard error of the mean** (SE_M). As stated earlier, one of the main purposes of descriptive

EXHIBIT 14.21	Excel output for sport fandom total score at Time 1.

SF Tot1	
Mean	23.5867
Standard Error	0.7570
Median	24.0000
Mode	21.0000
Standard Deviation	9.2709
Sample Variance	85.9488
Kurtosis	-0.7819
Skewness	-0.0944
Range	35.0000
Minimum	5.0000
Maximum	40.0000
Sum	3538.0000
Count	150.0000
Confidence Level(95.0%)	1.4958

statistics is to infer the findings to the population of interest. Since researchers typically do not have the resources to test the entire population to find the population mean (μ), we need to estimate the population mean from the sample mean. However, if we were to select multiple samples randomly from the population, we would find a different mean for each sample. In other words, there is some error associated with using the sample mean to estimate the population mean. The standard error of the mean is an estimate of the variability, or standard deviation, of these multiple sample means if they were drawn from the population of interest. We calculate it by dividing the sample standard deviation, or s, by the square root of the sample size (N or count). Based on the data in Exhibit 14.21, the standard error of the mean would be calculated as follows:

$$SE_M = \frac{s}{\sqrt{N}} = \frac{9.2709}{\sqrt{150}} = .7570$$

The standard error of the mean may be used to establish a **confidence interval (CI)** around the sample mean. The confidence interval is a range of values that has a certain level of probability of containing the true population mean. As discussed in the section on variability, if the scores in a data set are widely dispersed, then the sample mean may not be very representative of the data set, and in such a case the confidence interval will be larger. If the

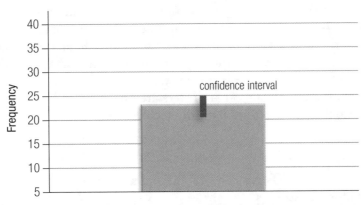

Mean Sport Fandom Total Score at Time 1 = 23.59

measure is more precise, with less variability, then the confidence interval will be smaller. Specifically, a 95% CI sets lower and upper ranges around the statistic (i.e., sample mean), which are functions of the standard error of the mean and the confidence interval for the standard normal distribution. We calculate these lower and upper ranges by subtracting and adding the 95% CI value (i.e., 1.50, from Exhibit 14.21) to the mean (23.59), respectively. Based on the descriptive statistics from Exhibit 14.21, the true population mean would lie between 22.09 and 25.09 with a probability of 95%. A bar graph may be used to show the mean, with error bars for the upper and lower CI (see Exhibit 14.22).

A sport manager would use this information to gain a better understanding of the actual level of sport fandom in the population of interest. Since the CI is only three points (25.09 − 22.09) on a 35-point scale (possible scores range from 5 to 40), the sport manager could reasonably conclude that the population mean is, like the sample mean, somewhere around a moderate level of sport fandom.

STANDARDIZED SCORES

R esearchers may collect data from study participants by using many different measures. Each of these measures may use different scales, making it difficult to interpret the data from the **raw scores**. For example, a person's sport fandom total score of, say, 30 (with possible scores ranging from 5 to 40) is calculated with a completely different scale than the number of tickets purchased by the participant over the past month, which can range from 0 to the total number of tickets available for purchase in that time interval. In order to understand how an individual participant's sport fandom score or number of tickets purchased (or any other measure) compares to the entire sample, we need to know the mean and standard deviation for each measure. There is a way to save time and facilitate interpretation of the data: we can *standardize* the scores, or convert each raw score to an equivalent standard score, such as a Z-score or a T-score. This is often helpful because it clarifies, for example, whether a sport fandom score of 30 is a low score or a high score, compared to others in the data set. When the population mean and standard deviation are known and the sample size is greater than 30, then Z-scores are usually recommended. If the population parameters are unknown and the sample size is less than 30, then T-scores are typically recommended.

Z-score

A Z-score distribution has a mean of 0.00 and a standard deviation of 1.00. The formula for a **Z-score** is

$$Z\text{-score} = \frac{(X - \mu)}{\sigma}$$

We can calculate it in the following manner:

- subtract the population mean (μ) from a participant's raw score *(X)*, and
- divide the result by the population standard deviation (σ).

If the population parameters are unknown, then you may use the sample mean and standard deviation.

For example, suppose a participant's raw score on the Sport Fandom Questionnaire is 33 (see cell H151 in Exhibit 14.23), the sample mean is 23.59 (cell H152), and the sample mean standard deviation is 9.27 (see cell H155). Also, this participant purchased 3 tickets last year (see cell J151) with a sample mean of 5.63 (see cell J152) and a sample mean standard deviation of 4.26 (see cell J155). To convert the participant's Sport Fandom raw score of 33 to a Z-score, we subtract the mean of 23.59, obtaining 9.41. Then, we divide 9.41 by the sample mean standard deviation, 9.27. The resulting Z-score is 1.02. A similar process would be done for tickets purchased.

$$\frac{(33 - 23.59)}{9.27} = 1.02$$

$$\frac{(3 - 5.63)}{4.26} = -0.62$$

We might report this finding as follows:

Sport Fandom Total scores and tickets purchased at Time 1 were calculated for a sample of 150 community members, and these raw scores were converted to Z-scores. A person with a raw Sport Fandom score of 33 and 3 tickets purchased would have an equivalent *Z*-score of 1.02 and −0.62, respectively. This *Z*-score indicates that the person's Sport Fandom score is above the mean for the entire sample by about 1 standard deviation, but that this person purchased fewer tickets last year compared to the entire sample by a little over one-half standard deviation.

The information provided in the report above indicates that the person's interest in sport is well above the average for the sample, but the person has purchased fewer tickets than would be expected on average in this community. This finding may indicate that the person lacks the financial ability to purchase more tickets or that the person has chosen not to purchase the tickets for some other reason(s). As a result of these findings, an analyst may seek a better understanding regarding why they have chosen not to purchase more tickets, or this person may be targeted to increase his or her awareness of ticket packages that decrease ticket costs. Regardless, this strategy should be beneficial to the agency to improve ticket purchases in the future.

We can use Excel to convert a raw score to a *Z*-score. Select an empty cell (e.g., M151) where you would like the *Z*-score to be placed (see Exhibit 14.23). Click on the *Formulas* tab and select *Insert Function*. In the pop-up

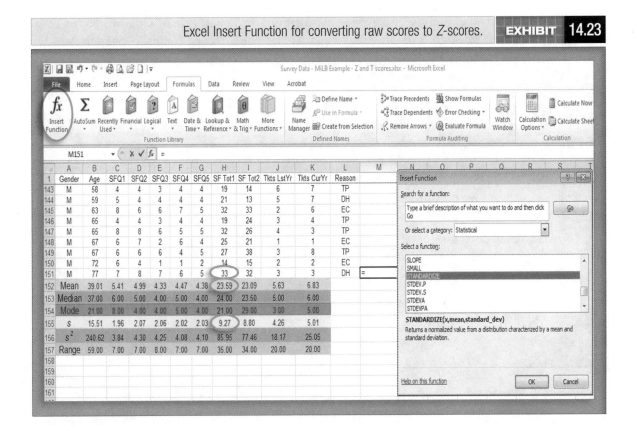

Excel Insert Function for converting raw scores to *Z*-scores.   **EXHIBIT 14.23**

box, select the *Statistical* category, and then scroll to the STANDARDIZE function. Click *OK*.

The Function Arguments box will require you to input the participant's raw score, the mean, and the standard deviation. Select the cells on the Excel spreadsheet where this information is located: H151, H152, and H155, respectively. Click *OK*, and the Z-score will be calculated (see Exhibit 14.24).

The Excel formula for the Z-score is: =STANDARDIZE(H151,H152, H155). If you wish to use this formula to convert multiple raw scores, then you will need to insert a dollar symbol ($) in front of the column and row designations for the cells that contain the mean and standard deviation. The dollar signs tell Excel that the mean is *always* to be found in cell H152, and the standard deviation is *always* to be found in cell H155. Without the dollar signs, Excel would assume that when it moves to the next row for the next value of *X*, it also needs to move to the next row for the next value of the mean, and likewise for the value of the standard deviation, resulting in erroneous calculations. Hence, the formula to calculate Z-scores for multiple raw scores will look like this:

=STANDARDIZE(H151,$H$152,$H$155).

You can copy and paste this formula into each cell in Column M, in rows 2 through 150, in order to calculate the Z-score for each participant. See Exhibit 14.25.

EXHIBIT 14.24	Function Arguments box for calculation of *Z*-scores.

Function Arguments

STANDARDIZE

X	H151	= 33
Mean	$H$152	= 23.58666667
Standard_dev	$H$155	= 9.270858338

= 1.015368048

Returns a normalized value from a distribution characterized by a mean and standard deviation.

Standard_dev is the standard deviation of the distribution, a positive number.

Formula result = 1.015368048

Help on this function   OK   Cancel

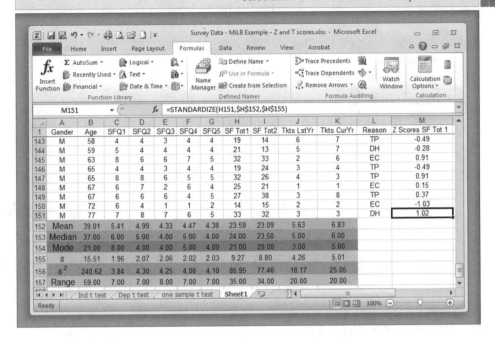

Calculation of *Z*-scores in Excel spreadsheet.   **EXHIBIT 14.25**

T-score

A *T*-score distribution has a mean of 50.00 and a standard deviation of 10.00. A **T-score** may be calculated from a *Z*-score by multiplying the *Z*-score by 10 and then adding 50. Specifically, the formula for the *T*-score is

$$T = (Z \times 10) + 50$$

A *Z*-score of 1.02 is equivalent to a *T*-score of 60.2. (10 x 1.02 + 50 = 60.2). This finding could be reported in the following manner:

> Sport fandom total scores at Time 1 were calculated for a sample of 150 community members, and these raw scores were converted to *T*-scores. A raw score of 33 would be equivalent to a *T*-score of 60.2. This *T*-score indicates that a score of 33 is above the mean for the entire sample by about 1 standard deviation.

Excel does not provide a function for *T*-scores, but you may create a formula. Suppose a participant's raw score has been converted to a *Z*-score, which is located in cell M2. Select an empty cell where you would like the *T*-score to be placed (i.e., N2; see Exhibit 14.26). At the top of the spreadsheet, in the f_x box, type in **=M2*10+50**. If you wish to use this formula to convert multiple *Z*-scores to *T*-scores, then copy and paste the cell with the formula to the rest of the cells in Column N. Remember, converting all relevant data to *T*-scores (or *Z*-scores) will allow a sport manager to make cross-comparisons of data that were originally scored with different scales.

| EXHIBIT | 14.26 | Calculation of *T*-scores in Excel spreadsheet. |

	A	B	C	D	E	F	G	H	I	J	K	L	M	N
1	Gender	Age	SFQ1	SFQ2	SFQ3	SFQ4	SFQ5	SF Tot1	SF Tot2	Tkts LstYr	Tkts CurYr	Reason	Z Scores SF Tot 1	T Scores SF Tot 1
2	F	18	7	7	4	5	6	29	29	1	3	EC	0.58	55.84
3	F	18	8	8	8	8	7	39	35	12	15	EC	1.66	66.63
4	F	19	2	2	2	2	1	9	8	2	1	EC	-1.57	34.27
5	F	20	8	5	4	3	4	24	29	9	13	TP	0.04	50.45
6	F	20	7	7	4	7	7	32	25	2	6	TP	0.91	59.08
7	F	20	6	6	7	6	6	31	10	4	3	EC	0.80	58.00
8	F	21	5	4	4	4	4	21	25	8	5	OF	-0.28	47.21
9	F	21	4	2	2	1	1	10	15	9	7	TP	-1.47	35.34
10	F	21	3	3	3	3	3	15	17	1	5	OF	-0.93	40.74
11	F	21	6	4	3	2	2	17	14	7	10	EC	-0.71	42.90

RESEARCH SCENARIO II

PRACTICE PROBLEM FOR DESCRIPTIVE STATISTICS

In this scenario, the analyst for a health club has surveyed 30 male and 30 female members by using a stratified sampling technique. Among the various questions, participants were asked, "On average, how frequently do you come to use the facility? _____ times per week." Participants were asked to provide a number to fill in the blank. The analyst will use this information to obtain descriptive statistics of male and female members and will provide these statistics to the owner of the health club so that she or he can better understand members' facility usage. When members use the facility infrequently, they are likely to discontinue their membership. The statistical information will help the owner determine whether action is needed to influence facility usage.

Questions

Use the data provided for Scenario II and the procedures discussed in this chapter to complete the following activities or answer the questions:

1. Calculate the value of the mean weekly facility usage for both men and women in this distribution.

2. What is the value of the mode for weekly facility usage for men and women?

3. Which score in the distribution is the median for weekly facility usage for men and women?

4. Calculate the variance and standard deviation for weekly facility usage for men and women.

5. What is the range for weekly facility usage for men and women?

6. What is the standard error of the mean for weekly facility usage for men and women?

7. What is the confidence level around the sample mean for weekly facility usage for men and women? What is the significance of the confidence level?

8. Given the statistics calculated above, how should the analyst advise the club owner about facility usage?

TALKING POINTS

Descriptive Statistics

- Measures of central tendency allow the analyst to describe a collection of scores or values quickly and to evaluate how any one particular score or value compares with the middle (or central) scores in a set of data.

- Measures of variability indicate how far apart (or widely dispersed) scores are in a data set and allow the analyst to evaluate how well a measure of central tendency represents the data.

- The data should be examined for skewness and kurtosis.

- The standard error of the mean may be used to establish a confidence interval (CI) around the sample mean that has a certain level of probability of containing the true population mean.

- Raw data scores may be converted to standardized Z-scores when the population mean and standard deviation are known and the sample size is greater than 30.

- Raw data scores may be converted to standardized T-scores when the population parameters are unknown and the sample size is less than 30.

CHAPTER

15

Correlation

EXECUTIVE SUMMARY Understanding how variables are related can help a sport manager identify variables to target in marketing and promotions or in other types of research (e.g., management style/traits, employee satisfaction, revenue). In a correlation analysis, we calculate the relationship between two or more variables. The most common correlation is the simple correlation, or Pearson's correlation, which quantifies the relationship between two variables. It is very important to keep in mind that, although the observation of correlations can be very useful, we cannot infer *causation* from a correlation.

WHAT IS A CORRELATION?

Correlation refers to the degree of the relationship between two or more variables that are measured on an interval or ratio scale. As mentioned above, the most common type of correlation is a *simple correlation,* also known as *bivariate correlation, inter-class correlation,* or *Pearson product-moment correlation coefficient.* We will discuss this type of correlation first and then discuss intra-class correlation and Cronbach's alpha.

SIMPLE CORRELATION

A simple correlation provides a quantitative value to the degree that two variables are linearly related to each other. For a simple correlation, the **test statistic**, or final calculated value of a statistical test, is r. The **correlation coefficient** or r value is a measure of the strength of the linear relationship between two variables. A correlation coefficient of 0 indicates that the variables are not related to each other, and an r value of +1 or –1 indicates that the two variables are perfectly correlated. In sport management, as in many other fields, however, the values never reach +1 or –1; they always fall somewhere in between. Values cannot exceed ±1.00.

If the r value is between 0 and +1, then this is considered a positive correlation. A positive correlation means that higher values on one variable are associated with higher values on the other variable, and vice versa. In other words, the values for both variables move in the same direction. For example, as a team's winning percentage increases, spectator attendance also increases. If the r value for a relationship is between 0 and –1, then this is considered a negative correlation. A negative correlation means that higher values on one variable are associated with lower values on the other variable. In this case, the values move in opposite directions. For example, an increase in employee satisfaction is associated with a decrease in employee absences.

The fact that a simple correlation identifies a linear relationship between two variables means that we can add a **best fit line** to a scatterplot of the data. This is simply a line that best represents the set of data. The strength of the correlation depends on how far the data points deviate from the best fit line, rather than falling directly on the slope of the line. Exhibit 15.1 provides examples of a positive correlation and a negative correlation, as well as a case where the variables are not related to each other.

Correlation Does Not Equal Causation

Although two variables may be related to each other, causation cannot be determined from a correlation alone. For example, in a survey of spectators at a sport event, an analyst may discover that sport fandom (a person's view of himself or herself as a sport fan) is correlated with spectator enjoyment. While it is possible that high levels of sport fandom cause high levels of enjoyment, it is also possible (perhaps even likely) that another variable or group of variables is the true causative factor for spectator enjoyment (e.g., who the fan attends the game with). Correlation is a necessary but not sufficient component for establishing causation. A rigorous, carefully controlled experimental study is the only method for providing evidence that one variable (i.e., the independent variable) causes an effect on another variable (i.e., the dependent variable).

EXHIBIT 15.1 Examples of positive, negative, and no-relationship correlations.

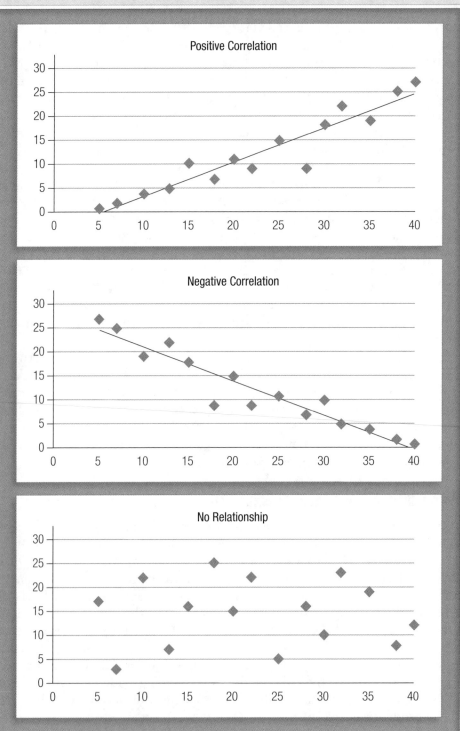

Calculating a Simple Correlation

Chapter 12 introduced Research Scenario I, in which you are studying attendance for a MiLB team by collecting data from 150 community participants. Suppose you have decided to calculate the correlation between sport fandom and the number of baseball tickets individual participants purchased last year. If these two variables are related, then you might consider developing marketing strategies and promotions that either target "hard core" fans or reach out to the community to foster sport fandom.

For this example, you will focus on the column of sport fandom total scores (column H) and the number of baseball tickets purchased last year (column J). You will use the Data Analysis ToolPak or StatPlus.

Excel is a bit inflexible on some issues, and in statistical analysis the software requires that the data be placed in contiguous (adjacent) columns. The quickest way around this issue is simply to copy and paste the data into new columns, so that the data you require are in side-by-side columns. For this example (see Exhibit 15.2), the data have been copied and placed into columns N (SF Tot1) and O (Tkts LstYr). The data in the original columns (H and J) have been retained. Copy and paste these columns in your own spreadsheet.

STEP 1

Click on the *Data* tab and on *Data Analysis* on the far right. In StatPlus, click on *Statistics* and then *Basic Statistics and Tables*.

STEP 2

The Data Analysis box should appear (see Exhibit 15.3). Select *Correlation* from the Analysis Tools menu. Click *OK*. In StatPlus, click on *Linear Correlation (Pearson)*.

STEP 3

Excel spreadsheet prepared for calculating a correlation.   **EXHIBIT 15.2**

| EXHIBIT | 15.3 | Excel's Data Analysis box for correlation. |

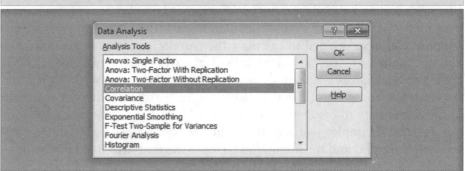

STEP 4   The Correlation box (see Exhibit 15.4) should appear. Place the cursor in the *Input Range* box, and then highlight the appropriate values in columns N and O on the spreadsheet. The input should read **$N$2:$O$151**, and the input should be Grouped By Columns. If an option appears for Labels in the First Row, then check this box. Under Output Options, select *New Worksheet Ply* and enter a title for the new worksheet (e.g., Correlation). If you wish, you may select Output Range or New Workbook, which will put the output on the current spreadsheet or in a new workbook, respectively. Click *OK*. In StatPlus, place the cursor in the *Variables* box and then highlight the appropriate values. Click *OK*.

   The output for the correlation should indicate that the correlation between sport fandom total scores and tickets purchased last year is 0.52987 (see Exhibit 15.5).

STEP 5   Unfortunately, Excel does not provide a *p* value for this correlational value. (Recall from Chapter 13 that the *p* value is the probability that a test statistic of

| EXHIBIT | 15.4 | Excel's Correlation box. |

EXHIBIT 15.5

Excel's output for correlation between sport fandom and tickets purchased.

	SF Tot1	Tkts LstYr
SF Tot1	1	
Tkts LstYr	0.52987	1

a size indicating a finding of significance would emerge from the data, assuming the null hypothesis is true.) Since the p value is not provided, you will need to use a table of critical values for correlation coefficients to find the r value, or critical r value, based on the tailness, degrees of freedom, and alpha level of your study. (These tables are widely available on the internet; e.g., www.radford.edu/~jaspelme/statsbook/Chapter%20files/Table_of_Critical_Values_for_r.pdf.) You will then compare your calculated r value obtained from Excel against the critical r value from the table to evaluate the statistical significance of your calculated r value. *Note:* To use the table of critical values, you will need to know whether the correlation is for a one-tailed or two-tailed distribution, the degrees of freedom (df), and the alpha level (α).

Tailness. First, you will need to know whether the correlation is *one-tailed* or *two-tailed*. Statistical tests, such as Pearson's r, use a probability distribution similar to the normal distribution (see Exhibit 15.6) to illustrate the calculated test statistic. For correlation, the central point of the distribution indicates that there is no relationship between the two variables ($r = 0$; the null hypothesis is true). As r values increase in absolute value, they will move toward the tails of the distribution.

The question, then, is How large does the test statistic, r, have to be to be considered statistically significant? Together with the alpha value, selection of either a one-tailed or two-tailed test will establish the cutoff value for statistical significance. For a **one-tailed statistical test**, we look to only one tail of the distribution to find the level of significance (e.g., $\alpha = .05$). In other words, the analyst is hypothesizing that the relationship between the variables lies in one direction only (either positive or negative). One-tailed tests are not very common, but they may be used when strong theoretical or empirical evidence suggests that the relationship will be either positive or negative. For a **two-tailed statistical test**, the level of significance is split in half (e.g., $\alpha = .05/2 = .025$), with half occurring on each tail of the distribution. In other words, the analyst is hypothesizing that the relationship between the variables may be either positive or negative. Two-tailed tests are much more common than one-tailed tests. They are typically used when little research exists on the variables of interest. For example, in

EXHIBIT **15.6** Distribution of correlational test statistic.

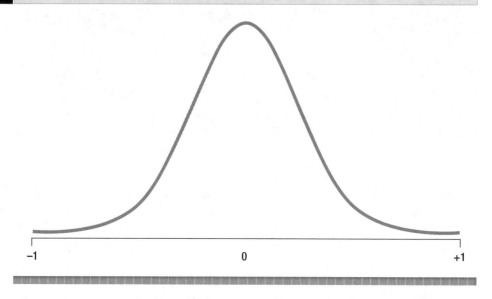

the MiLB scenario, you might use a one-tailed test when examining gender and sport fandom, as consistent empirical evidence holds that men report higher sport fandom scores than do women. However, you might use a two-tailed test when examining age and sport fandom, as there is little research available on this topic, and the findings have not been consistent. For the example of sport fandom and tickets purchased, a two-tailed test would be appropriate, because it is unknown whether the relationship between the two variables is positive or negative.

Degrees of freedom. Briefly, **degrees of freedom** (df) is the number of values used in the final calculation of a statistic that are free to vary. For example, if you know that the sum of sport fandom scores for 10 people equals 200, then you actually need to know only 9 scores, and then you can determine the 10th score by subtraction. In this case, the degrees of freedom is 9 ($N - 1$). The calculation of df will vary depending on the statistical test. Each parameter being estimated from the data set "costs" one degree of freedom, and the remaining degrees of freedom are used to estimate the variability. For our example, we have two parameters—fandom and tickets purchased. To calculate the degrees of freedom in this example, we start with the number of paired observations in the data set, i.e., the number of participants (150) that have data for both variables (fandom and tickets purchased). Then, we subtract 2, because we are examining the two variables in the correlation. Hence, for the example, df = $150 - 2 = 148$.

Alpha level. Alpha level was discussed in Chapter 13. To summarize, the alpha level controls for the probability of making a Type I error, and it is established by the analyst. The most common alpha levels are 0.05 and 0.01. As stated in Chapter 13, research for sport management purposes typically uses a 0.05 alpha level.

Interpreting the results: Statistical significance

Suppose that prior to analyzing the data, you have decided to use a two-tailed test with alpha = 0.05, and df = 148, for the reasons given above. Since most tables only report up to 100 df, in this case, you should use the df associated with ∞. Based on these criteria, the critical r value from the table of critical values is 0.087. In other words, this critical correlation coefficient of 0.087 has a p value equal to 0.05 based on the specified tailness, df, and alpha level. Calculated correlational values that are greater than the critical r value of 0.087 would have a p value (or probability that the correlation is a chance occurrence) that is less than 0.05. Calculated correlations that are less than the critical r value of 0.087 would have a p value that is greater than 0.05.

The next step is to compare the critical r value against the calculated r value, disregarding the sign (+ or −) of the calculated r value. If the calculated r value (i.e., 0.52987) is greater than the critical r value (0.087), as is the case for our example, then you reject the null hypothesis and conclude that the calculated r value is significant. This means that the two variables (fandom and tickets purchased) are significantly related to each other. If the calculated r value is less than the critical r value, then you do not reject the null hypothesis, and your conclusion is that the calculated r value is not significant.

If the df associated with the study is not specifically listed in the table (i.e., it falls between two df reported in the table), then you compare the calculated r value to both of the two values that it falls between. If the calculated r value is greater than the critical r value associated with the smaller df, you conclude that the r value is significant. If it is less than the critical r value associated with the larger of the df, you conclude that it is not significant. Occasionally, this procedure will not work because the calculated r value is somewhere between two listed critical r values that are far apart. In such a case, you must interpolate the critical value.

Interpolation example. Suppose you have df = 45 and calculated r = .27. For an alpha of 0.05 (two-tailed test), the table provides only critical r values for df = 40 (r = .304) and df = 60 (r = .250). In this case, you would interpolate a value for df = 45 as follows:

- First, calculate the difference between the two critical values: 0.304 − 0.250 = .054.
- Second, calculate the difference between the two df: 60 − 40 = 20.
- Third, divide the value from step 1 by the value from step 2: .054 / 20 = .0027.

- Fourth, subtract the study's df from the larger df: 60 − 45 = 15.
- Fifth, multiply the step 3 and 4 values: 15 x .0027 = .0405.
- Last, add the step 5 value to the smaller critical *r* value: 0.0405 + 0.25 = .2905.

In this example, since the calculated *r* value (0.27) is not larger than the interpolated critical *r* value (0.2905), you would conclude that the two variables are not significantly related or correlated with each other.

Calculators for statistical table entries. Another strategy for finding the *p* value is to use the Internet to find a calculator for statistical table entries (e.g., http:// vassarstats.net/tabs.html#r). These calculators are not as commonly available as the tables, but they are very easy to use. Simply fill in the required data, such as *N* (df + 2) and the calculated *r* value, and click on Calculate (see Exhibit 15.7). The calculator returns the *p* value for both a one-tailed and a two-tailed test. For the interpolation example, the *p* value (0.0664) is greater than the alpha (0.05), so you would conclude that the calculated *r* value is not significant. For the sport fandom/ticket purchase example, however, the *p* value (<.0001) is less than the alpha (0.05), so you would conclude that the calculated *r* value is significant.

Interpreting the results: Practical significance (meaningfulness)

The measure of meaningfulness for a simple correlation is the coefficient of determination. The **coefficient of determination** is the percent of variance that is shared between the two variables. The closer the data are to the best fit line (refer back to Exhibit 15.1), the higher the percentage of variation that is shared, resulting in a greater ability to use scores from one variable to understand (or predict) scores for the other variable. Calculation of the coefficient of determination is very simple. It is the square of the correlation coefficient, or r^2. For example,

EXHIBIT 15.7   Calculator for *p* values for the research scenario (left) and interpolation example (right).

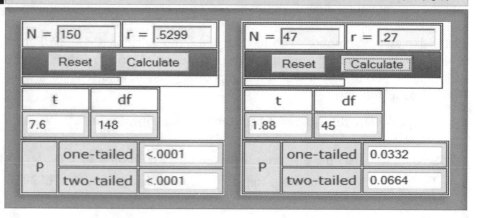

in the research scenario, the correlation coefficient between sport fandom total scores and tickets purchased last year was 0.5299, so the coefficient of determination is $r^2 = .5299^2 = 0.2808$. This means that about 28% of the variation in sport fandom total scores and tickets purchased last year is shared between these two variables, leaving about 72% of the variation in the two variables unexplained or explained by other variables. In other words, you would need to explore other variables (e.g., gender, income) to understand why some people are lower or higher on sport fandom or the number of tickets purchased last year.

Here is a general guideline for interpreting the coefficient of determination:

- $r^2 = .01$ is considered a small effect (1% shared variance),
- $r^2 = .09$ is considered a moderate effect (9% shared variance), and
- $r^2 = .25$ and above is considered a large effect (25% shared variance).

In general, most analysts want to find large effects, as this allows the analyst to target one of the variables (i.e., sport fandom) to see how much of an effect it can have on the other, related variable (e.g., ticket purchase intentions). In other situations, small effects may be desirable. For example, if age has a small effect on sport fandom, then marketing strategies designed to increase sport fandom may not need to take age into consideration.

Statistical statement

When researchers report the results of a study, they provide the findings of the statistical analysis in the Results section of the article. The standard way of reporting the results of a correlation consists of: 1) a brief restatement of the statistical tests and the variables involved and 2) the statistical statement, followed by 3) a brief description of the findings. The statistical statement includes the calculated r value (test statistic) and the p value associated with the test statistic.

For the research scenario, the results of the correlational analysis would be reported in a scholarly article in the following manner:

> In a sample of 150 community participants, the relationship between sport fandom total scores and the number of baseball tickets purchased last year was calculated by using a simple (Pearson) correlation. The correlation was significant, with $r = .5299$, $p < .05$. An increase in sport fandom scores was associated with an increase in tickets purchased last year, and a large proportion of variance was shared between the two variables ($r^2 = .28$).
>
> *Note:* If the correlation was not significant, then $p >$ would be used. For example, $r = .01$, $p > .05$. In some instances, the specific p value for the test statistic may be reported (e.g., $p = .14$). This may be done whether the test statistic is significant or not.

For a non-scholarly report, the results would be presented in the following manner:

> People in the local community (75 men and 75 women) were surveyed on how many tickets they purchased last year and whether they consider themselves to be sports fans

(i.e., sport fandom), which was rated on a scale from 5 to 40 (5 = not a sport fan at all, 40 = very much a sport fan). Sport fandom was found to be related to how many tickets they purchased last year. The more strongly people considered themselves to be sport fans, the more tickets they purchased. The relationship was strong and meaningful, indicating that future strategies that involve improving people's perceptions about sport fandom should be associated with an increase in tickets purchased.

As discussed in Chapter 3, to determine test–retest reliability the same measure is used on separate days (or trials) within a specified time period, such as the next day, a week later, or perhaps a month later. These trials are then correlated with each other, typically with an intra-class correlation. The time period is crucial, as the correlation between two trials is typically stronger for shorter time intervals than longer ones.

RESEARCH SCENARIO I

Calculating Intra-class Correlation

We will measure the test–retest reliability of the sport fandom total scores administered at Time 1 (column H) and approximately six months later, at Time 2 (column I). *Note:* This statistical test is not available in the free version of StatPlus.

STEP 1 Click on the *Data* tab and then on *Data Analysis* on the far right (see Exhibit 15.8).

STEP 2 The Data Analysis box should appear (see Exhibit 15.9). Select *Anova: Two-Factor Without Replication* from the Analysis Tools menu. Click *OK*. Note

EXHIBIT 15.8   Excel's Data tab and Data Analysis option for intra-class correlation.

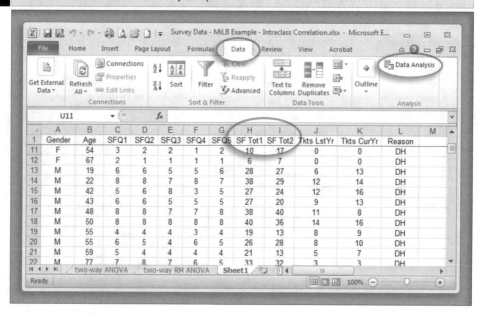

Excel's Data Analysis box for intra-class correlation.   **EXHIBIT** **15.9**

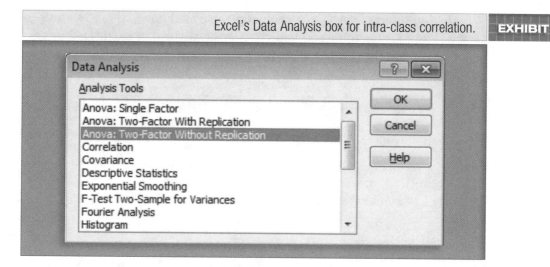

that you will use the ANOVA tool to obtain the information needed for calculating the ICC. The tool produces a summary table that provides information for the ICC, as well as for the Analysis of Variance statistical technique. The information related to ANOVA will be discussed in Chapter 18.

The Anova: Two-Factor Without Replication box (see Exhibit 15.10) should **STEP 3** appear. Place the cursor in the *Input Range* box, and then highlight the appropriate values in columns H and I. The input should read **$H$2:$I$151**. Leave the alpha at 0.05. Under Output Options, select *New Worksheet Ply, Output Range,* or *New Workbook,* and add a title if you are using a new worksheet (e.g., Intra-class Correlation). Click *OK.*

Excel's Anova Two-Factor Without Replication box for intra-class correlation.   **EXHIBIT** **15.10**

The output in the ANOVA summary table (Exhibit 15.11, rows 159 to 165) will provide the information necessary for calculating the intra-class correlation. The formula for calculating the ICC is:

$$ICC = \frac{(MSRows - MSError)}{[MSRows + (dfColumns)(MSError) + (dfColumns + 1)(MSColumns - MSError) / (dfRows + 1)]}$$

Type the following formula in cell B167 (see Exhibit 15.11):

=(D161-D163)/(D161+C162*D163+(C162+1)*(D162-D163)/(C161+1))

Exhibit 15.11 shows the results of the calculation (ICC = .8848).

Interpreting the results

Interpretation of an intra-class correlation is similar to interpretation of a Pearson's correlation, discussed earlier. Basically, a value approaching 1 indicates a relatively strong relationship or more stable measure, and a value approaching 0 indicates a relatively weak relationship or less stable measure. The test–retest reliability should be strong for shorter time intervals; however, a weaker test–retest reliability coefficient might be desirable for longer time intervals, as this may indicate that the measure is sensitive to change. Since sport fandom is a dispositional characteristic that is developed over

EXHIBIT 15.11 Intra-class correlation output in Excel spreadsheet.

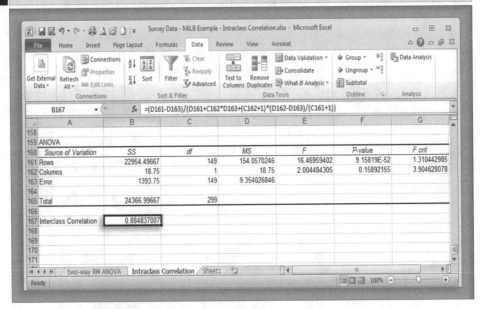

Source of Variation	SS	df	MS	F	P-value	F crit
Rows	22954.49667	149	154.0570246	16.46959402	9.15819E-52	1.310442985
Columns	18.75	1	18.75	2.004484305	0.15892155	3.904628078
Error	1393.75	149	9.354026846			
Total	24366.99667	299				

Interclass Correlation: 0.884837007

many years of a person's life, this variable would not be expected to change very much in a relatively short time interval of, say, six months. The intra-class correlation analysis supports this perspective, as sport fandom had a high test–retest reliability over the six months (ICC = .88). On the other hand, if mood were the variable of interest, we might expect it to be stable over several days, but we would not be surprised (and we might perhaps expect) that a person's mood six months later would be unrelated to the person's current mood state.

CRONBACH'S ALPHA

I f a measure includes several items (or questions) that are designed to tap into the same construct, e.g., fandom, then those items or questions should be highly correlated with each other. If they are highly correlated, then the measure is considered to have internal consistency. For example, the Sport Fandom Questionnaire has five questions to measure total sport fandom (see Chapter 12). Each of these questions is supposed to measure whether the respondent considers himself or herself to be a sport fan. Consequently, the respondent should provide similar ratings for each of these questions. As discussed in Chapter 13, the most commonly reported measure of internal consistency is the coefficient alpha, also known as Cronbach's alpha coefficient (α). A measure is considered to have good internal consistency, or reliability, when the coefficient alpha value is 0.70 or higher.

Calculating Cronbach's Alpha

RESEARCH SCENARIO I

The data for this example is provided in the Excel file associated with this book. We will measure the internal consistency of the five items (columns C through G) of the Sport Fandom Questionnaire at Time 1, using Cronbach's alpha coefficient. *Note:* This statistical test is not available in the free version of StatPlus.

Click on the *Data* tab and then on *Data Analysis* on the far right (see Exhibit 15.12). **STEP 1**

The Data Analysis box should appear (see Exhibit 15.13). Select *Anova: Two-Factor Without Replication* from the Analysis Tools menu. Click *OK*. **STEP 2**

The Anova: Two-Factor Without Replication box (see Exhibit 15.14) should appear. Place the cursor in the *Input Range* box, and then highlight the appropriate values in columns C through G on the spreadsheet. The input should read $C$2:$G$151. Leave the alpha value at 0.05. Under Output Options, **STEP 3**

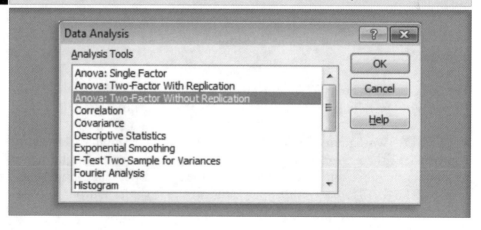

select *New Worksheet Ply* and enter a title for the new worksheet (e.g., Internal Consistency). Click *OK*.

As with the calculation of the ICC, the output in the ANOVA summary table (Exhibit 15.15, rows 162 to 168) will provide the information necessary for calculating the internal consistency with Cronbach's alpha. The formula for calculating the Cronbach's alpha is:

Cronbach's alpha = 1 − (MSError / MSRows)

EXHIBIT   15.13   Excel's Data Analysis box used in the calculation of Cronbach's alpha.

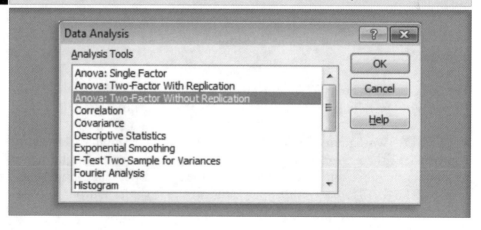

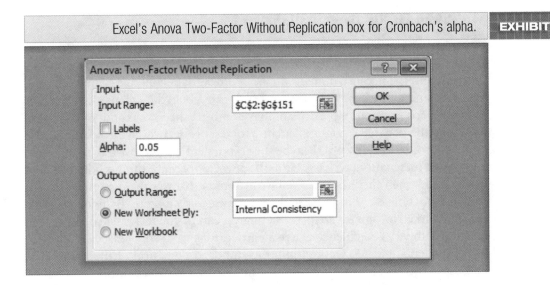

Excel's Anova Two-Factor Without Replication box for Cronbach's alpha.   **EXHIBIT 15.14**

Type the following formula in cell B170 (see Exhibit 15.15):

= 1 – (D166 / D164)

Exhibit 15.15 shows the results of the calculation (Cronbach's alpha = .9508). A Cronbach's alpha of 0.95 indicates that the five items on the Sport Fandom Questionnaire had high internal consistency at Time 1 and would be considered to provide a reliable measure of sport fandom.

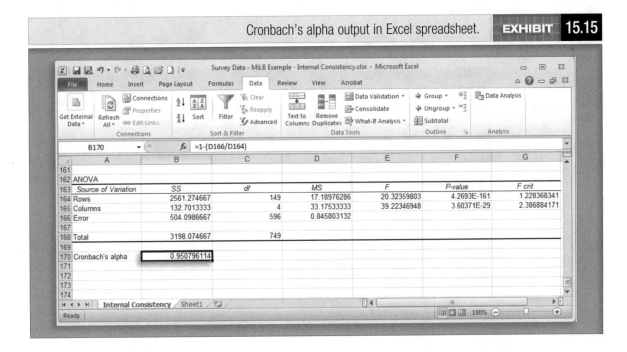

Cronbach's alpha output in Excel spreadsheet.   **EXHIBIT 15.15**

STANDARD ERROR OF MEASUREMENT

With regard to the **standard error of measurement (SEM)**, the most important point to understand is that most, if not all, measures have some error associated with them. Since humans are not perfect, data collected by humans and from humans, as well as the measurement devices created by humans, will not be error-free. For example, a participant may complete the Sport Fandom Questionnaire, and the researcher might calculate a total score. However, this score may not be the person's "true" score. Maybe the respondent's team lost the night before and, out of indignation, he has sworn off sports, or perhaps the test administrator was unclear when she provided the instructions. Whatever the reason, we can be certain that some error is associated with the calculated score. By understanding the standard error of measurement, an analyst can calculate a range of scores, indicating with 95% confidence where a participant's true score lies.

To calculate SEM, we multiply the standard deviation of the variable of interest by the square root of 1 minus the intra-class correlation:

$$SEM = s\sqrt{(1 - ICC)}$$

Recall that in the research scenario, the standard deviation of the results of the Sport Fandom Questionnaire at Time 1 is 9.2709, and the ICC is 0.8848. To find SEM in Excel, enter the following formula in cell N3 (see Exhibit 15.16):

= 9.2709*SQRT(1-0.8848)

The SEM value is 3.1466. We can now create a confidence interval to provide a range of scores within which a person's true score may lie (see Chapter

---

EXHIBIT 15.16   Excel formula for standard error of measurement.

14 for a discussion of CI). Recall that a confidence interval sets a lower and upper range around a statistic (e.g., a person's observed score). The CI is a function of the SEM and the chosen level of confidence (e.g., 95%) for the standard normal distribution. We determine the lower and upper ranges by subtracting and adding the CI value to the person's observed score. For a 95% CI, a respondent's true score is equal to the person's observed score +1.96 x SEM. Hence, if a person's measured sport fandom total score is 24, then the low score for the CI range would be 24 – 1.96 x 3.1466 = 17.83, and the high score for the range would be 24 + 1.96 x 3.1466 = 30.17. We would estimate with 95% confidence that the person's true sport fandom score lies somewhere between 17.83 and 30.17. In sport management, confidence intervals can help analysts decide on how "good" an estimate is for the value of the dependent variable of interest, such as an employee's job skills/traits or, in the case of our sport fandom/ticket purchase example, customer purchase intentions. The confidence interval provides a range of values (based on the measurement error) that contains the true value of the variable (such as a person's job performance aptitude or a customer's purchase intention) with the selected level of confidence.

PRACTICE PROBLEM FOR CORRELATION

**RESEARCH
SCENARIO II**

R ecall that in this scenario, members of a health club were surveyed with the following question: "On average, how frequently do you come to use the facility? _____ times per week." (We named this variable ExWeekT1.) Members were also asked their perceptions of the club's hours of operation (OpHours), with responses recorded on a Likert scale from 1 to 7 (1 = poor; 4 = average; 7 = excellent). You will examine whether the relationship (correlation) between facility usage and hours of operation is significant and whether this relationship is positive or negative.

Questions

1. What would a positive correlation between facility usage and hours of operation suggest? What would a negative correlation suggest?
2. What is the correlation between facility usage and hours of operation?
3. Should you conduct a one-tailed test or two-tailed test on the data? Why?
4. What are the degrees of freedom for this example?
5. What is the critical r value for this example, using alpha = .05?
6. Is the correlation between facility usage and hours of operation statistically significant? Why?
7. What is the practical significance?
8. How might you report the results in a scholarly article?
9. How might you report the results to the club's owner?

TALKING POINTS

Correlation

- Use a correlation to measure the degree of the linear relationship between two or more variables.
- Base a decision on the tailness and alpha level to be used in a correlation on theoretical and empirical evidence.
- Refer to a table of critical values for correlation or a statistical calculator to determine statistical significance.
- Use the coefficient of determination as a measure of meaningfulness for correlation.
- Use an intra-class correlation to determine the test–retest reliability of the same measure applied on separate occasions.
- Use Cronbach's alpha as a measure of the internal consistency, or reliability, of a multi-item scale of the same construct.
- Use the standard error of measurement to calculate a range of scores that indicate with 95% confidence where a respondent's true score lies.

16

Regression

EXECUTIVE SUMMARY With a regression analysis, we can predict the change in a dependent variable that will result from a change in a single independent variable or a group of independent variables. Regression analyses are very useful to sport managers for identifying key variables that contribute to important revenue and psycho-behavioral (e.g., employee/client satisfaction) variables.

WHAT IS A REGRESSION?

Regression is a statistical technique by which we examine (or predict) the change in scores on one dependent variable based on changes in or information about a single independent variable or a group of independent variables. Regression analysis makes use of the correlation between the independent and dependent variables. Correlation simply tells us the strength of the relationship between variables, whereas regression uses this information to create a prediction formula. A stronger correlation of the independent variable(s) with the dependent variable will allow for a better understanding (or prediction) of the change in the dependent variable.

Simple regression uses only one independent variable, and **multiple regression** uses two or more independent variables. As with correlation, a regression analysis examines the *linear* relationship(s) between the dependent variable and the independent variable(s). The test statistic for simple and multiple regression is R, and the R value will always be positive and range from 0 to 1. Since a simple regression involves just two variables (i.e., the dependent variable and the independent variable), the R value will be the same as the absolute value of r, or the correlation test statistic (see Chapter 15). *Multiple regression* refers to the correlation between a dependent variable and a combined set of independent variables. Interpretation of the multiple R is the same as interpretation of r. An example of simple regression may be use of years of prior job experience (independent variable) to predict potential job performance (dependent variable). Multiple regression would involve multiple independent variables, such as years of prior job experience, level of education, and age, to predict potential job performance.

The ability to predict future behavior can be quite important in sport management. Regression may be useful in identifying variables relevant to the prediction of future sport consumptive behaviors (e.g., tickets purchased, money spent at an event, sport viewing habits), spectator enjoyment, or employee satisfaction. For example, a sales team might use regression equations to identify individuals who are most likely to purchase tickets or memberships. Rather than have reps make a large number of cold calls to prospective buyers with the typical low success rate, a sales manager could scale down a large list to a smaller list of more likely buyers and allow the sales representatives to spend more time targeting key variables that might be attractive to the individual prospective buyer or client.

CALCULATING MULTIPLE REGRESSION

As a member of the front office of a MiLB team, you wish to use the data collected in a study of 150 community participants to identify variables that are important in the prediction of sport consumptive behaviors. The results of this analysis may be useful in marketing and promotional efforts, as well as for more targeted efforts by the organization's sales team. Although this type of analysis typically uses interval- and ratio-scaled measures, categorical- (or nominal-) scaled variables, such as gender, may be used, but they will have to be dummy-coded. **Dummy coding** simply refers to assigning a quantitative value to each category. Various coding schemes may be used, such as 0 and 1 or –1 and +1. If more than two categories exist, then 1, 2, 3, etc. may be used.

For this example, the dependent variable is the number of tickets purchased last year (column J). The independent variables are gender (column A), age (column B), and sport fandom (column H). We will use the Data Analysis ToolPak or StatPlus.

As before, we must place the data in contiguous columns. Copy and paste the **STEP 1** data into new columns so that the required data appear side by side. In the spreadsheet in Exhibit 16.1, we have copied the data into column N (Gender), column O (Age), column P (SF Tot1), and column Q (Tkts LstYr). The data in the original columns (A, B, H, and J) have been retained.

The categorical variable of gender must be dummy-coded. In this example, **STEP 2** men will be assigned a 1 and women will be assigned a 0. Highlight the first cell in the new Gender column (cell N2), select the *Formulas* tab, and, from the *Logical* function drop-down menu, select *IF* (see Exhibit 16.1).

The Function Arguments box should appear. Place the cursor in the *Logical Test* **STEP 3** box and then highlight the first cell in the original column for Gender (cell A2). Next, complete the logical statement and the values to be assigned depending on whether the logical statement is true or false (see Exhibit 16.2). Click *OK*.

The value in cell N2 should now be 0. Copy and paste the formula to the rest **STEP 4** of the cells in column N. All cells with an F in column A (for women) should be 0s in column N, and all cells with an M in column A (for men) should be 1s in column N.

| Excel Formulas tab and IF function for dummy coding gender. | **EXHIBIT** | **16.1** |

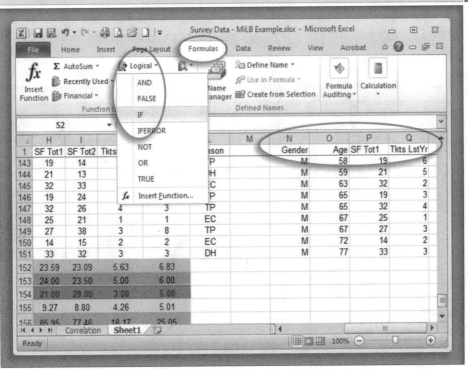

EXHIBIT 16.2   Excel's Function Arguments box for dummy coding gender.

Function Arguments

IF

Logical_test	A2="F"	= TRUE
Value_if_true	0	= 0
Value_if_false	1	= 1

= 0

Checks whether a condition is met, and returns one value if TRUE, and another value if FALSE.

Value_if_false is the value that is returned if Logical_test is FALSE. If omitted, FALSE is returned.

Formula result = 0

Help on this function   OK   Cancel

STEP 5   Click on the *Data* tab and then on *Data Analysis* on the far right (see Exhibit 16.3). In StatPlus, click on *Statistics*, then *Regression*.

STEP 6   The Data Analysis box should appear. Select *Regression* from the Analysis Tools menu (see Exhibit 16.4). Click *OK*. In StatPlus, select *Linear Regression*.

STEP 7   The Regression box should appear (see Exhibit 16.5). Place the cursor in the *Input Y Range* box (this box is for the dependent variable), and then highlight

EXHIBIT 16.3   Excel's Data tab and Data Analysis for regression.

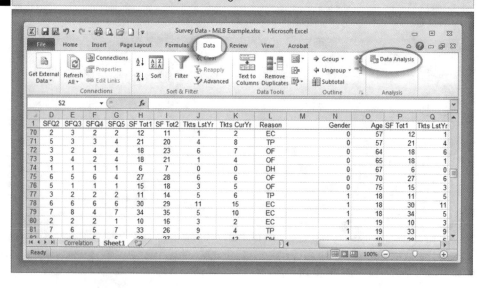

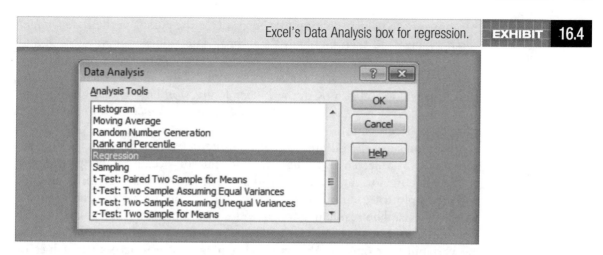

Excel's Data Analysis box for regression.   **EXHIBIT**   **16.4**

Excel's Regression box.   **EXHIBIT**   **16.5**

the appropriate values in column Q. The input should read **$Q$2:$Q$151**. Next, place the cursor in the *Input X Range* box (this box is for the independent variables), and then highlight the appropriate values in columns N, O, and P. The input should read **$N$2:$P$151**. Select *Labels* if the column has them, and select *Residuals, Residuals Plot,* and *Line Fit Plots.* Click *OK.* In StatPlus, place the cursor in the *Dependent Variables* box and then highlight the appropriate values (column Q). Next, place the cursor in the *Independent Variables* box and then highlight the appropriate values (columns N, O, and P). In *Advanced Options*, select *Residual Plots* and *Line Fit Plots*, and then click *OK*. In *Preferences*, make sure the alpha value is 5%, then click *OK*. Once this is done, click *OK* in the *Linear Regression* box. Under Output Options, select *New Worksheet Ply, Output Range*, or *New Workbook* and enter a title (e.g., Regression).

Residuals are the differences between predicted and actual scores on the dependent variable. The Residual function is useful because it will provide the predicted score for each person on the dependent variable. A **residuals plot** is a scatterplot of each independent variable on the X-axis and the residuals on the Y-axis. The residuals plot provides visual evidence as to whether the assumption of homoscedasticity has been met. **Homoscedasticity** exists when the variability of one variable is consistent or uniform across the values of the other variable. In other words, the number and deviations of data points should be similar above and below the 0 line. See the SF Tot1 residual plot in Exhibit 16.6. The residual plot for age looks a little different because there are only two values for gender (0 = women; 1 = men), but the variability above and below 0 is the same for both genders (see Exhibit 16.6).

If the homoscedasticity assumption has not been met, then the data may be transformed to reduce heteroscedasticity. **Heteroscedasticity** exists when the variability of one variable is *not* consistent or uniform across the values

---

EXHIBIT 16.6 Excel's summary output of the regression analysis with gender, age, and sport fandom included in the model.

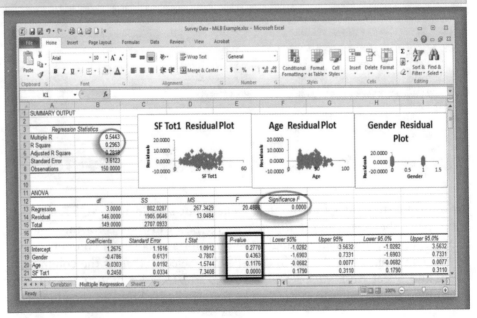

of the other variable. For example, the residual plot may show that (1) more points appear above 0 than below 0, or vice versa, and/or (2) the points are more spread out in some areas and less so in other areas. Transformation of data is beyond the scope of this book.

Line fit plots are scatterplots of the actual and predicted scores of the dependent variable for each value of the independent variable. These plots provide visual evidence of a linear relationship; if a linear relationship exists, the plot should look oval in shape. For Research Scenario I, we could create a line fit plot for sport fandom, age, and gender (see Exhibit 16.7 for a line fit plot with sport fandom as the independent variable).

Interpreting the Results: Statistical Significance

The summary output for regression (Exhibit 16.6) provides an Analysis of Variance summary table. ANOVA will be discussed in detail in Chapter 18. For the purpose of regression, you need to focus only on the outlined areas in Exhibit 16.6, which are R, R^2, Significance F, and p values for each independent variable. The R value (0.5443) indicates the strength of the relationship between the dependent variable (tickets purchased last year) and the combined set of independent variables (age, gender, and sport fandom at Time 1). Since the test statistic for regression, R, is interpreted in the same way as r (see Chapter 15), the coefficient of determination is the same: it equals the square of the

Line fit plot for actual and predicted tickets purchased in the previous year with sport fandom as the independent variable.	EXHIBIT 16.7

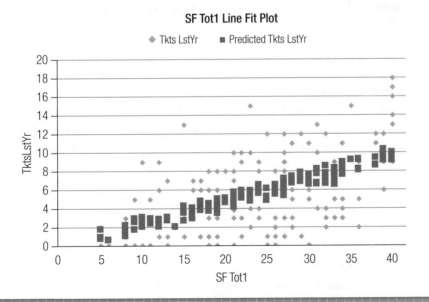

multiple correlation coefficient, or R^2. The R^2 value of 0.2963 indicates that about 30% of the variance in number of tickets purchased can be accounted for by the combination of age, gender, and sport fandom at Time 1, leaving 70% of the variance to be explained by other factors. This would lead you to conclude that the independent variables are important but that other factors also influence ticket purchases. The Significance F value indicates whether the regression model with three independent variables is significant at a certain probability level. If the Significance F value is less than the established alpha (e.g., 0.05), then the model is significant. Looking at the p values for each independent variable, only SF Tot1 (i.e., sport fandom total scores at Time 1) has a significant p value (i.e., less than the alpha level of 0.05); thus, you should conclude that only fandom significantly contributes to the prediction of the dependent variable (ticket purchases). This three-variable example illustrates the fact that as an analyst, you want to be parsimonious, by using the fewest variables possible for prediction.

In this example, you would also want to perform a second regression—a simple regression, in which you will use only one independent variable to predict a dependent variable. To perform this regression, we will remove gender and age from the regression analysis in order to determine the R and R^2 values that result when the total sport fandom score at Time 1 is the only independent variable included in the model.

Exhibit 16.8 gives the summary output for this second, simple regression analysis. Although this output indicates multiple regression, this is simply how Excel displays the output, and you should understand the value labeled "Multiple R" to be the R statistic. Therefore, the summary output provides the R (0.5299) and R^2 (0.2808) values. Notice that the R value is the same as the r value calculated for the simple correlation example in Exhibit 15.4; this occurs because the analysis is now using only one independent variable. Recall that a correlation examines the relationship between two variables, and a regression analysis with one dependent variable and one independent variable is the same as a correlation. Thus, we interpret the R value in the same way as the r value.

The summary output also provides the information that we need to create the regression (prediction) formula. Since we are using regression to estimate the linear relationship between the dependent variable and an independent variable (or a set of independent variables), the regression formula is the same as the formula for a straight line:

$$Y = a + bX$$

where

Y = predicted value for the dependent variable

a = intercept (or constant)

b = slope of the regression line (or regression coefficient)

X = observed score on the independent variable

EXHIBIT   16.8

Excel's summary output of the regression analysis with only sport fandom included in the model.

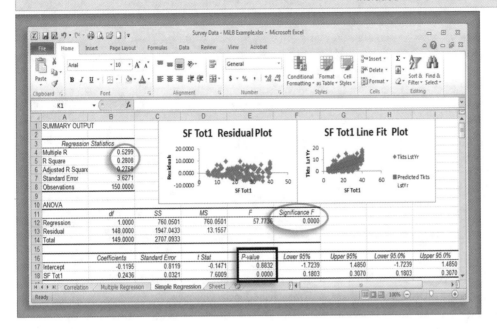

Note that the formula for multiple regression is just an extension of the one for simple regression, derived by adding the additional independent variables and associated regression coefficients to the simple regression formula:

$$Y = a + bX_1 + bX_2 + \ldots + bX_i$$

Based on the information from the summary output in Exhibit 16.8, the regression formula for the research scenario data would be:

$$Y = -.1195 + (.2436)X$$

This regression formula indicates that each unit increase in a person's sport fandom total score is associated with a 0.2436 increase in the number of tickets purchased. Stated another way, we predict that every four-point increase in a person's sport fandom score will result in roughly one additional ticket purchase.

If you selected the Residuals box when you conducted the regression analysis, then Excel will provide prediction scores for number of tickets purchased. Alternatively, you may use the Insert function to create a formula to provide this information. To create the formula, choose an empty column (e.g., column R), highlight the first cell, and insert the following function:

$$= P2{*}0.2436-0.1195$$

See Exhibit 16.9. Note that cell P2 contains the X (or independent variable) score used in the formula. Copy and paste this formula down the column.

EXHIBIT 16.9 Excel formula to predict number of tickets purchased based on sport fandom score.

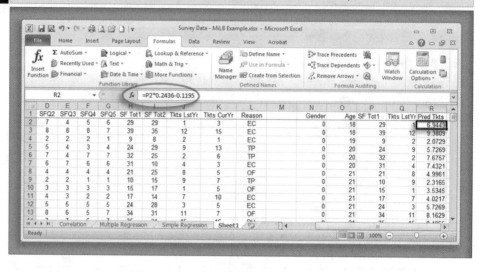

As an example of how this information can be useful, if a person has a sport fandom score of 29, the predicted number of tickets purchased in a year is 6.94. An analyst might use this type of information to tailor ticket packages that may be of interest to potential ticket purchasers who have sport fandom scores in certain ranges.

Interpreting the Results: Practical Significance (Meaningfulness)

The measure of meaningfulness for simple and multiple regression is the *coefficient of determination*. The **coefficient of determination** is the percentage of variance in the dependent variable that is explained by the independent variable (or a combined set of independent variables). Since the test statistic for regression is R, which is interpreted the same way as r, the coefficient of determination is the square of the multiple correlation coefficient, or R^2. As reported in Exhibit 16.8, the correlation coefficient between sport fandom total scores and tickets purchased last year was 0.5299; hence, the coefficient of determination is $r^2 = .5299^2 = 0.2808$. Since sport fandom accounts for 28% of the variation in tickets purchased, other variables, such as income or distance from the stadium, should be explored to try to explain more of the variation in number of tickets purchased.

Statistical Statement

The results just discussed would be reported in a scholarly article in the following manner:

> A simple regression was used to predict the number of tickets purchased last year based on a person's sport fandom score. The regression coefficient was significant [F(1,

148) = 57.77, $p < .0001$], with $R = .5299$ and $R^2 = .2808$. A person's predicted number of tickets purchased is: $Y = -.1195 + (.2436)X$. Each one-point increase in a person's sport fandom score is associated with a 0.2436 increase in the number of tickets purchased.

Note that the numbers in parentheses next to *F* are the degrees of freedom for the *F* test statistic. These numbers, along with the *F* value of 57.77, appeared in the ANOVA summary table in Exhibit 16.8. Chapter 18 discusses ANOVA.

For a non-scholarly report, the results would be presented in the following manner:

People in the local community (75 men and 75 women) were surveyed on how many tickets they purchased last year and whether they considered themselves to be sport fans (i.e., sport fandom), which was rated on a scale from 5 to 40 (5 = not a sport fan at all, 40 = very much a sport fan). Sport fandom was found to be related to how many tickets these individuals purchased last year. The stronger a person's feeling of being a sport fan, the more tickets the person was likely to have purchased. Thus, a person's sport fandom score can be used to predict how many tickets the person will purchase in the next year. A person's predicted number of tickets purchased is: $Y = -.1195 + (.2436)$ X. Each one-point increase in a person's sport fandom score is associated with a 0.2436 increase in the number of tickets purchased; hence, an increase of four points in sport fandom would predict an increase of approximately one ticket. For example, Fan X, who had a low/moderate sport fandom score of 18, can be predicted to purchase 4.27 (or 4) tickets, whereas Fan Y, who had a high sport fandom score of 30, can be predicted to purchase 7.19 (or 7) tickets. The relationship was strong and meaningful, indicating that future marketing and promotional strategies that increase individuals' perception of their sport fandom should be associated with an increase in tickets purchased, as well.

PRACTICE PROBLEM FOR REGRESSION

Suppose you wish to use the data gathered from health club member surveys to identify variables that are associated with facility usage, as measured by the reported number of times per week (ExWeekT1) that members come to use the club. In a multiple correlation, the dependent variable will be ExWeekT1, and the independent variables will be gender, marital status (single, married), and income (low: <$35,000, middle: $35,000–$70,000, high: >$70,000). Before starting this analysis, remember to (1) place the relevant data in contiguous columns and (2) dummy code the independent variables. Code males (M) as 1 and females (F) as 0, code Single members (S) as 1 and married members (M) as 0, and code high-income members (H) as 2, middle-income members (M) as 1, and low-income members (L) as 0.

Questions

1. Perform a multiple regression using gender, marital status, and income to predict facility usage, with alpha = .05.

2. Plot the residuals. Has the assumption of homoscedasticity been met?
3. What is the R value?
4. What is the F value?
5. What is the p value?
6. What is the statistical significance of the results?
7. What is the squared multiple correlation coefficient (R^2)?
8. Are the results meaningful?
9. How would you write up the results for a scholarly article?
10. How would you report the results to the health club's owner?

TALKING POINTS

Regression

- Use regression to predict scores on a dependent variable based on one or more independent variables that are correlated with the dependent variable.

- In simple regression, predictions are based on one independent variable; in multiple regression, predictions are based on more than one independent variable.

- Regression analysis provides an R value, which is the correlation between the dependent and the independent variable(s).

- The coefficient of determination, or R^2, measures the meaningfulness of the association between the dependent variable and the independent variable(s).

- The regression analysis provides the constant and regression coefficients to be used in the prediction formula.

17

t-Tests

EXECUTIVE SUMMARY A *t*-test allows us to examine the difference between two means. A *t*-test may evaluate the difference between two independent sample group means, or it may evaluate the difference between two means from the same sample group. We can calculate measures of meaningfulness to interpret the results of *t*-tests. A finding might be considered statistically significant but might not be meaningful.

WHAT IS A *t*-TEST?

A *t*-test is a statistical technique that we can use to study the difference between two means measured on interval or ratio scales. The two most common types of *t*-tests are the independent *t*-test and the dependent *t*-test. In all *t*-tests, the test statistic is *t*. The independent variable refers to the classification of the two sample groups (e.g., gender), and the dependent variable is the interval- or ratio-scaled measure on which the two groups are being compared (e.g., fandom). The use of *t*-tests in sport management is limited only by the imagination of the analyst.

INDEPENDENT *t*-TEST

An independent *t*-test compares the means from two independent (different) sample groups. Of all the *t*-tests, this one is probably the most frequently used. The independent variable that serves to distinguish the two sample groups might be a simple dichotomous variable, such as gender, or it might be defined based on complex distinguishing criteria identified by the analyst. For example, the length of employment at a sport organization could define two groups: experienced and inexperienced employees. Season ticket holder status (yes/no), athletic status (athlete/non-athlete), or age groups (younger/older) are just a few other possible dichotomous groups that could be examined. Remember, a participant in one group cannot also belong to the other group. The two groups must be independent of each other.

RESEARCH SCENARIO I

Performing an Independent *t*-Test

Suppose you wish to use the data collected in the study of 150 community participants to determine whether men and women differ on sport fandom. In this case, the dependent variable will be sport fandom scores at Time 1 (column H), and gender is the independent variable. Column H contains the scores for both men and women.

STEP 1   Before you perform the independent *t*-test, you should check the data regarding the assumptions for parametric tests. In particular, check the two sample groups (men, women) for equal variances. Unequal variances could indicate that the sample means are not good estimates of the data, thus making comparisons between the means invalid (see Chapter 13). Select *Data* and then *Data Analysis* on the far right. When the Analysis Tools box appears, select *F-Test Two-Sample for Variances* (see Exhibit 17.1). Click *OK*. In StatPlus, click on *Statistics*, then *Basic Statistics and Tables*. Select *F-Test for Variances*.

STEP 2   In the F-Test Two-Sample for Variances box (see Exhibit 17.2), place the cursor in the *Variable 1 Range* box. In this box, you will specify the scores for one of the sample groups being compared. Women will be variable 1, so highlight the appropriate values in column H corresponding to women's scores only (i.e., cells H2 to H76). The Variable 1 Range should read **$H$2:$H$76**. Next, place the cursor in the *Variable 2 Range* box. In this box, you specify the scores for the other sample group (i.e., men), so highlight the appropriate values in column H corresponding to men's scores (i.e., cells H77 to H151). The Variable 2 Range should read **$H$77:$H$151**. Under Output Options, select *New Worksheet Ply* and enter a title (e.g., *t*-test variance). Click *OK*. In StatPlus, place the cursor in the *Variable #1* box and then highlight the appropriate values for variable 1 (H2 to H76). Next, place the cursor in the *Variable #2* box and highlight the appropriate values for variable 2 (H77 to

| | Excel's Data tab and Data Analysis option for testing sample variances. | **EXHIBIT** | **17.1** |

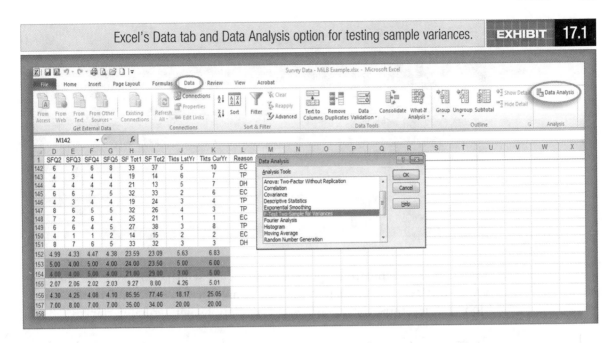

| | Excel's F-Test Two-Sample for Variances box. | **EXHIBIT** | **17.2** |

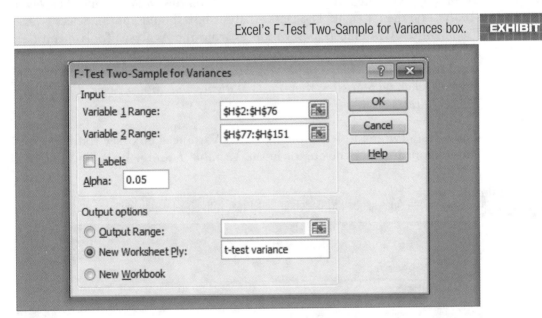

H151). Deselect *Labels in First Row,* since the heading in the first row was not highlighted. For Preferences, make sure alpha is 5%. Click *OK.*

As shown in Exhibit 17.3, the variances are nearly identical for women and men: 80.85 and 79.74, respectively. The *p* value is not significant (.48 > .05), so we would not reject the null hypothesis of equal variances for sport fandom scores at Time 1. Remember, the assumption for use of parametric

EXHIBIT 17.3 Excel's output for F-Test Two-Sample for Variances.

F-Test Two-Sample for Variances		
	Variable 1	Variable 2
Mean	21.1067	26.0667
Variance	80.8533	79.7387
Observations	75.0000	75.0000
df	74.0000	74.0000
F	1.0140	
P(F<=f) one-tail	0.4763	
F Critical one-tail	1.4695	

tests is that the spread in sport fandom scores will be the same for men and women. We can conclude that the two sample variances (for men and women) do not differ; thus, they come from distributions with equal variances.

STEP 3 To proceed with the independent *t*-test, click on the *Data* tab and then *Data Analysis* on the far right. The Data Analysis box should appear. Select *t-Test: Two-Sample Assuming Equal Variances* from the Analysis Tools menu (see Exhibit 17.4). Note that if the variances were found not to be equal, then you would select *t-Test: Two-Sample Assuming Unequal Variances*. Click *OK*. In StatPlus, click on *Statistics*, then *Basic Statistics and Tables*. Select *Comparing Means (t-Test)*.

STEP 4 The *t*-Test: Two-Sample Assuming Equal Variances box (see Exhibit 17.5) should appear. Place the cursor in the *Variable 1 Range* box. Since women

EXHIBIT 17.4 Excel's Data Analysis box for independent *t*-test with equal variances.

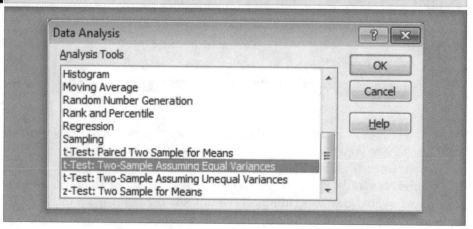

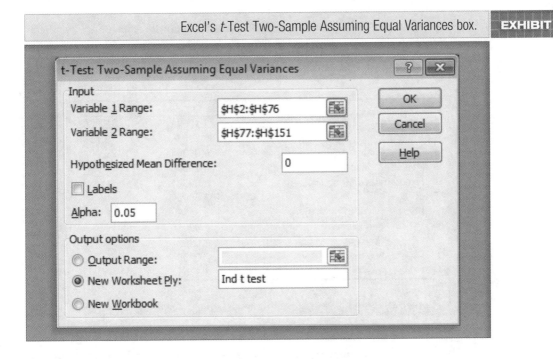

Excel's *t*-Test Two-Sample Assuming Equal Variances box. **EXHIBIT** **17.5**

will be variable 1, highlight the values in column H corresponding to women's scores only. The *Variable 1 Range* should read **$H$2:$H$76**. Next, place the cursor in the *Variable 2 Range* box. Highlight the appropriate values for men in column H. The *Variable 2 Range* should read **$H$77:$H$151**. For *Hypothesized Mean Difference,* you may enter 0, or you may leave it blank, because Excel will assume a 0 value. Remember that the null hypothesis states that there will be no difference between the two means. Select an alpha level of 0.05. Under Output Options, select *New Worksheet Ply* and enter a title for the new worksheet (e.g., Ind *t*-test). Click *OK*. In StatPlus, in the *Compare Means* box, place the cursor in the *Values* box for variable 1 and then highlight the values in column H for women. Next, place the cursor in the *Values* box for variable 2 and highlight the values for men. Hypothesized Mean Difference should be 0, and alpha should be 5%. In the pull-down menu for *t*-Test Type, select *Two-Sample t-Test Assuming Equal Variances (homoscedastic)*. Click *OK*.

Interpreting the results: Statistical significance

Exhibit 17.6 gives Excel's output, including the mean and variance for the women ($M = 21.12$, $s^2 = 80.85$) and men ($M = 26.07$, $s^2 = 79.74$). Note that when we report these summary statistics, the conventional method is to provide the standard deviation for each group instead of the variance. We can find the standard deviation easily, by taking the square root of the variance ($s_{women} = \sqrt{80.85} = 8.99$; $s_{men} = \sqrt{79.74} = 8.93$).

| EXHIBIT | 17.6 | Excel's summary output for *t*-Test: Two-Sample Assuming Equal Variances. |

	A	B	C
1	t-Test: Two-Sample Assuming Equal Variances		
2			
3		*Variable 1*	*Variable 2*
4	Mean	21.1067	26.0667
5	Variance	80.8533	79.7387
6	Observations	75.0000	75.0000
7	Pooled Variance	80.2960	
8	Hypothesized Mean Difference	0.0000	
9	df	148.0000	
10	t Stat	-3.3896	
11	P(T<=t) one-tail	0.0004	
12	t Critical one-tail	1.6552	
13	P(T<=t) two-tail	0.0009	
14	t Critical two-tail	1.9761	
15			

Ind t test / Correlation / Multi

The number of observations (N, shown in cell A6 of Exhibit 17.6) refers to the total number of scores in the entire sample and is the sum of the sample sizes for groups 1 and 2 ($N = n_1 + n_2 = 75 + 75 = 150$). The **pooled variance** (cell A7) is basically the weighted average of the two sample variances, and this value should always be somewhere between the two sample variances. To calculate the degrees of freedom for an independent *t*-test, we add the sample sizes and subtract the number of variables under consideration: $(n_1 + n_2) - 2 = 150 - 2 = 148$. We evaluate the test statistic (t) based on the t distribution associated with the degrees of freedom in the study, which is a function of the sample sizes. The further the calculated t value moves away from 0, the less likely it is that the calculated t value is a chance occurrence. The calculated t value may have a positive or negative sign, but this simply indicates which group mean is higher. The sign would have been opposite had men been considered variable 1 and women variable 2. In other words, it is the absolute value of t that we evaluate for significance. The decision on the alpha level and tailness of the study assigns the cutoff value (or critical t value) that the test statistic must exceed in order to be considered significant.

To review the difference between one-tailed and two-tailed tests, with a one-tailed test, the entire alpha (e.g., 0.05) will be put on one side (or tail) of the distribution; when we select the one-tailed test we are assuming that the difference between the two sample means will lie in one direction only. In other words, we know that one group will have a higher mean than the other group. With a two-tailed test, the alpha is split and placed in both tails of the distribution (e.g., .05/2 = .025). Now, we are assuming that the difference between the two sample means may lie in either direction. In other words, it is unknown which group will have a higher mean.

Since studies are typically done to gain new information, a two-tailed test is more common. A one-tailed test is more powerful than a two-tailed test, but its use requires strong empirical or theoretical evidence. You will notice that the Excel summary output provides *p* values and critical *t* values for one-tailed (cell A12) and two-tailed (cell A14) tests. In the sport fandom example, we are performing a two-tailed test because we do not know which gender will have the higher mean. In this example, the calculated *t* value would be considered significant because the probability of this test statistic being due to chance is less than 1 in 1,000 (i.e., $p < .0009$). Stated another way, the absolute calculated *t* value (cell A10) exceeded the two-tailed critical *t* value at the *a priori* alpha level ($\alpha = .05$) that we selected as the level of significance (3.3896 > 1.9761).

Interpreting the results: Practical significance (meaningfulness)

We can calculate two measures of meaningfulness for an independent *t*-test. Although both measures may be reported, one measure will usually suffice. The more common measure of meaningfulness for an independent *t*-test is called **effect size** (or Cohen's *d*). Effect size is the standardized difference between the two means as a function of the pooled standard deviation (Exhibit 17.6, cell A7). We calculate it by finding the difference between the two means and dividing by the pooled standard deviation (s_p). *Note:* The Excel output provides the pooled variance (s_p^2), so we must take the square root of this value to obtain the pooled standard deviation.

$$s_p = \sqrt{s_p^2} = \sqrt{80.2960} = 8.96$$

$$d = \frac{(M_1 - M_2)}{s_p} = \frac{(21.11 - 26.07)}{8.96} = -.55$$

Exhibit 17.7 gives Cohen's general guidelines for interpreting the absolute effect size. The significant difference in sport fandom means between men and women was about one-half of a standard deviation ($d = -.55$), and this difference was moderate in magnitude and would be considered meaningful. Small

Cohen's general guidelines for interpreting the absolute effect size.	**EXHIBIT**	**17.7**

$d = .20$ is considered a small effect,

$d = .50$ is considered a moderate effect, and

$d = .80$ and above is considered a large effect.

effects are typically not considered very meaningful, while large effects are often considered very meaningful.

The second measure of meaningfulness that we may calculate for an independent *t*-test is r^2, which is interpreted in the same way as it was for correlation: it is the proportion of total variation of the dependent variable that is accounted for (or explained by) the independent variable (see Chapter 15). This measure is a function of the calculated *t* value and the sample sizes. The general formula for r^2 is

$$r^2 = \frac{t^2}{(t^2 + df)}$$

For the sport fandom example,

$$r^2 = \frac{-3.3896^2}{(-3.3896^2 + 148)} = \frac{11.4894}{159.4894}$$

$$r^2 = .0720$$

Hence, about 7% of the total variation in sport fandom scores is accounted for by gender. Based on the statistical results and the effect size, the difference in means is meaningful, but r^2 shows that it only accounts for 7% of the variance in sport fandom scores. We conclude that, while gender is an important variable, other variables should be examined to help account for the 93% of the variance that is left unexplained.

Statistical statement

For the sport fandom example, the results would be reported in a scholarly article in the following manner:

> An independent *t*-test was used to evaluate whether sport fandom would differ between women and men. The calculated *t* value was significant, with $t(148) = -3.3896$, $p < .0001$. The mean score for men ($M = 26.07$, $s = 8.93$) was significantly higher compared to the mean for women ($M = 21.11$, $s = 8.99$). This gender effect was moderate in magnitude ($d = -.55$) and accounted for 7% of the variance in sport fandom scores as measured by r^2.

For a non-scholarly report, the results would be presented in the following manner:

> People from the local community were surveyed on whether they considered themselves to be sport fans (i.e., sport fandom), which was rated on a scale from 5 to 40 (5 = not a sport fan at all, 40 = very much a sport fan). Equal numbers of men and women were selected from the local community, and we tested to see if the 75 men and 75 women had different ratings. Men were rated higher on sport fandom (average = 26.07) compared to women (average = 21.11), but we considered the difference in these overall ratings as moderate. As a result, we decided that, while there is a gender difference in sport fandom, marketing or promotional efforts to increase perceptions of being a sport fan may be effective for both genders, but especially for women.

DEPENDENT *t*-TEST

A *dependent t-test* compares the means from two samples that are related. Although this *t*-test is not quite as common as the independent *t*-test, it is still a widely used statistical test. The most common application of this test is in a pre–post test study. In this type of study, the participants are measured on the variable of interest before an intervention (treatment), and then the same participants are measured again on the same variable after the intervention. In reality, an intervention does not necessarily need to have occurred or been implemented; a researcher may simply measure participants again after some time has passed to see if there is any change in the measure. In sport management, an analyst might measure the effectiveness of a marketing campaign by surveying the same respondents or examining sales numbers before and after its implementation. Did it result in more client satisfaction or revenue? Or an analyst might ask, after a change in managers, do employees work well under the new management style? Has productivity increased from last month or last year? As you can see, there are many applications for a dependent *t*-test in the sport industry.

Performing a Dependent *t*-Test

RESEARCH SCENARIO I

After previous analyses identified sport fandom as an important variable, the front office of the MiLB team created new marketing and promotional efforts with the hope of increasing the number of tickets purchased by community members. Prior to the start of the baseball season, 150 community participants were measured on the number of tickets they purchased last year. After the end of the baseball season, the same community participants were assessed on the number of tickets they purchased for the current season. The results of this analysis will determine whether the new strategies were effective or not. Note that this study was not anonymous, and participant contact information was collected with the first survey. If the first survey had been anonymous, then it would be impossible to match the data at both time points. Since this is a hypothetical scenario, we are assuming that all 150 participants completed the survey at both time points. In reality, this may not occur, and an analyst would use the data from only those participants who completed the survey at both times.

For this test, the dependent variable is number of tickets purchased, and time is the independent variable, with last year being Time 1 (column J) and after the current season being Time 2 (column K).

Click on the *Data* tab and then *Data Analysis* on the far right. The Data Analysis box should appear. Select *t-Test: Paired Two Sample for Means* from the Analysis Tools menu (see Exhibit 17.8). This option is appropriate for a dependent *t*-test. The other options are appropriate for independent *t*-tests. Click *OK*. In StatPlus, click on *Statistics*, then *Basic Statistics and Tables*. Select *Comparing Means (T-Test)*.

STEP 1

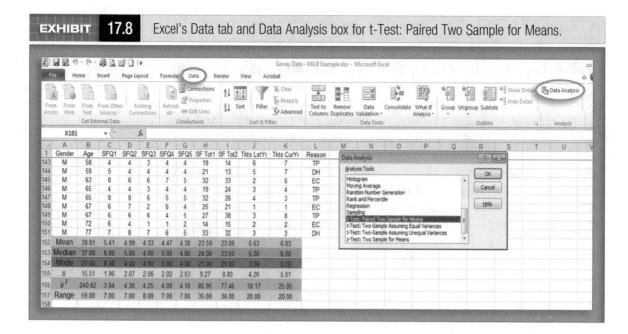

EXHIBIT 17.8   Excel's Data tab and Data Analysis box for t-Test: Paired Two Sample for Means.

STEP 2   The *t*-Test: Paired Two Sample for Means box (see Exhibit 17.9) should appear. Place the cursor in the *Variable 1 Range* box. Since the number of tickets purchased for last year's season (Time 1) will be variable 1, highlight the appropriate values in column J (cells J1 to J151). Next, place the cursor in the *Variable 2 Range* box. Highlight the values for the number of tickets pur-

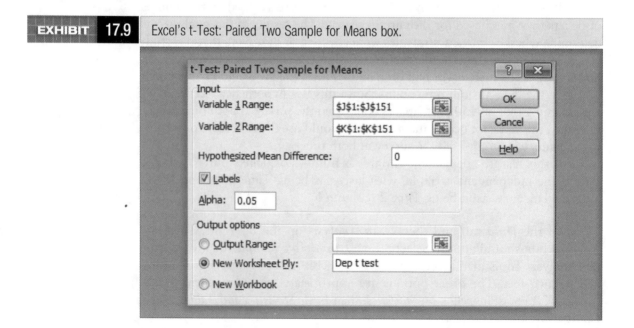

EXHIBIT 17.9   Excel's t-Test: Paired Two Sample for Means box.

chased after this year's season (Time 2) in column K (cells K1 to K151). For Hypothesized Mean Difference, you may enter 0, or you may leave it blank, because Excel will assume a 0 value (i.e., the null hypothesis). Since the first row of column headings was highlighted for each variable, place a check in the Labels box. Select the alpha level of 0.05. Under Output options, select *New Worksheet Ply* and enter a title (e.g., Dep t-test). Click *OK*. In StatPlus, in the Compare Means box, place the cursor in the *Values* box for variable 1 and then highlight the appropriate values (column J for tickets purchased last year). Next, place the cursor in the *Values* box for variable 2 and then highlight the appropriate values (columns K for tickets purchased this year). Hypothesized Mean Difference should be 0, and alpha should be .05. In the pull-down menu for T-Test Type, select *Paired Two Sample T-Test*. Click *OK*.

Interpreting the results: Statistical significance

As shown in Exhibit 17.10, the mean and standard deviation at Time 1 are $M = 5.63$, $s = 4.26$ and at Time 2 are $M = 6.83$, $s = 5.01$. As stated earlier, we calculate the standard deviation by taking the square root of the variance. The observations number refers to the total number of *paired* scores for the entire sample (i.e., 150 participants reported values at both assessment points). If some participants had data only at Time 1 or at Time 2, then those participants would not be included in the analysis at all, because a participant must have data at both times. Since the dependent *t*-test factors in the correlation of Time 1 and Time 2 values, the Pearson correlation is reported in the output. Because there is only one sample group (being tested twice), when we calculate the degrees

Excel's summary output for *t*-Test: Paired Two Sample for Means.   **EXHIBIT 17.10**

	A	B	C
1	t-Test: Paired Two Sample for Means		
2			
3		Tkts LstYr	Tkts CurYr
4	Mean	5.6267	6.8333
5	Variance	18.1684	25.0526
6	Observations	150.0000	150.0000
7	Pearson Correlation	0.8650	
8	Hypothesized Mean Difference	0.0000	
9	df	149.0000	
10	t Stat	-5.8820	
11	P(T<=t) one-tail	0.0000	
12	t Critical one-tail	1.6551	
13	P(T<=t) two-tail	0.0000	
14	t Critical two-tail	1.9760	

Dep t test / Correlation / Multipl

of freedom for a dependent *t*-test, we subtract one from the sample size rather than two. Hence, for this example, df = $N - 1 = 150 - 1 = 149$. Excel provides the calculated *t* value, along with the *p* values and critical *t* values for one-tailed and two-tailed tests (see the independent *t*-test example for more information on these terms). In this example, the calculated *t* value would be considered significant, because the probability of this test statistic being due to chance was, at minimum, less than 1 in 10,000 (i.e., $p < .0001$). Stated another way, the absolute calculated *t* value exceeded the two-tailed critical *t* value at the *a priori* alpha level ($\alpha = .05$) that was selected as the level of significance ($5.8820 > 1.9761$).

Interpreting the results: Practical significance (meaningfulness)

As stated previously, we can calculate two measures of meaningfulness for a dependent *t*-test. The first measure, the effect size (or Cohen's *d*), was discussed in the independent *t*-test example. For a dependent *t*-test, rather than use a pooled standard deviation, we use the standard deviation at pre-test, because this value more closely estimates the variance in the population that has not received the intervention (see Exhibit 17.10, cell B5). Note that the output provides the variance (s^2) at pre-test (Time 1), so we take the square root of this value to obtain the standard deviation.

$$s = \sqrt{s^2} = \sqrt{18.1684} = 4.26$$

$$d = \frac{(M_1 - M_2)}{s} = \frac{(5.63 - 6.83)}{4.26} = -.28$$

We disregard the sign of *d*. The significant difference in number of tickets purchased last season and for the current season was about one-quarter of a standard deviation ($d = -.28$), and this difference was small in magnitude and would not be considered meaningful. Refer back to Exhibit 17.7 for guidelines for interpreting the absolute effect size.

The second measure of meaningfulness that we can calculate for a dependent *t*-test is called *percent improvement or change*. This measure is the difference between the post-test and pre-test means (or average gain) divided by the pre-test mean. The general formula for percent change is:

$$\% \text{ change} = \frac{(\text{post-test mean} - \text{pre-test mean})}{\text{pre-test mean}}$$

In our example,

$$\% \text{ change} = \frac{(6.8333 - 5.6267)}{5.6267} = \frac{1.2066}{5.6267}$$

$$\% \text{ change} = .2144$$

Hence, there was a 21% improvement in tickets purchased for the current season compared to last season. There are no established guidelines for interpreting percent improvement. Each analyst must interpret this finding based on local and national trends for his or her agency. A 21% improvement may be considered very good if local or national trends are around 5%, or it may not be considered very good if local or national trends are exceeding 60%.

Statistical statement

For the example, the results would be reported in a scholarly article in the following manner:

> A dependent *t*-test was used to compare the number of MiLB baseball tickets purchased for last season and this season in a sample of 150 community participants. The calculated *t* value was significant, with $t(149) = -5.8820$, $p < .0001$. The mean number of tickets purchased for this season ($M = 6.83$, $s = 5.01$) was significantly higher than the mean number of tickets purchased for last season ($M = 5.63$, $s = 4.26$). Although the effect may be considered small according to conventional standards ($d = .28$), the new marketing and promotional strategies seem to have contributed, in part, to a meaningful increase in tickets purchased (21% improvement).

For a non-scholarly report, the results would be presented in the following manner:

> We surveyed a group of 150 people from the local community on how many MiLB baseball tickets they purchased for last season and this season. The average number of tickets purchased for this season (average = 6.83) was significantly higher than the average number of tickets purchased for last season (average = 5.63). Although the difference of a little more than one ticket may be considered small, the new marketing and promotional strategies seem to have contributed, in part, to a meaningful increase in tickets purchased (21% improvement), which compares favorably to the increase in ticket sales reported by other regional minor league teams for the same season.

PRACTICE PROBLEMS FOR *t*-TESTS

Independent *t*-Test

RESEARCH SCENARIO II

In this scenario, you will use an independent *t*-test to examine whether men and women differed in their perceptions about the hours of operation of the health club, as measured on a Likert scale (1 = poor, 4 = average, 7 = excellent). The results of this analysis will help the owner of the health club decide whether the hours of operation or perhaps the club's programming at select times in the day should be changed to accommodate the needs of men and women.

The dependent variable is the perception of the hours of operation (Op Hours), and the independent variable is gender. Use alpha = .05.

Questions for Independent *t*-Test

1. Test the data for assumption of equal variances. What are the variances in the scores for men and women regarding their perceptions of the hours of operation?

2. Did the data meet the assumption of equal variances? Explain.

3. Decide whether the analyst should use a one-tailed or two-tailed *t*-test to analyze this data, and explain your choice.

4. What are the mean and standard deviation for women and for men?

5. What is the *t* statistic? What is its significance?

6. What are the observations? Explain what the observations refer to.

7. What is the degrees of freedom? How is this calculated?

8. What is the *p* value?

9. What is the critical *t* value?

10. Are the results of the *t*-test statistically significant? Why or why not?

11. Using the formula for Cohen's *d*, what is the effect size for this data? Is the effect size meaningful? Why or why not?

12. How would you report the results of the *t*-test in a scholarly article?

13. How would you report them to the health club's owner?

Dependent *t*-Test

You will examine whether changes in the hours of operation for the health club have resulted in an increase in the frequency of weekly visits to the health club. A sample of 60 members was surveyed prior to changes in the hours of operation. Since this was not an anonymous survey, the same members were surveyed again about one month later. You will perform a dependent *t*-test to examine whether the frequency of weekly visits changed over this one-month span.

The dependent variable is facility usage (frequency of weekly visits to the health club). Time is the independent variable. Facility usage was measured before (ExWeekT1) and after (ExWeekT2) changes in the hours of operation. Use alpha = .05.

Questions for Dependent *t*-Test

1. Should you use a one-tailed or two-tailed *t*-test? Explain your choice.

2. What are the mean, variance, and standard deviation for Time 1 and for Time 2?

3. What is the Pearson correlation for the Time 1 and Time 2 values?

4. What is the degrees of freedom?

5. What are the *t* statistic and critical *t* values for this data?

6. Are the results of the dependent *t*-test statistically significant? Why or why not?

7. Based on percent improvement, are the results meaningful? Why or why not?

8. How would you report the results in a scholarly article?

9. How would you report the results to the health club's owner?

TALKING POINTS

t-Tests

- An independent *t*-test compares the means from two independent (or different) sample groups.

- A dependent *t*-test compares the means from two samples that are related.

- Effect size (or Cohen's *d*) is the most common measure of meaningfulness and should be used for both types of *t*-test.

- Another measure of meaningfulness, r^2, is an alternative measure for independent *t*-tests.

- Percent improvement, or change, is an alternative measure of meaningfulness for dependent *t*-tests.

Analysis of Variance

EXECUTIVE SUMMARY With analysis of variance, we can examine the differences among multiple means on one dependent variable. We can use ANOVA to compare means with one independent variable (one-way ANOVA) or to compare means from multiple independent variables (factorial ANOVA). With factorial ANOVA, we can also evaluate the interaction of the independent variables.

WHAT IS ANOVA?

A nalysis of variance (ANOVA) is a statistical technique used to examine the differences among means on one dependent variable that is measured with an interval or ratio scale. We will discuss two main types of ANOVA procedures: one-way ANOVA and factorial ANOVA. The *t*-test provides a statistical test for comparing two means, but ANOVA is a more general procedure that allows for a comparison of multiple means. In fact, a *t*-test is just a special case of ANOVA that is limited to two means. The terms *one-way* and *factorial* refer to the number of independent variables that are being examined. In ANOVA we call the independent variable the *factor*.

Each factor may have multiple levels (that is, we can have two or more groups, conditions, or measurement times). The term *repeated measures,* as in "one-way ANOVA with repeated measures," indicates that the same measure was collected multiple times (repeatedly). This situation is similar to a dependent *t*-test, which focuses on a measure that is collected twice in a study. Regardless of the type of ANOVA test, the test statistic is *F*. We will discuss *F* in detail later in this chapter.

ONE-WAY ANOVA

A one-way ANOVA compares the means from two or more independent sample groups on one dependent variable. The term *one-way* means that only one independent variable (or factor) is being examined. The independent variable may have multiple levels (or groups). As with the use of *t*-tests, ANOVA in sport management research is limited only by the imagination of the analyst. For example, we could create multiple groups based on the length of employment at a sport organization (independent variable): experienced (> 6 months), less experienced (1–5 months), and novice employees (< 1 month). We could compare these individuals on a particular dependent variable of interest, such as a measure of productivity (e.g., average calls or sales made) or job satisfaction. Other multi-level groups that we could examine include age (young/middle/older), education (high school/some college/college degree/graduate degree), exerciser status (regular exerciser/infrequent exerciser/sedentary), venue size (small/medium/large), and departments in a sport organization (administration/facilities/marketing/sales/operations). As with independent *t*-tests, a participant in one group cannot also belong to another group.

Performing a One-Way ANOVA

RESEARCH SCENARIO I

As a member of the front office of a MiLB team, you wish to use the data collected in the study of 150 community participants to determine whether the number of tickets purchased differs according to various age groups (young = 18–29 yrs; middle = 30–49 yrs; older = 50+ yrs). The dependent variable is tickets purchased last year (column J). Age is the independent variable.

STEP 1

Before you can perform the one-way ANOVA to see whether number of tickets purchased differs by age group, you must complete two tasks: data reorganization and Levene's test for the assumption of homogeneity of variances (or equal variances) in a three-or-more-group scenario. This is a test of the assumption for use of parametric tests that the spread (or variance) in number of tickets purchased last year will be the same for each of the age groups. Testing for this assumption was first discussed in Chapter 17 in the independent *t*-test example. As discussed there, Excel includes an option to test for this assumption in a two-group/sample scenario, called the F-Test Two Sample for Variances. Unfortunately, Excel does not include a built-in analysis for Levene's test, which tests the assumption in a three-or-more-group scenario. We will follow a procedure to perform this test "manually."

First, organize the data with the three age groups serving as new column headings: Young (column O), Middle (column P), and Older (column Q). Copy and paste the number of tickets purchased into the appropriate columns (see Exhibit 18.1). For example, copy and paste the number of tickets purchased from cells J2 through J26 (young women) and J77 through J101 (young men) to the new Young column (column O). Repeat this process for the age groups Middle and Older (see Exhibit 18.1). Also, use the Average function to display the mean at the end of each column (cells O52 through Q52).

STEP 2   Before conducting Levene's test to check for homogeneity of variances, create three new columns to represent the absolute values of the residuals of the variable. Enter Res-Y, Res-M, and Res-O as headings in columns R, S, and T, respectively. The **residuals** are the absolute values of the differences between the raw scores and the sample mean. To calculate them in Excel, we will create a formula that subtracts the sample mean from the raw score and takes the absolute. For the Res-Y column, the appropriate raw scores appear in column O, and the mean is found in cell O52. In cell R2, we enter the following function: =ABS(O2-$O$52). See Exhibit 18.2. Highlight the cell and drag it down the column to copy and paste this function to the remaining cells in the column.

EXHIBIT   18.1   Reorganizing data by age group for average number of tickets purchased.

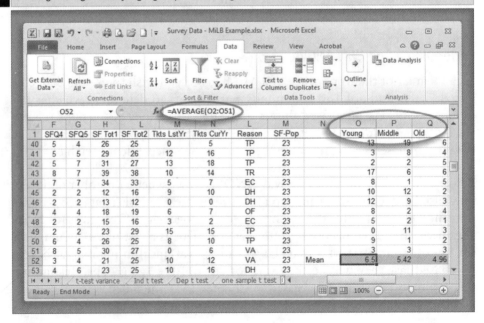

Residuals calculation for Levene's test for homogeneity of variances.   **EXHIBIT** **18.2**

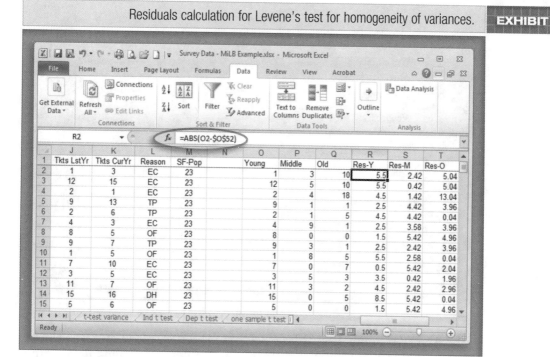

	J	K	L	M	N	O	P	Q	R	S	T
1	Tkts LstYr	Tkts CurYr	Reason	SF-Pop		Young	Middle	Old	Res-Y	Res-M	Res-O
2	1	3	EC	23		1	3	10	5.5	2.42	5.04
3	12	15	EC	23		12	5	10	5.5	0.42	5.04
4	2	1	EC	23		2	4	18	4.5	1.42	13.04
5	9	13	TP	23		9	1	1	2.5	4.42	3.96
6	2	6	TP	23		2	1	5	4.5	4.42	0.04
7	4	3	EC	23		4	9	1	2.5	3.58	3.96
8	8	5	OF	23		8	0	0	1.5	5.42	4.96
9	9	7	TP	23		9	3	1	2.5	2.42	3.96
10	1	5	OF	23		1	8	5	5.5	2.58	0.04
11	7	10	EC	23		7	0	7	0.5	5.42	2.04
12	3	5	EC	23		3	5	3	3.5	0.42	1.96
13	11	7	OF	23		11	3	2	4.5	2.42	2.96
14	15	16	DH	23		15	0	5	8.5	5.42	0.04
15	5	6	OF	23		5	0	0	1.5	5.42	4.96

Formula bar: R2 — f_x =ABS(O2-$O$52)

Sheet tabs: t-test variance / Ind t test / Dep t test / one sample t test

Repeat this process for the Res-M and Res-O columns, making sure to select the appropriate reference cells.

To conduct Levene's test, select *Data* and then *Data Analysis* on the far right. **STEP 3** In the Analysis Tools box, select *Anova: Single Factor* (see Exhibit 18.3). Click *OK*. In StatPlus, click on *Statistics*, then *Analysis of Variance (ANOVA)*. Select *One-way ANOVA (simple)*.

Excel's Data Analysis box for Levene's test *(Anova: Single Factor).*   **EXHIBIT** **18.3**

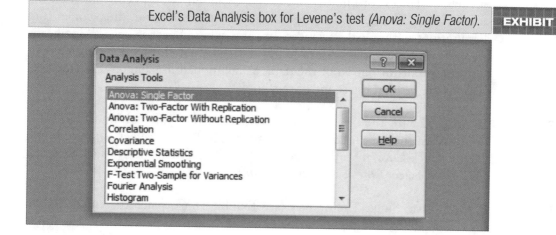

EXHIBIT **18.4**   Excel's Anova: Single Factor box, used for Levene's test.

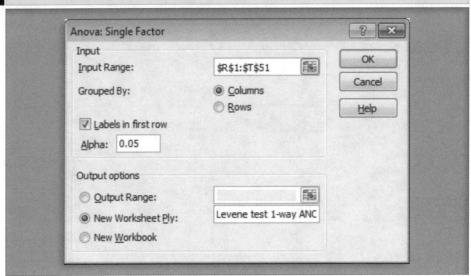

STEP 4   In the ANOVA: Single Factor box (see Exhibit 18.4), place the cursor in the *Input Range* box and highlight the residual values in columns R, S, and T. The Input Range box should read **$R$1:$T$51**. Be sure to select *Grouped By Columns* and the *Labels* box, because the first row contains the column headings. Select the alpha level of 0.05. Under Output Options, select *New Worksheet Ply* and enter a title for the new worksheet (e.g., Levene test 1-way ANOVA). Click *OK.* In StatPlus, in the *ANOVA* box, place the cursor in the *Variables* box and then highlight the appropriate residual values in columns R, S, and T. In *Preferences,* make sure the alpha is .05. Click *OK.*

In Exhibit 18.5, the variances appear in cells E5 through E7, and the *p* value is not significant (.58 > .05), so we would not reject the null hypothesis of equal variances for number of tickets purchased. We can conclude that the sample variances for the three age groups do not differ and, thus, come from distributions with equal variances. In cases where Levene's test is significant (*p* < .05) and the variances are found not to be equal, then we may have to perform a transformation of the data, as mentioned in Chapter 17. Transformations are beyond the scope of this book.

STEP 5   To proceed with the one-way ANOVA, select the *Data* tab and then *Data Analysis* on the far right. In the *Analysis Tools* box, select *Anova: Single Factor.* Click *OK.* In StatPlus, click on *Statistics,* then *Analysis of Variance (ANOVA).* Select *One-way ANOVA (simple).*

STEP 6   In the Anova: Single Factor box (see Exhibit 18.6), place the cursor in the *Input Range* box and highlight the values in columns O, P, and Q. The Input

EXHIBIT 18.5

Excel output for Levene's test of homogeneity of variances.   **EXHIBIT** 18.5

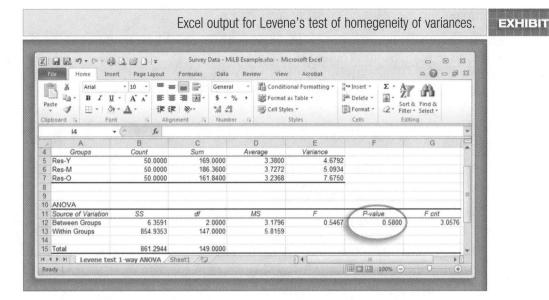

Range box should read **$O$1:$Q$51**. Be sure to select *Grouped By Columns* and the *Labels* box, because the first row contains the column headings. Select the alpha level of 0.05. Under Output Options, select *New Worksheet Ply* and enter a title for the new worksheet (e.g., 1-way ANOVA). Click *OK*. In StatPlus, in the ANOVA box, place the cursor in the *Variables* box and then highlight the appropriate values in columns O, P, and Q. In *Preferences*, make sure the alpha is .05. Click *OK*.

Excel's ANOVA: Single Factor box, used for one-way ANOVA.   **EXHIBIT** 18.6

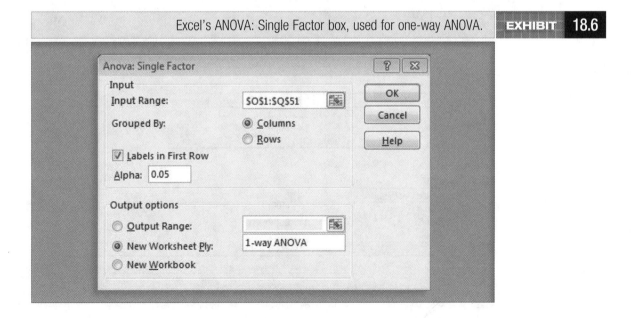

Interpreting the results: Statistical significance

The summary output, shown in Exhibit 18.7, provides the mean and variance for each group: Young (M = 6.50, s^2 = 16.34), Middle (M = 5.42, s^2 = 19.27), and Older (M = 4.96, s^2 = 18.37). As discussed in Chapter 17, when we report these summary statistics, the conventional method is to provide the standard deviation for each group instead of the variance. To find the standard deviation, take the square root of each variance (column E in Exhibit 18.7), as follows:

$$s_{young} = \sqrt{s^2} = \sqrt{16.34} = 4.04$$

$$s_{middle} = \sqrt{19.27} = 4.39$$

$$s_{older} = \sqrt{18.37} = 4.29$$

Count (column B in the summary table) refers to the sample size (n) within each group. Between Groups (Row 12) refers to the true variance associated with the group differences. The degrees of freedom (df, cell C12) equals $k - 1$,

---

EXHIBIT 18.7   Excel's summary output for one-way ANOVA.

where k = the number of groups. Within Groups (row 13) refers to the error variance associated with the measures, and df (cell C13) equals $N - k$, where N is the total sample size and k is the number of groups ($150 - 3 = 147$). The test statistic (F) is the ratio of true variance over error variance and is evaluated based on the F distribution associated with the degrees of freedoms in the study. The **F distribution** is a probability distribution based in inferential statistics, especially ANOVA, that we use when examining the ratio of the variances for two normally distributed populations. The F value is a random variable with an F distribution. The farther the calculated F value moves away from 1.00, the less likely it would be that the calculated F value is a chance occurrence.

The F value (or test statistic) is $F(2, 147) = 1.74$. Whenever an F value is reported, the degrees of freedom for the between groups and the within groups are noted in parentheses, followed by the calculated F value. The p value for the calculated F value indicates that the F value is not significant, because the probability of this test statistic being due to chance is about 18 times in 100, which is greater than the alpha level ($p = .1797 >$ alpha $= .05$). Stated another way, the absolute calculated F value does not exceed the critical F value at the *a priori* alpha level ($\alpha = .05$) that was selected as the level of significance ($1.7368 < 3.0576$).

If the F value had been considered significant, follow-up (also called post hoc) tests would be necessary. Why? The F test indicates only whether there is at least one significant difference among the means (actually, all possible combinations of the means), and not which one or combination is significant. To find out which difference is significant, we can perform several different post hoc tests. One type of post hoc test would be to conduct several different independent t-tests (see Chapter 17) on all possible pairings. In a three-group situation, there would be three different possible pairs: groups 1 and 2, groups 1 and 3, and groups 2 and 3.

Interpreting the results: Practical significance (meaningfulness)

We can calculate two measures of meaningfulness for a one-way ANOVA. Although both measures may be reported, one measure will usually suffice. The more widely reported measure of meaningfulness for one-way ANOVA is called **eta-squared** (η^2), and it provides the proportion of total variation of the dependent variable that is accounted for (or explained by) the independent variable. This measure is very easy to calculate; it is based on sum of squares (SS) values provided in the ANOVA table. The sum of squares between groups ($SS_{Between}$) quantifies the variability *between* the comparison groups, and the sum of squares total (SS_{Total}) quantifies the *total* variability in the observed data. The general formula for η^2 is:

$$\eta^2 = \frac{SS_{Between}}{SS_{Total}}$$

For our example,

$$\eta^2 = \frac{62.4933}{2707.0933} = .0231$$

From this calculation, the MiLB front office can conclude that about 2% of the total variation in number of tickets purchased can be accounted for by age. This figure confirms that the effect of age on ticket purchases is not significant.

The second measure of meaningfulness that we can calculate for a one-way ANOVA is called **omega-squared** (ω^2), and this measure also refers to the proportion of total variation of the dependent variable that is accounted for (or explained by) the independent variable. This measure is more accurate than η^2, which tends to overestimate slightly. Omega-squared is calculated based on SS values and mean square within groups (MS_{Within}) values, provided in the ANOVA table in cells B12, B15, and D13. We use the following formula:

$$\omega^2 = \frac{[SS_{Between} - (df_{Between})(MS_{Within})]}{(SS_{Total} + MS_{Within})}$$

In our example,

$$\omega^2 = \frac{[62.4933 - (2)(17.9905)]}{(2707.0933 + 17.9905)}$$

$$\omega^2 = \frac{[62.4933 - (35.981)]}{2725.0838}$$

$$\omega^2 = \frac{26.5123}{2725.0838} = .0097$$

Less than 1% of the total variation in number of tickets purchased can be accounted for by age. Based on the results of the statistical and practical significance analyses, this measure confirms that the age group difference in means is not meaningful at all and that other variables should be examined to help account for the 99% of the variance that is left unexplained.

If we needed to conduct post hoc tests, we could calculate effect sizes for any significant findings that resulted from the independent t-tests. The section on practical significance for independent t-tests covers calculation of effect size (see Chapter 17).

Statistical statement

For the example, the results would be reported in a scholarly article in the following manner:

A one-way ANOVA was performed to determine whether the number of tickets purchased differed by age groups (young = 18–29 yrs; middle = 30–49 yrs; older = 50+ yrs). The calculated F value was not significant, with $F(2, 147) = 1.74$, $p = .1797$, in samples of young ($M = 6.50$, $s = 4.04$), middle ($M = 5.42$, $s = 4.39$), and older ($M = 4.96$, $s = 4.29$) community participants. Measures of meaningfulness indicated that age group accounted for less than 1% of the variance in number of tickets purchased, as measured by ω^2.

For a non-scholarly report, the results would be presented in the following manner:

We surveyed 150 people from the local community on the number of tickets they purchased last year. Equal numbers of participants were selected from three age groups (young = 18–29 yrs; middle = 30–49 yrs; older = 50+ yrs), and we tested whether age groups differed in the number of tickets purchased. Average number of tickets purchased per person did not differ significantly among the age groups: young (6.50), middle (5.42), and older (4.96).

ONE-WAY ANOVA WITH REPEATED MEASURES

A one-way **ANOVA with repeated measures** compares the means from two or more samples that are related. The most common situation is when one sample group is measured two or more times on the same dependent variable. The independent variable is the time of measurement. For example, we could measure participants' attitudes or feelings about a sport team multiple times across a season or across multiple years with the same sample of fans, season ticket holders, or community residents. A sport manager could evaluate changes in workplace productivity (e.g., tickets sold, sponsorship sales, new memberships) or employee satisfaction across time (e.g., weekly, monthly, annually). Although the changes might simply result from the passage of time, the manager might implement purposeful changes (e.g., different interventions, conditions, marketing strategies) and evaluate the effects of these changes in the sample.

Performing a One-Way ANOVA with Repeated Measures

We will use the same scenario presented in Chapter 17 for a dependent *t*-test, in order to illustrate that a one-way ANOVA with repeated measures will result in the same findings as obtained with a dependent *t*-test. The number of measures can easily be extended to three or more, as will be noted in the steps below.

Prior to the start of the baseball season, 150 community participants were measured on the number of tickets they purchased last year. After the end of the baseball season, the same participants were assessed on the number of tickets they purchased for the current season. The results of this analysis will determine whether new marketing strategies created with fandom in mind were effective or not.

The dependent variable is number of tickets purchased. Time is the independent variable, with tickets purchased last year being Time 1 (column J) and after the current season being Time 2 (column K). *Note:* This statistical test is not available in the free version of StatPlus.

RESEARCH SCENARIO I

STEP 1 Click on the *Data* tab and then *Data Analysis* on the far right. The Data Analysis box should appear. Select *Anova: Two-Factor Without Replication* from the Analysis Tools menu (see Exhibit 18.8). We select this option because there is only one measurement for each level of the independent variable. Click *OK*.

STEP 2 The Anova: Two-Factor Without Replication box (see Exhibit 18.9) should appear. Place the cursor in the *Input Range* box and highlight the values in columns J and K that give the number of tickets purchased last year and this year, respectively. The Input Range box should read **$J$2:$K$151**. Select the alpha level of 0.05. Under Output Options, select *New Worksheet Ply* and enter a title for the new worksheet (e.g., One-way RM ANOVA). Click *OK*.

Note that the number of columns included at this step in this analysis could easily have involved many more measurement time points. This example has only two measures, but if there were more measures, then we would have highlighted all of the appropriate columns.

EXHIBIT 18.8 Excel's Data Analysis box for one-way ANOVA with repeated measures.

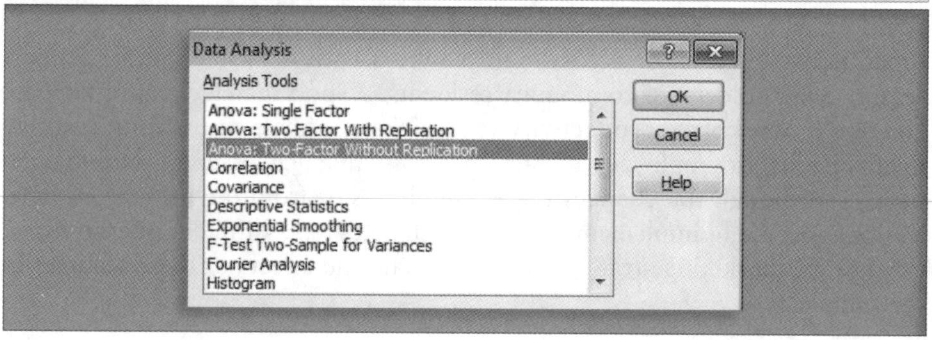

EXHIBIT 18.9 Excel's Anova: Two-Factor Without Replication box, used for one-way ANOVA with repeated measures.

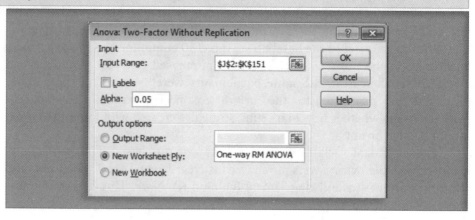

Interpreting the results: Statistical significance

The summary output shown in Exhibit 18.10 provides the mean and standard deviation for number of tickets purchased last year (see cells D155 and E155 of the output: $M = 5.63$, $s = 4.26$) and number of tickets purchased this year (see cells D156 and E156 of the output: $M = 6.83$, $s = 5.01$). As stated earlier, we calculate the standard deviation by taking the square root of the variance. In the ANOVA table, disregard the effect for rows (row 161) and focus on the effect for columns (row 162), which is the time effect (or true variance). The time effect, or true variance, reflects the difference in number of tickets purchased last year and this year. The degrees of freedom for time equals $T - 1$, where $T =$ the number of times of measurement: df $= 2 - 1 = 1$. When we calculate the error variance, df $= (T - 1)(N - 1)$, where N equals the total sample size: df $= (2 - 1)(150 - 1) = 149$. As before, the test statistic (F) is the ratio of true variance over error variance and is evaluated based on the F distribution associated with the degrees of freedom in the study. The further the calculated F value moves away from 1.00, the less likely it is that the calculated F value is a chance occurrence.

The ANOVA table provides the F value: $F(1, 149) = 34.5979$. As stated earlier, whenever an F value is reported, the degrees of freedom for the true variance and error variance are noted in parentheses, followed by the calculated F value. The p value for the calculated F value is also provided. In this example, the p value indicates that the F value is significant, because the probability of this test statistic being due to chance is less than 1 in 10,000 (i.e., $p < .0001$), which is less than the alpha level of 0.05. Stated another way, the absolute calculated F value exceeded the critical F value at the *a priori* alpha level ($\alpha = .05$) that was selected as the level of significance ($34.5979 > 3.9046$).

Since the F value is significant, we would need to conduct post hoc tests in situations with three or more measures. With a repeated measures design involv-

---

Excel's summary output for one-way ANOVA with repeated measures.   **EXHIBIT** 18.10

	A	B	C	D	E	F	G
154	SUMMARY	Count	Sum	Average	Variance		
155	Column 1	150.0000	844.0000	5.6267	18.1684		
156	Column 2	150.0000	1025.0000	6.8333	25.0526		
157							
158							
159	ANOVA						
160	Source of Variation	SS	df	MS	F	P-value	F crit
161	Rows	5969.6300	149.0000	40.0646	12.6933	0.0000	1.3104
162	Columns	109.2033	1.0000	109.2033	34.5979	0.0000	3.9046
163	Error	470.2967	149.0000	3.1564			
164							
165	Total	6549.1300	299.0000				

ing three or more measures, we could perform several dependent t-tests on all possible group pairings. For more information on post hoc tests, see the discussion in the one-way ANOVA example. For a two-measure effect, post hoc tests are not necessary. Can you see why? The F test indicates that there is at least one significant difference among the measures involved, and the only possible difference in a two-measure situation is the difference between those two measures.

As discussed earlier, a t-test is just a special case of ANOVA. The F value and t value are related ($F = t^2$). In our example, the dependent t-test returned a t value of 5.8820, and the one-way ANOVA with repeated measures returned an F value of 34.5979. Notice that

$$t^2 = 5.8820^2 = 34.5979 = F$$

Interpreting the results: Practical significance (meaningfulness)

A measure of meaningfulness for a one-way ANOVA with repeated measures is **partial eta-squared** (η_p^2), which is interpreted in the same way as eta-squared (that is, it refers to the proportion of total variation of the dependent variable that is explained by the independent variable). This measure is very easy to calculate; it is based on sum of squares values provided in the ANOVA table, as follows:

$$\eta_p^2 = \frac{SS_{Effect}}{SS_{Effect} + SS_{Error}}$$

For our example,

$$\eta_p^2 = \frac{SS_{Effect}}{SS_{Effect} + SS_{Error}}$$

$$\eta_p^2 = \frac{109.2033}{(109.2033 + 490.2967)}$$

$$\eta_p^2 = \frac{109.2033}{579.50} = .1884$$

About 19% of the total variation in number of tickets purchased can be accounted for by time (i.e., last season to the current season). "Time" represents any intervening factors, such as new marketing and promotional strategies that influence the variance in number of tickets purchased across these two time points. Based on the statistical results and the effect size, we conclude that the difference in means is meaningful and accounts for 19% of the variance in number of tickets purchased. So, time (or, in reality, the intervening factors that occurred during this time interval), is an important variable, but other variables should be examined to help account for the 81% of the variance that is left unexplained.

If post hoc tests had been necessary, we could have calculated the effect sizes or percent changes among significant pairwise differences.

Statistical statement

For the example, the results would be reported in a scholarly article in the following manner:

> A one-way ANOVA with repeated measures was performed to compare the number of MiLB baseball tickets purchased last season and this season in a sample of 150 community participants. The calculated F value was significant, with $F(1, 149) = 34.5979$, $p < .0001$, $\eta_p^2 = .1884$. The mean number of tickets purchased for this season ($M = 6.83$, $s = 5.01$) was significantly higher than the mean number of tickets purchased for last season ($M = 5.63$, $s = 4.26$). The new marketing and promotional strategies contributed, in part, to a meaningful increase in tickets purchased (21% improvement), with the passage of time accounting for about 19% of the variance.

For a non-scholarly report, the results would be presented in the following manner:

> We surveyed a group of 150 people from the local community on how many MiLB baseball tickets they purchased for last season and this season. The average number of tickets purchased for this season (average = 6.83) was significantly higher than the average number of tickets purchased for last season ($M = 5.63$). Although the difference of a little more than one ticket may appear small, the new marketing and promotional strategies seem to have contributed, in part, to a meaningful increase in number of tickets purchased (21% improvement).

FACTORIAL ANOVA

A factorial ANOVA compares the effects of two or more independent variables on one dependent variable. If a factorial ANOVA includes two independent variables (IVs), it is referred to as a two-way ANOVA. Three IVs make a three-way ANOVA, and so forth. Each independent variable may have multiple levels (or groups). Given the complexity of sport organizations and the factors involved, factorial ANOVA is often preferred over one-way ANOVA because it allows the analyst to examine the effects of multiple independent variables simultaneously. However, the inclusion of too many variables makes interpretation difficult, so it is important to be parsimonious. In other words, the analyst should carefully review available research and select a few important independent variables to examine that are believed to have an effect on the dependent variable.

For example, an analyst could examine the effects of age and gender on a particular variable of interest, such as a measure of productivity (e.g., average number of calls or sales) or job satisfaction. Factorial ANOVA calculates the effect of each independent variable, while controlling for the other independent variables. The effect of each independent variable is called the **main effect**. For example, we might want to consider how age alone affects the number of sales calls per hour. To study this main effect, we would group men and women together for each age group and compare the means for each age group. In

Exhibit 18.11, the bar graph illustrates a significant main effect for age group, with young people being more productive on calls per hour than middle-aged and older individuals. Gender does not enter into this comparison. However, we could also consider how gender alone affects the number of calls per hour. To study this main effect, we would group men of all ages together and women of all ages together, and then we would compare the means for men and women. In Exhibit 18.12, the bar graph illustrates a non-significant main effect for gender; men and women have the same average number of calls per hour.

Additionally and perhaps more importantly, factorial ANOVA also calculates the interaction of the independent variables. This is called the **interaction effect**. Perhaps the effect of age on the number of calls per hour varies by gender (e.g., young men might be more productive than young women, but the reverse might be true with older individuals). When we plot the data on a line graph, the data lines will not be parallel when there is a significant interaction effect (see Exhibit 18.13). When the interaction effect is not significant, the data lines will be parallel.

EXHIBIT 18.11 Significant main effect for age on number of calls per hour.

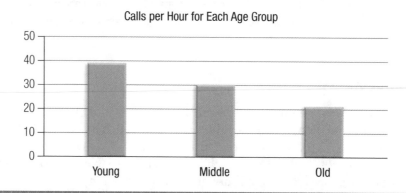

EXHIBIT 18.12 No significant main effect for gender on number of calls per hour.

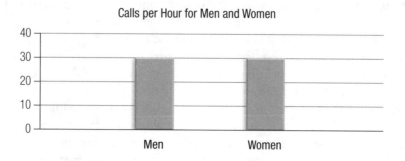

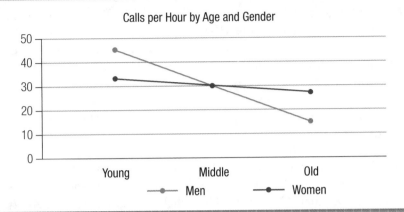

Age (young/middle/older), education (high school/some college/college degree/graduate degree), exerciser status (regular exerciser/infrequent exerciser/sedentary), venue size (small/medium/large), and departments in a sport organization (administration/facilities/marketing/sales/operations) are just a few other multilevel groups that could be examined. The important point to remember is that a participant in one group cannot also belong to another group.

Performing a Two-Way (Factorial) ANOVA

RESEARCH SCENARIO I

As a member of the front office of a MiLB team, you wish to use the data collected in the study of 150 community participants to determine whether the number of tickets purchased differs by gender or age group (young = 18–29 yrs; middle = 30–49 yrs; older = 50+ yrs). In particular, you are interested in whether potential gender differences are larger or smaller in certain age groups. The dependent variable is number of tickets purchased last year (column J). Gender is one independent variable, and column J contains the scores for both men and women. Age is the second independent variable.

STEP 1

Before we can perform the two-way ANOVA, we must check the data regarding the assumptions for parametric tests, particularly for homogeneity of variances. See the discussion of the independent t-test (two levels) or one-way ANOVA (multiple levels) for more information about checking for homogeneity of variances.

STEP 2

We will also have to reorganize the data, a process described in step 1 of the one-way ANOVA example. We will create three new column headings: Young (column O), Middle (column P), and Older (column Q). Then, we will group together the scores for men and for women (see Exhibit 18.14). Copy and paste the number of tickets purchased from cells J2 through J26 (young women) and J77 through J101 (young men) to the new Young column (column O) in cells O2 through O26 and O27 through O51, respectively. Repeat this process for the Middle and Older age groups (Exhibit 18.14). If you are using StatPlus, you will not have to reorganize the data, but you will need to dummy code the independent variables (i.e., gender and age). See Chapter 16 for an example of dummy coding. Make sure to copy and paste the age and gender data into different columns. Then you may proceed with dummy coding. For gender, code men as 0 and women as 1. Young participants will be coded as 1, middle age as 2, and older as 3.

STEP 3 To proceed with the two-way ANOVA, select the *Data* tab and then *Data Analysis* on the far right. In the Analysis Tools box, select *Anova: Two-Factor With Replication*. Click *OK*. In StatPlus, click on *Statistics*, then *Analysis of Variance (ANOVA)*. Select *Two-way ANOVA*.

STEP 4 In the Anova: Two-Factor With Replication box (see Exhibit 18.15), place the cursor in the *Input Range* box and highlight columns N, O, P, and Q (including the headings). The Input Range box should read **$N$1:$Q$51**. Rows per sample refers to the number of observations (or participants) in each group

EXHIBIT 18.14 New columns for average number of tickets purchased by age group.

	A	B	C	D	E	F	G	H	I	J	K	L	M	N	O	P	Q
1	Gender	Age	SFQ1	SFQ2	SFQ3	SFQ4	SFQ5	SF Tot1	SF Tot2	Tkts LstYr	Tkts CurYr	Reason			Young	Middle	Old
2	F	18	7	7	4	5	6	29	29	1	3	EC		Women	1	3	10
3	F	18	8	8	8	8	7	39	35	12	15	EC			12	5	10
4	F	19	2	2	2	2	1	9	8	2	1	EC			2	4	18
5	F	20	8	5	4	3	4	24	29	9	13	TP			9	1	1
6	F	20	7	7	4	7	7	32	25	2	6	TP			2	1	5
7	F	20	6	6	7	6	6	31	10	4	3	EC			4	9	1
8	F	21	5	4	4	4	4	21	25	8	5	OF			8	0	0
9	F	21	4	2	2	1	1	10	15	9	7	TP			9	3	1
10	F	21	3	3	3	3	3	15	17	1	5	OF			1	8	5
11	F	21	6	4	3	2	2	17	14	7	10	EC			7	0	7
12	F	21	4	5	5	5	5	24	28	3	5	EC			3	5	3
13	F	21	8	8	6	5	7	34	31	11	7	OF			11	3	2
14	F	21	8	7	7	6	7	35	34	15	16	DH			15	0	5
15	F	22	3	3	1	1	1	9	9	5	6	OF			5	0	0
16	F	22	7	6	5	5	5	28	22	2	6	EC			2	12	4
17	F	22	4	3	6	4	4	21	20	5	9	OF			5	13	0
18	F	23	7	7	4	4	5	27	26	8	13	EC			8	10	16
19	F	24	5	4	2	3	3	17	15	6	8	OF			6	5	0
20	F	24	5	4	3	5	4	21	22	7	5	TP			7	9	1
21	F	25	1	1	1	1	1	5	6	0	0	EC			0	0	4
22	F	25	6	5	5	3	3	22	23	10	12	EC			10	6	6
23	F	26	4	3	5	5	5	22	19	6	5	DH			6	3	1
24	F	28	4	7	5	5	7	28	26	11	13	TP			11	15	0
25	F	28	8	7	8	6	7	36	35	9	14	EC			9	8	6
26	F	29	4	5	5	7	6	27	26	10	7	EC			10	0	3
27	F	30	5	1	1	1	1	9	6	3	3	OF		Men	5	12	3
28	F	31	6	5	4	3	3	21	22	5	4	TP			11	5	11
29	F	31	4	4	3	3	3	17	20	4	8	TP			5	4	14
30	F	31	4	3	4	3	3	17	23	1	2	EC			3	2	5

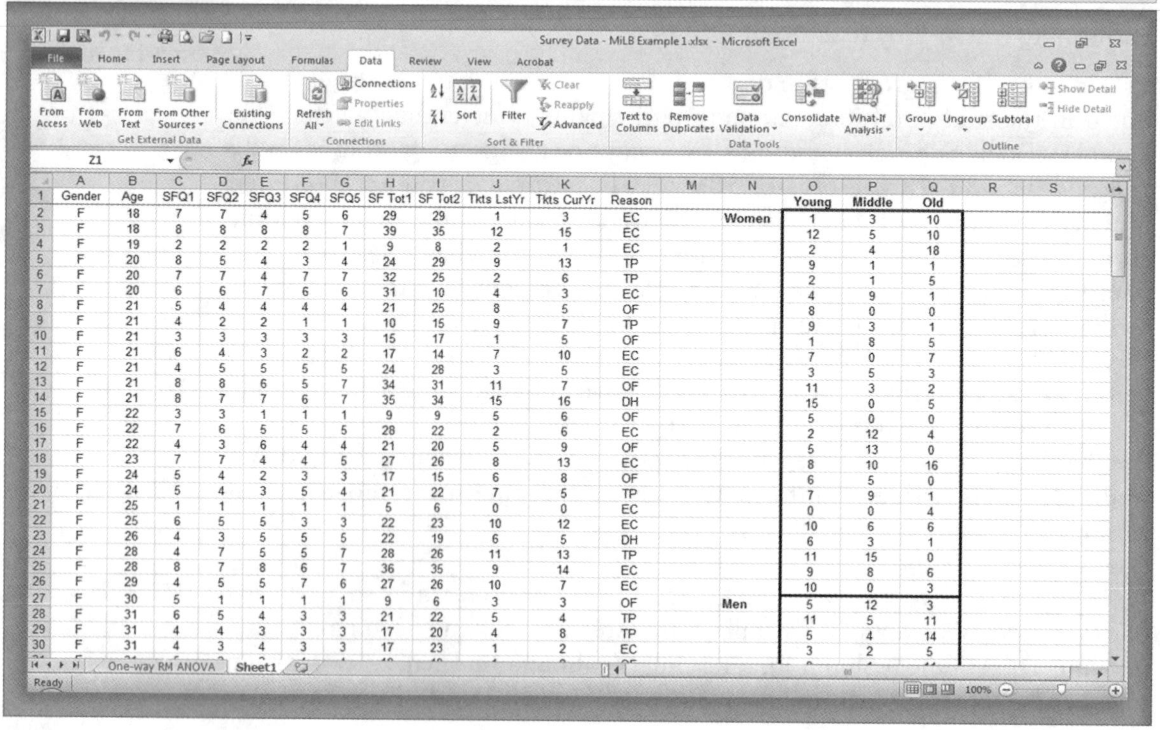

(i.e., 25). Select the alpha level of 0.05. Under Output Options, select *New Worksheet Ply* and enter a title (e.g., Two-way ANOVA). Click *OK*. In StatPlus, in the ANOVA box, place the cursor in the *Response* box and then highlight the appropriate values for the dependent variable (i.e., number of tickets purchased last year). Next, place the cursor in the *Factor #1* box and highlight the appropriate values in the dummy-coded gender column. Finally, place the cursor in the *Factor #2* box and highlight the appropriate values in the dummy-coded age column. In Preferences, make sure the alpha is .05. Click *OK*.

Interpreting the results: Statistical significance

As shown in Exhibit 18.16, the summary output provides the mean and variance for men and women in each age group, as well as the marginal statistics (i.e., the means and variances averaged across the levels of the other factor). Under "Source of Variation," the main effect (true variance) for gender is found in the row labeled Sample. This indicates whether a significant difference exists between the marginal mean for women (found in cell E7) and for men (in cell E13). The degrees of freedom (df_{gender}) equals $g - 1$, where g is the number of gender groups. The main effect for age is found in the row labeled Columns. This indicates whether any significant differences exist among the marginal means for the three age groups (in cells B19, C19, and D19). The degrees of freedom (df_{age}) equals $a - 1$, where a is the number of age groups. The interaction effect (true variance) for gender x age, found in the row labeled Interaction, indicates whether the pattern of mean gender differences is similar across the three age groups (cells B7, B13, C7, C13, D7, and D13). The degrees of freedom (df_{Int}) equals df_{gender} x df_{age}. Within Group refers to the error variance associated with

EXHIBIT	18.16	Excel's summary output for two-way ANOVA.

	A	B	C	D	E	F	G
1	Anova: Two-Factor With Replication						
2							
3	SUMMARY	Young	Middle	Old	Total		
4	*Women*						
5	Count	25.0000	25.0000	25.0000	75.0000		
6	Sum	163.0000	123.0000	109.0000	395.0000		
7	Average	6.5200	4.9200	4.3600	5.2667		
8	Variance	15.7600	20.3267	23.3233	20.1171		
9							
10	*Men*						
11	Count	25.0000	25.0000	25.0000	75.0000		
12	Sum	162.0000	148.0000	139.0000	449.0000		
13	Average	6.4800	5.9200	5.5600	5.9867		
14	Variance	17.5933	18.4933	13.4233	16.2025		
15							
16	*Total*						
17	Count	50.0000	50.0000	50.0000			
18	Sum	325.0000	271.0000	248.0000			
19	Average	6.5000	5.4200	4.9600			
20	Variance	16.3367	19.2690	18.3657			
21							
22							
23	ANOVA						
24	Source of Variation	SS	df	MS	F	P-value	F crit
25	Sample	19.4400	1.0000	19.4400	1.0709	0.3025	3.9068
26	Columns	62.4933	2.0000	31.2467	1.7213	0.1825	3.0589
27	Interaction	11.0800	2.0000	5.5400	0.3052	0.7375	3.0589
28	Within	2614.0800	144.0000	18.1533			
29							
30	Total	2707.0933	149.0000				

the measures, and $df_{Error} = (N - 1) - (df_{gender} + df_{age} + df_{Int})$, where N is the total sample size. For completeness, $df_{Total} = df_{gender} + df_{age} + df_{Int} + df_{Error}$ (or, more simply, $N - 1$). The test statistic *(F)* and associated p value are given for each main effect and interaction effect. As you may recall, whenever an F value is reported, the degrees of freedom for the true variance and the error variance are noted in parentheses, followed by the calculated F value for that effect.

In the table, the F value for gender, $F(1, 144) = 1.07$, is not significant ($p = .30$), which means that men and women did not differ in the number of tickets purchased last year. The F value for age, $F(2, 144) = 1.72$, is also not significant ($p = .18$), which means that young, middle, and older age groups did not differ in the number of tickets purchased last year. The F value for gender x age, $F(2, 144) = .31$, is also not significant ($p = .74$), which means that the difference in the number of tickets purchased last year by men and women did not differ across young, middle, and older age groups. None of the effects were considered significant because the probability of these test statistics being due to chance was, at minimum, 18 times in 100, which is greater than the alpha level of 0.05. Stated another way, the absolute calculated F values did not exceed the critical F values at the *a priori* alpha level ($\alpha = .05$) that was selected as the level of significance.

If the F value had been found significant, we would have conducted post hoc tests, including independent t-tests for all possible pairwise group comparisons to identify exactly where the significant differences occurred. Suppose that the main effect for age *was* significant. The values stated in the following paragraph are hypothetical, to illustrate how a researcher would write a statement for the main effect of age with a significant finding.

> The F value for age was significant, with $F(2, 144) = 14.84$, $p < .01$. Follow-up independent t-tests showed that young participants purchased more ($p < .05$) tickets last year ($M = 8.30$, $s = 4.00$) than middle-aged ($M = 5.50$, $s = 3.00$) and older ($M = 4.90$, $s = 3.50$) community participants. The magnitude of these differences was large, with $d = .80$ and $d = .91$, respectively. Middle-aged and older participants did not differ from each other, with $p > .05$, $d = .18$. This finding may be useful for several reasons. First, the fan base seems to encompass younger individuals, so services should certainly cater to this population to ensure that younger individuals continue purchasing tickets. Second, the findings may be informative to the marketing team, as they reveal an opportunity for growth in middle-aged and older demographics.

For more information about follow-up testing, see the section on one-way ANOVA in this chapter.

Interpreting the results: Practical significance (meaningfulness)

We can calculate two measures of meaningfulness for a two-way ANOVA: eta-squared (η^2) and omega-squared (ω^2). See the section on one-way ANOVA for more information on these measures. Following are the calculations for this example:

- Gender main effect:

$$\eta^2 = \frac{SS_{Gender}}{SS_{Total}} = \frac{19.4400}{2707.0933} = .0072$$

$$\omega^2 = \frac{[SS_{Gender} - (df_{Gender})(MS_{Within})]}{(SS_{Total} + MS_{Within})}$$

$$\omega^2 = \frac{[19.4400 - (1)(18.1533)]}{(2707.0933 + 18.1533)} = .0005$$

- Age main effect:

$$\eta^2 = \frac{SS_{Age}}{SS_{Total}} = \frac{62.4933}{2707.0933} = .0231$$

$$\omega^2 = \frac{[SS_{Age} - (df_{Age})(MS_{Within})]}{(SS_{Total} + MS_{Within})}$$

$$\omega^2 = \frac{[62.4933 - (2)(18.1533)]}{(2707.0933 + 18.1533)} = .0096$$

- Gender x age interaction:

$$\eta^2 = \frac{SS_{Int}}{SS_{Total}} = \frac{11.0800}{2707.0933} = .0041$$

$$\omega^2 = \frac{[SS_{Int} - (df_{Int})(MS_{Within})]}{(SS_{Total} + MS_{Within})}$$

$$\omega^2 = \frac{[11.0800 - (2)(18.1533)]}{(2707.0933 + 18.1533)} = .0000$$

Based on the omega-squared measure of meaningfulness, less than 1% of the total variation in number of tickets purchased can be accounted for by either gender, age, or the interaction of gender and age. Based on the results of the statistical and practical significance analyses, the age and gender group difference in means is not meaningful at all, and other variables should be examined to help account for the 99% of the variance that is left unexplained.

If post hoc tests had been required, we would have conducted independent *t*-tests and then calculated effect sizes for any significant findings that resulted. See the section on practical significance for independent *t*-tests in Chapter 17 for information about the calculation of effect size.

Statistical statement

For the example, the results would be reported in a scholarly article in the following manner:

A two-way ANOVA was performed to determine whether the number of tickets purchased differed by gender or age groups (young = 18–29 yrs; middle = 30–49 yrs; older = 50+ yrs). The main effects and the interaction effect were not significant: gender, $F(1, 144) = 1.07$, $p = .30$; age, $F(2, 144) = 1.72$, $p = .18$; gender x age, $F(2, 144) = .31$, $p = .74$. The reported means of number of tickets purchased by women and men in each age group were similar: young ($M_{Women} = 6.52$, $s = 3.97$; $M_{Men} = 6.48$, $s = 4.19$), middle ($M_{Women} = 4.92$, $s = 4.51$; $M_{Men} = 5.92$, $s = 4.30$), and older ($M_{Women} = 4.36$, $s = 4.83$; $M_{Men} = 5.56$, $s = 3.66$). Measures of meaningfulness indicated that gender, age, and the interaction of gender and age each accounted for less than 1% of the variance in number of tickets purchased, as measured by ω^2.

For a non-scholarly report, the results would be presented in the following manner:

We surveyed a group of 150 people from the local community on the number of tickets purchased last year. Equal numbers of men and women members of three age groups (young = 18–29 yrs; middle = 30–49 yrs; older = 50+ yrs) were selected, and we tested to see if men and women from different age groups differed in the number of tickets purchased. The average number of tickets purchased did not differ for men and women in each of the age groups: young (women = 6.52; men = 6.48), middle (women = 4.92; men = 5.92), and older (women = 4.36; men = 5.56).

PRACTICE PROBLEMS FOR ANOVA

One-Way ANOVA

For this scenario, you have surveyed 60 members using a stratified sampling technique to ensure equal samples of low-income (<$35,000), middle-income ($35,000 to $70,000), and high-income (>$70,000) members. You performed a one-way ANOVA to examine whether income influenced participants' perceptions about the club's hours of operation, as measured on a Likert scale (1 = poor, 4 = average, 7 = excellent). The dependent variable is the perception of the hours of operation (OpHours), and the independent variable is income. The results of this analysis will help the club's owner decide whether to change the club's hours of operation or perhaps the programming at select times in the day to accommodate the needs of members at varying income levels. Before starting this one-way ANOVA analysis, remember to reorganize the data, with the three income groups serving as new column headings. Use .05 as the alpha.

Questions for One-Way ANOVA

1. What are mean, variance, and standard deviation for each of the three income groups?
2. What is the degrees of freedom for the between groups, and how is this calculated?
3. What is the degrees of freedom for the within groups, and how is this calculated?
4. What is the F value (test statistic) for the data? How is it calculated?
5. Are the results of the one-way ANOVA statistically significant? Why or why not?
6. What post hoc tests should be performed on this data?
7. What are the results of the post hoc tests?
8. Based on eta-squared, are the results of the one-way ANOVA meaningful? Why or why not?
9. What are the effect sizes from the post hoc tests? Explain the practical significance of the effect sizes you found.
10. How would you report the results in a scholarly article?
11. How would you report the results to the health club's owner?

Two-Way ANOVA

For this scenario, you have surveyed 60 of the club's members using a stratified sampling technique to ensure equal samples of men and women in low-income (<$35,000), middle-income ($35,000 to $70,000), and high-income (>$70,000) groups. You performed a two-way ANOVA to examine whether gender and/or income influenced participants' perceptions about the club's hours of operation, as measured on a Likert scale (1 = poor, 4 = average, 7 = excellent). In particular, you are interested in whether potential gender differences are larger or smaller in certain income groups. The results of this analysis will help the health club's owner decide whether to change the hours of operation or perhaps the programming at select times in the day to accommodate the needs of members of different genders or income levels.

The data set for this example is provided in the Excel file associated with this book. The dependent variable is the perception of the hours of operation (OpHours), and the two independent variables are gender and income. Before starting this two-way ANOVA analysis, remember to reorganize the data with the three income groups serving as new column headings and the ratings for men and women together within each income column (see the first example of two-way ANOVA discussed earlier in this chapter).

Questions for Two-Way ANOVA

1. What are the mean, variance, and standard deviation for men and for women in each income group?

2. What are the marginal mean, variance, and standard deviation for women and for men? How are these values used?

3. What are the marginal mean, variance, and standard deviation for each income level? How are these values used?

4. What is the degrees of freedom for gender, and how is this calculated?

5. What is the degrees of freedom for income, and how is this calculated?

6. What does the interaction effect or true variance for gender x income reflect?

7. What is the degrees of freedom for the interaction, and how is this calculated?

8. To what does Within (Groups) refer in this output table? What is the degrees of freedom associated with it, and how is this calculated?

9. What is the F value (test statistic) for the data?

10. Are the results of the two-way ANOVA statistically significant? Why or why not?

11. What post hoc tests should be performed on the data?

12. What are the results of the post hoc tests?

13. Based on eta-squared, are the results of the two-way ANOVA meaningful? Why or why not?

14. What are the effect sizes from the post hoc tests? Explain the practical significance of the effect sizes you found.

15. How would you report the results in a scholarly article?

16. How would you report the results to the health club's owner?

ANOVA

- A one-way ANOVA compares the means from two or more independent sample groups on one dependent variable.

- A one-way ANOVA with repeated measures compares the means from two or more samples that are related.

- A factorial ANOVA compares the effects of two or more independent variables on one dependent variable.

- When an F value is significant, follow-up (post hoc) tests will identify which pairwise differences are significant.

- Eta-squared (η^2) and omega-squared (ω^2) are measures of meaningfulness for F values in one-way and factorial ANOVAs.

CHAPTER

Chi-square Tests

EXECUTIVE SUMMARY We can use a chi-square (χ^2) test to examine the differences between observed and expected frequencies in categorical data. A chi-square test can show whether the frequencies within the category levels are similar to what would have been expected based on chance or some other source of information. The analysis may involve one or two classification (categorical) variables, with each classification variable having two or more levels (categories).

WHAT IS A χ^2 TEST?

A chi-square test is a statistical technique that we can use to examine the difference between observed and expected frequencies of data in two or more categories. The test statistic is χ^2. This test is an example of a nonparametric statistical test, which means we can use it to analyze data collected with either nominal or ordinal measures. If the expected frequencies are unknown, then they may be distributed equally across all categories based on chance occurrence. Alternatively, the analyst may assign the expected frequencies to the categories based on an external source of information or a theoretical rationale.

200

You might recall from Chapter 13 that no assumptions are required about the data distribution for nonparametric tests. However, each category should have at least one observation (or count), and no more than 20% of the categories should have fewer than five observations. This is the only nonparametric test we will cover in this book, and it is the most commonly used one. The two types of χ^2 tests are the goodness of fit test and the test of independence.

CHI-SQUARE TEST OF GOODNESS OF FIT

A chi-square test of goodness of fit, also called one-way classification, compares the observed and expected frequencies of data that fall within each category of a single variable. For example, an analyst might use this test to examine a sample's response to a question with a categorical response format, such as, "Would you recommend this service to a friend? Yes or no." As another example, an analyst might compare the observed frequencies of men and women in upper management in a sport organization against the expected frequencies based on the overall percentages of men and women in the entire organization. Or, a researcher might examine the number of products sold within certain price ranges to determine whether the observed frequencies are significantly different from the expected frequencies established by prior historical sales figures or by corporate headquarters.

Performing a χ^2 Test of Goodness of Fit

RESEARCH
SCENARIO I

As an analyst for a MiLB team, you know that an accurate understanding of the reasons why people attend a game will provide useful data for marketing the team and for game-day operations. Prior to the start of the baseball season, 150 community participants were measured on their *primary* reason for attending a game last year. Participants selected one of six possible reasons: event cost, distance from home, teams playing, home team's record, venue appearance, and opportunity to be with friends. The results of this analysis will identify the predominant reason(s) for attendance.

The data set for this example is provided in the Excel file associated with this book. The classification variable is reason (column L). During data entry, participant responses were coded in the following manner: event cost (EC), distance from home (DH), teams playing (TP), home team's record (TR), venue appearance (VA), and opportunity to be with friends (OF).

We can use Excel to count the frequency of responses, which is helpful when a data set is large. First, we must sort the data in column L. Highlight one of the cells in the column. Click on the *Home* tab, select *Sort & Filter* on the far right, and then select *Sort A to Z*. The coded reasons in column L should now be sorted in alphabetical order.

STEP 1

STEP 2   Create six new column headings, one for each of the possible responses, in cells O1 to T1. In column N, we will enter descriptive row titles for the statistics necessary for computing the χ^2 test statistic. Enter these titles in column N: Observed Frequency (O), Expected Frequency (E), O-E, $(O-E)^2$, and $(O-E)^2/E$. Skip one row, and then enter three more row titles: Chi-Square: $\sum(O-E)^2/E$, df, and p value. See Exhibit 19.1.

STEP 3   To provide a count for the DH category in column O, you can either count the number of DH responses yourself and input the count by hand or let Excel count the responses for you. To use Excel, place the cursor in cell O2. Click on the *Formulas* tab at the top, and *Insert Function* on the left. The Insert Function box should appear (see Exhibit 19.2).

STEP 4   From the Select a Category drop-down menu, select *Statistical*. Highlight *CountA* in the Select a Function box. Click *OK*.

STEP 5   The *Function Arguments* box should appear (see Exhibit 19.3). Place the cursor in the *Value1* box. Highlight the cells in column L that contain the DH codes (L2 through L22). Click *OK*. The observed frequency (count) for DH will appear in cell O2 (it should be 21). Repeat steps 3 through 5 to obtain a count for each coded category, placing the counts in the appropriate cells.

| EXHIBIT | 19.1 | New column and row headings for chi-square test of goodness of fit. |

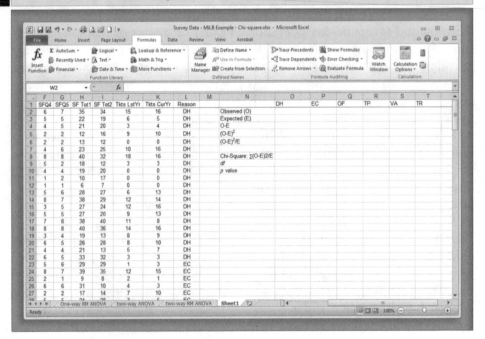

Excel's Insert Function box for frequency count. **EXHIBIT** 19.2

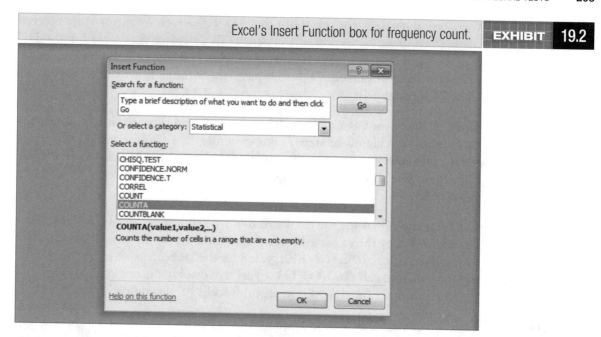

Excel's Function Arguments box for frequency count. **EXHIBIT** 19.3

Assign the expected frequency for each category in cells O3 through S3. Since   **STEP 6**
the TR category had zero observations, it will be omitted from the analysis
(that is, we will perform the analysis as if the TR category did not exist). We
will calculate expected frequencies based on chance occurrence, because no
other information or theoretical rationale is available regarding how participants would be expected to select each response. To do this, we divide the total
number of observations by the number of categories (omitting the TR category), resulting in an expected frequency of 30 for each category (150 / 5 = 30).

STEP 7   Calculate the values for the row titled "O–E," which is simply the observed frequency minus the expected frequency. To calculate the value for the DH category (cell O4), enter the following formula into the cell: =O2–O3. The result, –9, will be displayed. Copy and paste the formula for the other categories (cells P4 through S4).

STEP 8   Now, calculate the values for the $(O–E)^2$ row. To do this, we simply square the O–E values calculated in step 7. For example, to calculate the $(O–E)^2$ value for the DH category, enter the formula =O4^2 into cell O5. Excel will display the result, 81. Copy and paste the formula for the other categories (cells P5 through S5).

STEP 9   Calculate the values for the $(O–E)^2/E$ row by dividing the $(O–E)^2$ values calculated in step 8 by the expected frequency, found in row 3 for each column. For example, to calculate the $(O–E)^2/E$ value for the DH category, enter the following into cell O6: =O5/O3. Excel will display the result, 2.7. Copy and paste the formula for the other categories (cells P6 through S6).

STEP 10   Now we can calculate the chi-square test statistic. The formula is $\sum(O–E)^2/E$. That is, the χ^2 test statistic is calculated by taking the sum ($\sum$) of all the values from step 9. In cell O8, enter the formula =SUM(O6:S6). The result should be 42.60. See Exhibit 19.4.

STEP 11   The degrees of freedom is equal to $c – 1$, where c is the number of category columns. The df may be calculated by hand (5 – 1) or by using the Excel formula =COUNT(O2:S2)-1, which should result in df = 4.

STEP 12   We can obtain the p value for the χ^2 test statistic by using the chi-square test function. To do this in Excel, place the cursor in cell O10. Click on the *Formulas* tab at the top, and *Insert Function* on the left. The Insert Function box should appear. (See Exhibit 19.5.)

EXHIBIT 19.4   Excel calculation of chi-square test of goodness of fit.

	O8		f_x	=SUM(O6:S6)									
	F	G	H	I	J	K	L	M	N	O	P	Q	R	S	T
1	SFQ4	SFQ5	SF Tot1	SF Tot2	Tkts LstYr	Tkts CurYr	Reason			DH	EC	OF	TP	VA	TR
2	6	7	35	34	15	16	DH		Observed (O)	21	49	28	46	6	0
3	5	5	22	19	6	5	DH		Expected (E)	30	30	30	30	30	
4	4	5	21	20	3	4	DH		O-E	-9	19	-2	16	-24	
5	2	2	12	16	9	10	DH		$(O-E)^2$	81	361	4	256	576	
6	2	2	13	12	0	0	DH		$(O-E)^2/E$	2.7	12.03333	0.133333	8.533333	19.2	
7	4	6	23	25	10	16	DH								
8	8	8	40	32	18	16	DH		Chi-Square: $\sum(O-E)2/E$	42.6					
9	5	2	18	12	3	3	DH		df	4					
10	4	4	19	20	0	0	DH		p value	1.25266E-08					
11	1	2	10	17	0	0	DH								
12	1	1	6	7	0	0	DH								

Excel's Insert Function box for obtaining a *p* value for a chi-square test of goodness of fit.   **EXHIBIT 19.5**

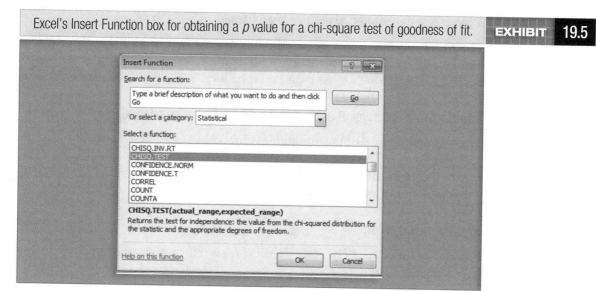

From the Select a Category drop-down menu, select *Statistical*. Highlight **STEP 13**
CHISQ.TEST in the Select a Function box. Click *OK*.

The Function Arguments box should appear. Place the cursor in the *Actual_range*   **STEP 14**
box (see Exhibit 19.6). Highlight the spreadsheet cells that contain the observed
frequencies (O2 through S2). Next, place the cursor in the *Expected_range* box.
Highlight the cells that contain the expected frequencies (O3 through S3). Click
OK. The resulting *p* value for the χ^2 test statistic is 0.00000001253, which
displays in the Function Arguments box as 1.25266E-08. We can state this more
simply as $p < .0001$.

Excel's Function Arguments box for obtaining a *p* value for a chi-square test   **EXHIBIT 19.6**
of goodness of fit.

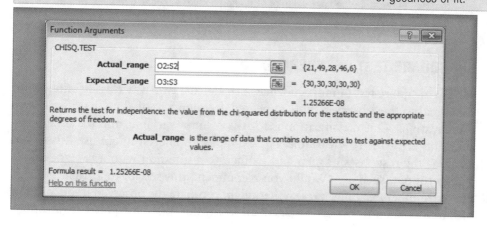

Interpreting the results: Statistical significance

The χ^2 test statistic was equal to 42.60. The p value indicates that this result is significant, because the probability of this statistic being due to chance is about 1 in 100,000,000, which is less than the alpha level ($p \approx .00000001 <$ alpha $= .05$).

Interpreting the results: Practical significance (meaningfulness)

There is no measure of meaningfulness for a chi-square test of goodness of fit. The measures of meaningfulness that do exist for chi-square work by measuring the strength of the relationship between two variables. However, the chi-square test of goodness of fit evaluates only one classification variable.

Statistical statement

For the example, the results would be reported in a scholarly article in the following manner:

> A sample of 150 community participants was measured on their *primary* reason for attending a game last year. The chi-square test of goodness of fit was significant, with χ^2 (4, $N = 150$) = 42.60, $p < .0001$. The two predominant reasons for attending a game were cost of the event (49) and teams playing (46). These were followed by opportunity to be with friends (28), distance from home (21), and appearance of the venue (6).

Note that the χ^2 statistical statement includes the df and N within the parentheses. This information lets the reader know the levels of the classification variable (minus 1) and the sample size that were used in the analysis.

For a non-scholarly report, the results would be presented in the following manner:

> We surveyed a group of 150 people from the local community on their *primary* reason for attending a game last year. The two predominant reasons for attending a game were cost of the event (49) and teams playing (46). These were followed by opportunity to be with friends (28), distance from home (21), and appearance of the venue (6). Strategies that aim to promote the cost-value of attending a MiLB baseball game, as well as the teams that are playing, should be targeted in the future.

CHI-SQUARE TEST OF INDEPENDENCE

A chi-square test of independence, also called a **two-way classification**, compares the observed and expected frequencies of data based on two classifications. One classification is for the column variable, and the other classification is for the row variable. For example, an analyst might use this test to examine the responses of men and women to a question with a categorical response format, such as, "Would you recommend this service to a friend? Yes or no." In another example, a researcher might compare the observed frequencies of men and women in upper management at several different sport organizations within a league. With a chi-square analysis, a marketing manager might examine the numbers of products sold within certain price ranges to determine whether the observed frequencies are significantly different for different age groups.

Performing a χ^2 Test of Independence

RESEARCH SCENARIO I

As an analyst for a MiLB team, you want to identify whether attendees' predominant reason or reasons for attending a game are related to gender. For this analysis, the classification (column) variable is reason (column L), and gender is the row variable. Open a fresh copy of the spreadsheet, or delete the contents of the cells that contain the goodness of fit calculation. You may save a copy of the spreadsheet first, if you wish.

First, we must sort the data in column L, if this has not already been done. Highlight one of the cells in the column. Click on the *Home* tab, select *Sort & Filter* on the far right, and then select *Sort A to Z*. The coded reasons in column L should now be sorted in alphabetical order.

STEP 1

As with the goodness of fit calculation, we will create six new column headings, one for each of the possible responses, in cells O1 to T1. Then, in column N, we will enter descriptive row titles for the statistics necessary for computing the χ^2 test of independence test statistic. Enter the titles in column N as shown in Exhibit 19.7.

STEP 2

| New column and row headings for chi-square test of independence. | **EXHIBIT** | **19.7** |

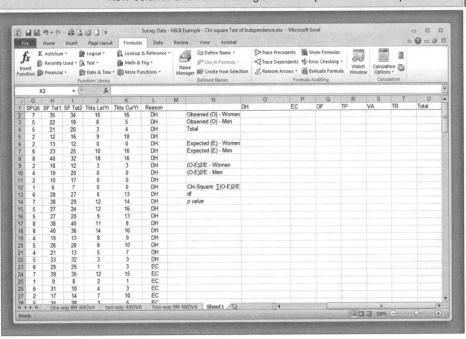

STEP 3   To obtain a count of observations for the DH category, place the cursor in cell O2. Click on the *Formulas* tab at the top, and *Insert Function* on the left. The Insert Function box should appear (see Exhibit 19.8).

STEP 4   From the Select a Category drop-down menu, select *Statistical*. Highlight *CountA* in the Select a Function box. Click *OK*.

STEP 5   The Function Arguments box should appear (see Exhibit 19.9). Place the cursor in the *Value1* box. Highlight the cells in column L that contain the

EXHIBIT 19.8   Excel's Insert Function box for frequency count.

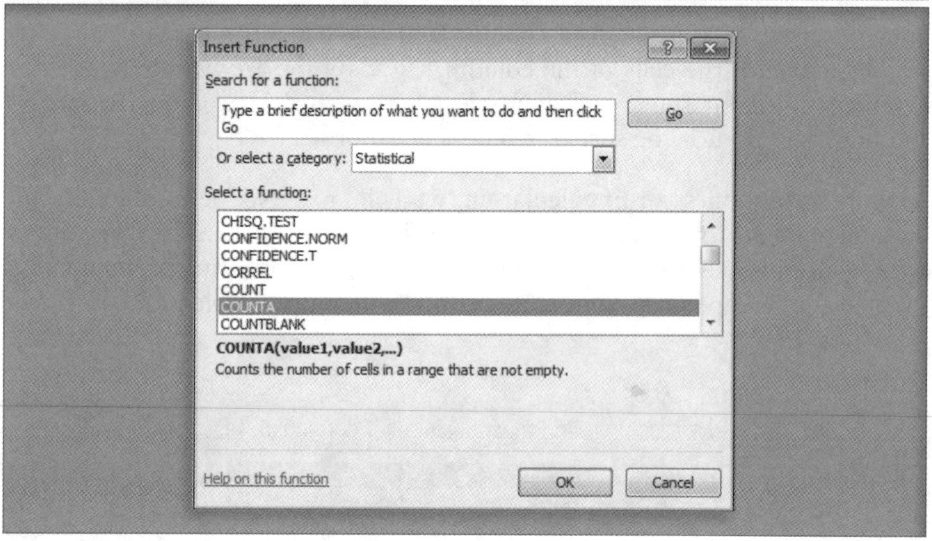

EXHIBIT 19.9   Excel's Function Arguments box for frequency count.

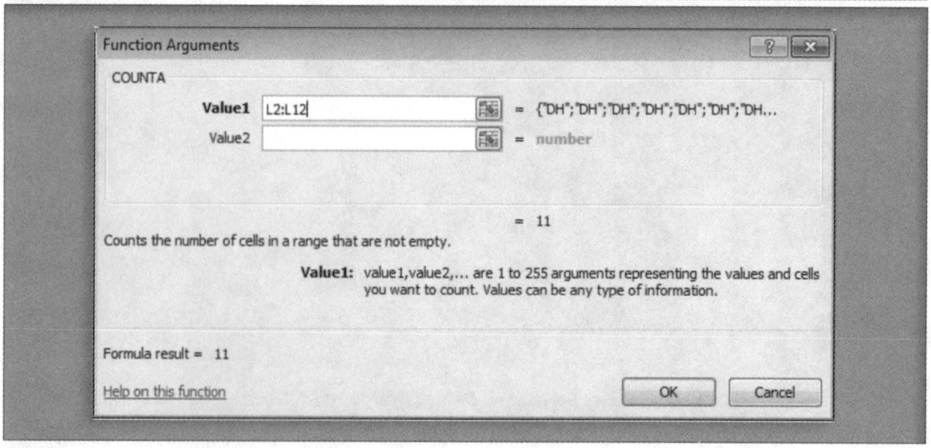

DH codes for women (L2 through L12). Click *OK*. The observed frequency, or count, for DH for women will be displayed; it should be 11. Repeat steps 3 through 5 to obtain counts for each coded category for the women and men.

Assign the expected frequency for each category for women and men in cells O6 through S7. As with the goodness of fit calculation, since the TR category has zero observations, it will be omitted from the analysis. We will calculate expected frequencies based on chance occurrence, because no other information or theoretical rationale is available regarding how participants are expected to select each categorical response. To calculate the expected value for women who selected the DH response, we multiply the total number of observations for DH (in cell O4) by the total number of women in the sample (in cell U2) and divide this value by the grand total of participants in the sample (in cell U4). The Excel formula for cell O6 is =(O4*$U$2)/$U$4. Copy and paste this formula into cells O6 through S6. The formula for men is =(O4*$U$3)/$U$4. Copy and paste this formula into cells O7 through S7.   **STEP 6**

Enter formulas to calculate the value of $(O-E)^2/E$ for women and men for each category. In cell O9, enter the formula =(O2-O6)^2/O6. Copy and paste this formula into cells P9 through S9 and cells O10 through S10.   **STEP 7**

We calculate the chi-square test statistic by using the formula $\sum(O-E)^2/E$. In the spreadsheet, the χ^2 test statistic is simply the sum of all ten values from Step 7. In cell O12, enter the formula =SUM(O9:S10). Excel should display 13.2999, the χ^2 test statistic (see Exhibit 19.10).   **STEP 8**

Excel calculation of chi-square test of independence.   **EXHIBIT   19.10**

O12			fx	=SUM(O9:S10)								
G	H	I	J	K	L	M	N	O	P	Q	R	S	T	U
1 SFQ5	SF Tot1	SF Tot2	Tkts LstYr	Tkts CurYr	Reason			DH	EC	OF	TP	VA	TR	Total
2 7	35	34	15	16	DH		Observed (O) - Women	11	24	21	15	4	0	75
3 5	22	19	6	5	DH		Observed (O) - Men	10	25	7	31	2	0	75
4 5	21	20	3	4	DH		Total	21	49	28	46	6	0	150
5 2	12	16	9	10	DH									
6 2	13	12	0	0	DH		Expected (E) - Women	10.5	24.5	14	23	3		
7 6	23	25	10	16	DH		Expected (E) - Men	10.5	24.5	14	23	3		
8 8	40	32	18	16	DH									
9 2	18	12	3	3	DH		(O-E)2/E - Women	0.023809524	0.010204	3.5	2.782609	0.333333		
10 4	19	20	0	0	DH		(O-E)2/E - Men	0.023809524	0.010204	3.5	2.782609	0.333333		
11 2	10	17	0	0	DH									
12 1	6	7	0	0	DH		Chi-Square: ∑(O-E)2/E	13.29991127						
13 6	28	27	6	13	DH		df	4						
14 7	38	29	12	14	DH		p value	0.009899651						

STEP 9 The degrees of freedom equals $(c - 1)(r - 1)$, where c is the number of category columns and r is the number of rows. You may calculate the df by hand $[(5 - 1)(2 - 1) = 4 \times 1 = 4]$ and type the result in cell O13, or you may enter the following formula in cell O13: **=(COUNT(O2:S2)-1)*(COUNT(O2:O3)-1)**, which should result in df = 4.

STEP 10 We can obtain the p value for the χ^2 test statistic by using Excel's chi-square test function. Place the cursor in cell O14. Click on the *Formulas* tab at the top, and *Insert Function* on the left. The Insert Function box should appear (see Exhibit 19.11).

STEP 11 From the Select a Category drop-down menu, select *Statistical*. Highlight *CHISQ.TEST* in the Select a Function box. Click *OK*.

STEP 12 The Function Arguments box should appear (see Exhibit 19.12). Place the cursor in the *Actual_range* box. Highlight the cells that contain the observed frequencies for both women and men (O2 through S3). Next, place the cursor in the *Expected_range* box. Highlight the cells that contain the expected frequencies for both women and men (O6 through S7). Click *OK*. Excel will display the p value for the χ^2 test statistic, 0.009899. We can state this more simply as $p < .01$.

EXHIBIT 19.11   Excel's Insert Function box for obtaining p value for a chi-square test of independence.

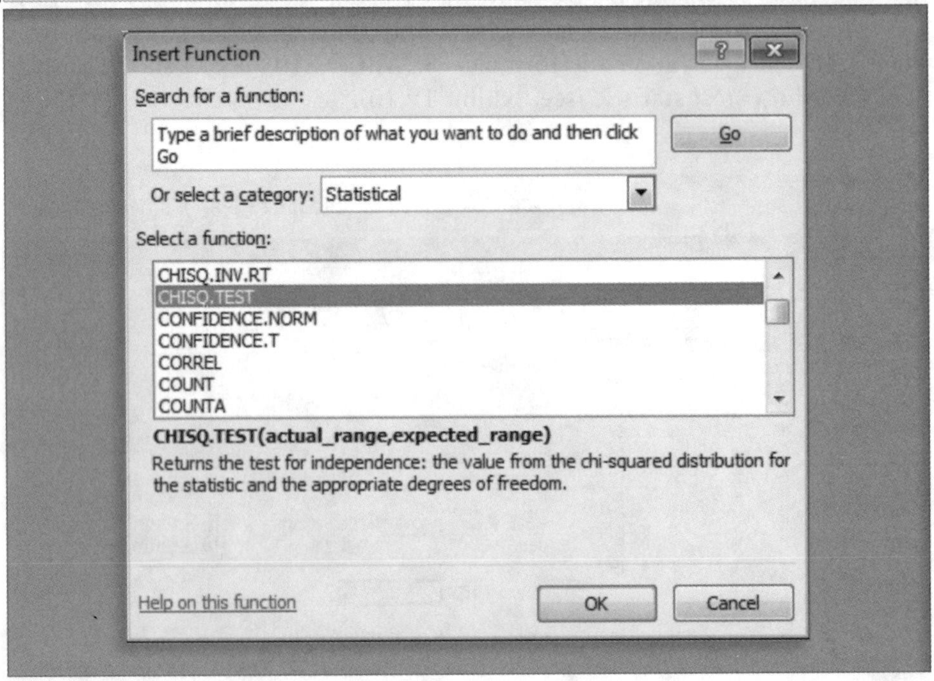

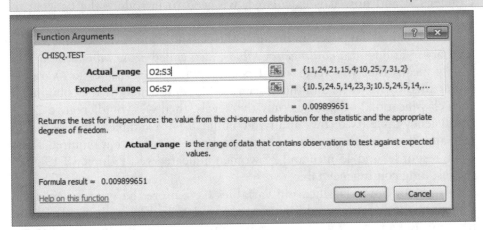

EXHIBIT 19.12

Excel's Function Arguments box for obtaining a *p* value for a chi-square test of independence.

Interpreting the results: Statistical significance

The χ^2 test statistic is equal to 13.30. The *p* value indicates that that result is significant, because the probability of this test statistic being due to chance is less than 1 in 100, which is less than the alpha level ($p < .01 <$ alpha $= .05$). This finding indicates that some reasons for attending a game are more frequently selected than others. A marketing team might focus future strategies on the cost-value of attending a MiLB baseball game, because this was the reason for attendance most frequently cited by men and women alike (women = 24; men = 25). Strategies highlighting the team's playing would be more effective for men (women = 15; men = 31), while strategies focusing on opportunity to be with friends would be more effective for women (women = 21; men = 7). Other reasons were selected less often: distance from home (women = 11; men = 10), and appearance of the venue (women = 4; men = 2).

Interpreting the results: Practical significance (meaningfulness)

The measure of meaningfulness for χ^2 is the **phi coefficient** (ϕ). The phi coefficient measures the strength of association (correlation) between the two classification variables. We can calculate phi by dividing the chi-square value by the grand total of observations (or total sample size) and then taking the square root of this value:

$$\phi = \sqrt{\frac{\chi^2}{N}}$$

Another measure of meaningfulness for χ^2 is **Cramer's V**. Cramer's V is also a measure of the strength of association between the two classification variables. However, it is used when there are more than two categories for at least one of the classification variables. To further explain when we use Cramer's V and how it is calculated, we need to introduce the concept of contingency tables.

For nominal data, we can organize the classification variables and associated observations into *contingency tables*, also called *cross tabulations*. This simply means that we create a matrix table with one classification variable represented by the rows and the other variable represented by the columns. If each classification variable has only two levels, then we would create a 2 x 2 contingency table (two rows and two columns). For example, suppose the 75 men and 75 women in our example were asked a question that required a yes-or-no response, and 45 men and 25 women indicated yes. Exhibit 19.13 gives the resulting contingency table.

If one or both classification variables have more than two levels, then the contingency table would be larger than 2 x 2; that is, the table would have more than two rows and/or more than two columns. In this situation, we can calculate Cramer's V. We do this by first dividing the chi-square value by the product of the grand total (or N, which is the total sample size) and M, where M refers to the smaller value of $c - 1$ or $r - 1$. Once this value is calculated, we then take the square root. In the research scenario example, the two classification variables are gender (two levels) and reason (five levels). This example would result in a 2 x 5 contingency table (see Exhibit 19.14).

EXHIBIT 19.13   2 x 2 contingency table of men's and women's responses to a yes/no question.

	YES	NO	TOTAL
Women	45	30	75
Men	25	50	75
Total	70	80	150

EXHIBIT 19.14   2 x 5 contingency table of men's and women's primary reason for attending a game.

	DISTANCE FROM HOME	EVENT COST	OPPORTUNITY TO BE WITH FRIENDS	TEAMS PLAYING	VENUE APPEARANCE	TOTAL
Women	11	24	21	15	4	75
Men	10	25	7	31	2	75
Total	21	49	28	46	6	150

Since this example requires a contingency table larger than 2 x 2, we can use Cramer's V. The general formula for Cramer's V is:

$$V = \sqrt{\frac{\chi^2}{NM}}$$

$$V = \sqrt{\frac{13.2999}{150}}$$

$$V = \sqrt{.08867}V = .2978$$

Note that $c - 1 = 4$ and $r - 1 = 1$. Hence, $M = 1$, because $r - 1 = 1$ is the smaller value.

The phi coefficient and Cramer's V are both estimates of the strength of the association between variables (e.g., their correlation). We can interpret the values as follows:

- ϕ or $V = .10$ is considered a small effect,
- ϕ or $V = .30$ is considered a moderate effect, and
- ϕ or $V = .50$ and above is considered a large effect.

In general, an analyst wants to find large effects, as this allows him or her to target one of the variables (e.g., gender) to see how much of an effect it might have on the other variable (e.g., ticket purchase intentions). See Chapter 15 for more discussion of interpretation of measures of meaningfulness between variables.

Statistical statement

For the example, the results would be reported in a scholarly article in the following manner:

> We surveyed a sample of 150 community participants on their *primary* reason for attending a game last year. The chi-square test of independence was significant, with χ^2 (4, $N = 150$) = 13.30, $p < .01$. The two predominant reasons for attending a game were cost of the event (women = 24; men = 25) and teams playing (women = 15; men = 31). These were followed by opportunity to be with friends (women = 21; men = 7), distance from home (women = 11; men = 10), and appearance of the venue (women = 4; men = 2). However, gender was related to reasons for attending a game, with more men selecting teams playing and more women selecting opportunities to be with friends. The strength of the relationship between gender and reasons for attending a game was large ($\phi = .2978$), which suggests that teams may wish to consider gender in future strategies for increasing ticket sales.

Note that the χ^2 statistical statement includes the df and N values within the parentheses.

For a non-scholarly report, the results would be presented in the following manner:

> We surveyed a group of 150 people from the local community on their *primary* reason for attending a game last year. Equal numbers of men and women were selected from

the community, and we tested to see if men and women would have similar reasons for attending a game. The two predominant reasons for attending a game were cost of the event (women = 24; men = 25) and teams playing (women = 15; men = 31). These reasons were followed by opportunity to be with friends (women = 21; men = 7), distance from home (women = 11; men = 10), and appearance of the venue (women = 4; men = 2). However, gender was related to reasons for attending a game, with more men selecting teams playing and more women selecting opportunities to be with friends. Future strategies that aim to promote the cost-value of attending a MiLB baseball game should be equally effective for men and women. Highlighting which teams are playing will be more effective with men, while highlighting opportunities to be with friends will be more effective with women.

RESEARCH SCENARIO II

PRACTICE PROBLEM FOR χ^2 TEST OF INDEPENDENCE

For this scenario, you have surveyed 30 male and 30 female members of your health club, using a stratified sampling technique. Among the various survey questions, participants were asked, "How does our health club stack up to your expectations?" Participants could select from the following options: (A) Exceeds expectations, (B) Meets expectations, and (C) Below expectations. A chi-square test of independence will allow you to determine whether men and women responded in the same way to this question. The classification variable is expectations (Expect). Gender will be the row variable. The results of this analysis will help the owner of the health club decide whether the club is meeting the expected needs of both men and women members.

Questions

1. What is the value of the χ^2 test statistic?
2. Are the results of the chi-square test of independence statistically significant? Why or why not?
3. Based on either the phi coefficient or Cramer's V, are the results of the chi-square test of independence meaningful? Why or why not?
4. How would you report the results in a scholarly article?
5. How would you report the results to the health club's owner?

TALKING POINTS

Chi-square

- A chi-square test of goodness of fit compares the observed and expected frequencies of data that fall within each category of a single variable.
- A chi-square test of independence compares the observed and expected frequencies of data based on two classifications.

- The phi coefficient is a measure of meaningfulness that calculates the strength of the association between two classification variables that have two levels in a chi-square test of independence.

- Cramer's V is a measure of meaningfulness that calculates the strength of the association between two classification variables that have more than two levels in a chi-square test of independence.

Note on Protecting Participants and Research Data

EXECUTIVE SUMMARY All research involving humans and animals is subject to review by a qualified body charged with protecting the subjects from cruel, harsh, or dangerous conditions. All institutions that require research of their faculty, as well as many private organizations and companies that conduct research, have review boards that oversee the methods and analyses in the interest of shielding participants from harmful conditions.

REVIEWS OF DATA COLLECTION METHODS AND ANALYSES

E ach college or university that supports research and inquiry and most organizations, such as manufacturers, brands, drug companies, and teaching hospitals, that conduct research on humans or animals have independent boards that determine whether the inquiry or research is being conducted according to the conventions and regulations that protect subjects from unethical treatment. Many of the rules of research involving living beings were instituted as a result of unprincipled medical and behavioral research that was conducted on humans and vertebrate animals during wartime. These boards have various names, such as the Human Subjects Review Board (HSRB), Institutional Review Board (IRB), Institutional Animal Care and Use Committee (IACUC), and the Institutional Biosafety Committee (IBC). However, each board has the same function: to assist investigators in complying with federal, state, local, and institutional/organizational regulations and policies. In essence, the review board protects the humans and vertebrate animals from unreasonable and dangerous research conditions and monitors the use of living beings that are to be placed in treatment conditions.

REVIEW BOARD OPERATIONS

T he boards are usually made up of industry researchers, faculty, administrators, and qualified community members (e.g., nurses, physicians, attorneys). They report to a central institutional or organizational administrator, such as a vice president for research. Boards examine all proposals involving humans, animals, and certain biomedical materials and subsequently approve the proposed procedures for a specified amount of time. It is not unusual for boards to require investigators to submit to several rounds in the proposal process, because they may require additional in-depth information in order to make a decision regarding the safety of participants.

There are typically two types of review processes. A full board review would be required when investigators are using humans in situations in which they may be hurt. Examples of these investigations include when a manufacturer or brand is testing humans on a track or treadmill while they wear a new track shoe design, or when children under the age of 18 are used in any situation and cannot judge their safety for themselves. An expedited or exempt review would be required when participants will not be subjected to any physical danger and when no psychological harm is involved, such as when sport fans complete a survey for a team's marketing department.

Under most circumstances, any participating subject or other interested party may review the research activities of any public or private institution and, under certain conditions, any private organization. For instance, members of the media often request information about ongoing research under the Freedom of Information Act or state or local "sunshine" laws—laws requiring governmental bodies to open their records or meetings to the public. When requested to do so, boards usually must share the proposals that they evaluate and any related forms that have been submitted. Individual investigators usually do not have to share incomplete results or data from work in progress, particularly if a study is funded externally and results have to be private.

Private results can often be kept confidential. Research data are often kept private because a company or other funding agency wants to keep the results in house. Imagine if an investigator was granted $150,000 by an equipment company to determine whether a new leg exercise machine designed for home use was more effective than regular weight training in building leg muscles and increasing speed. However, after eight months of testing, research indicated that participants who used the machine had increased their muscle mass and strength no more than a group that used weight training and that they did not increase their speed significantly more than the weight training group. The equipment company would likely request that the investigator send the data to them and not disseminate it in any form, and the company might even instruct the investigator to destroy the data sets.

Thus, arguments can be made about the ethical use of research results. If a company funds a project, do the results belong to that company, or to the investigator's organization, or to the investigator? If the project was completed at a state-assisted institution with state-funded equipment in state-funded venues, does the public have the right to view the results? Numerous ethical and moral issues arise from proposed and completed research, as well as from questions about external funding and the free flow of information. However, research review boards exist to pre-screen research for the safety of the participants and rarely, if ever, enter into ownership of research results.

PROTECTING AND STORING DATA

If results of a research project are disseminated through presentation or publication, the data set from the project usually has to be protected and saved for a certain number of years, as defined by rules or operating codes of the field or by the requirements of the institution or organization that sponsored the research or provided facilities. Data sets are saved so that interested parties can have access to them, in case questions arise or another investigator or analyst wants to replicate the project and did not get ample information from the published or presented report of the project. Data are usually stored both in hard copy and digitally.

TALKING POINTS

- Official inquiry and research are usually monitored by a nonpartisan body of qualified professionals.
- Participants in research must be protected from unprincipled methods.
- External funding presents unique issues, particularly in regard to campus-based inquiry.
- Data are public if the results are disseminated, and research results should be kept for a specified period of time, as defined by the review board, organization, or institution.

Afterword

BY BILL SUTTON

T here has never been a time when research and analysis have played a more crucial role in the sport industry. Data-driven decision making is the operative buzzword in this decade and will continue to be so far into the future. When I came to my current position at the University of South Florida in 2012, one of the first changes I proposed for our MBA/MS curriculum was the addition of a sport business analytics course. I was convinced that such a course would provide the types of knowledge that our graduates will need in order to find employment in this very fertile area of opportunity. Students who were not interested in becoming analysts would nevertheless have the opportunity to better comprehend how data is used to make decisions, enabling them to become better leaders in whatever field of endeavor they ultimately chose.

The faculty at USF has been pleased with the success of this course, and we have added an applied marketing research course so that students can become involved in research design and learn the types of data to be generated to allow for decision making. In April 2015, we offered a sport business analytics conference, sponsored by Ticketmaster, to help share this knowledge and expertise with students and faculty from other institutions who may have similar interests.

Why were these curriculum changes important to me, and why did we implement them as required courses? The answer is simple: the industry is demanding this type of knowledge and skill set, and as a graduate program director, part of my responsibility is training students to meet the needs of the industry. I have worked as Vice President for Team Marketing and Business Operations for the NBA, and I own a successful consulting practice, Bill Sutton & Associates. In my time in the industry, I have seen a real movement toward embracing research and analysis. All of my clients have analytics or business strategy departments, as they are sometimes called. A number of my clients also use analytics on the sport or player side, to evaluate talent or to help develop strategy to be used to improve player or team performance. These departments can range from two or three individuals to as many as seven or eight at the team level, and even larger at the league level. There is a clearly defined and now-articulated need for students emerging from sport business programs to have an understanding of research, analytics, forecasting, and modeling. It is also imperative that faculty recognize this need and adapt or alter their curricula accordingly.

I am excited that two noteworthy academicians and researchers, Dr. Cuneen and Dr. Tobar, have taken the opportunity and the time to develop a worthwhile textbook that also incorporates software to help students understand how to frame questions; to collect, analyze, and interpret data; and to validate that data before making decisions. Now that such a textbook has been developed, and given the number of students securing employment in the area of analytics and research (not only with teams, but also with research firms specializing in the sport industry, such as Turnkey Sports), it is my further hope that more academic programs will begin offering such courses and will work with sport organizations in their local communities and markets to provide the class a "laboratory" through which they can collect data from populations associated with the sport product, analyze that data, and propose solutions or alternatives based on their findings to improve organizational efficiency, performance, and profitability.

I have been fortunate to have utilized this approach for the majority of my academic life and work as a practitioner. I can assure you that it is some of the most effective learning I have witnessed—for both the students and the professor. This book is an excellent resource that should help any professor embark on such an integrated learning journey.

Dr. Wm. A. (Bill) Sutton

FOUNDING DIRECTOR
SPORT AND ENTERTAINMENT MS/MBA GRADUATE PROGRAM
UNIVERSITY OF SOUTH FLORIDA, TAMPA, FLORIDA

Appendix A

SURVEY DATA: MiLB SCENARIO I

GENDER	AGE	SFQ1	SFQ2	SFQ3	SFQ4	SFQ5	SF TOT1	SF TOT2	TKTS LSTYR	TKTS CURYR	REASON
F	18	7	7	4	5	6	29	29	1	3	EC
F	18	8	8	8	8	7	39	35	12	15	EC
F	19	2	2	2	2	1	9	8	2	1	EC
F	20	8	5	4	3	4	24	29	9	13	TP
F	20	7	7	4	7	7	32	25	2	6	TP
F	20	6	6	7	6	6	31	10	4	3	EC
F	21	5	4	4	4	4	21	25	8	5	OF
F	21	4	2	2	1	1	10	15	9	7	TP
F	21	3	3	3	3	3	15	17	1	5	OF
F	21	6	4	3	2	2	17	14	7	10	EC
F	21	4	5	5	5	5	24	28	3	5	EC
F	21	8	8	6	5	7	34	31	11	7	OF
F	21	8	7	7	6	7	35	34	15	16	DH
F	22	3	3	1	1	1	9	9	5	6	OF
F	22	7	6	5	5	5	28	22	2	6	EC
F	22	4	3	6	4	4	21	20	5	9	OF
F	23	7	7	4	4	5	27	26	8	13	EC
F	24	5	4	2	3	3	17	15	6	8	OF
F	24	5	4	3	5	4	21	22	7	5	TP

GENDER	AGE	SFQ1	SFQ2	SFQ3	SFQ4	SFQ5	SF TOT1	SF TOT2	TKTS LSTYR	TKTS CURYR	REASON
F	25	1	1	1	1	1	5	6	0	0	EC
F	25	6	5	5	3	3	22	23	10	12	EC
F	26	4	3	5	5	5	22	19	6	5	DH
F	28	4	7	5	5	7	28	26	11	13	TP
F	28	8	7	8	6	7	36	35	9	14	EC
F	29	4	5	5	7	6	27	26	10	7	EC
F	30	5	1	1	1	1	9	6	3	3	OF
F	31	6	5	4	3	3	21	22	5	4	TP
F	31	4	4	3	3	3	17	20	4	8	TP
F	31	4	3	4	3	3	17	23	1	2	EC
F	31	5	3	3	4	4	19	19	1	2	OF
F	31	8	7	6	8	7	36	35	9	9	EC
F	32	2	2	1	2	1	8	9	0	0	EC
F	33	4	5	3	4	5	21	20	3	4	DH
F	34	4	4	4	4	4	20	7	8	9	VA
F	34	5	4	4	4	4	21	23	0	2	OF
F	34	6	4	3	5	5	23	22	5	4	EC
F	36	3	2	2	2	2	11	13	3	3	EC
F	37	3	2	2	2	2	11	13	0	0	OF
F	38	6	6	5	5	4	26	25	0	5	TP
F	39	7	7	5	5	5	29	26	12	16	TP
F	40	7	7	5	5	7	31	27	13	18	TP
F	41	8	8	8	8	7	39	38	10	14	TR
F	41	7	6	7	7	7	34	33	5	7	EC
F	45	2	2	4	2	2	12	16	9	10	DH
F	45	4	4	1	2	2	13	12	0	0	DH
F	45	4	4	2	4	4	18	19	6	7	OF
F	48	4	5	2	2	2	15	16	3	2	EC

GENDER	AGE	SFQ1	SFQ2	SFQ3	SFQ4	SFQ5	SF TOT1	SF TOT2	TKTS LSTYR	TKTS CURYR	REASON
F	49	8	6	5	2	2	23	29	15	15	TP
F	49	6	6	4	6	4	26	25	8	10	TP
F	49	8	6	3	8	5	30	27	0	6	VA
F	50	5	4	5	3	4	21	25	10	12	VA
F	50	4	4	5	4	6	23	25	10	16	DH
F	50	8	8	8	8	8	40	32	18	16	DH
F	51	1	1	1	1	1	5	19	1	0	OF
F	51	4	4	4	5	3	20	21	5	4	EC
F	51	2	2	0	3	1	8	6	1	6	OF
F	51	3	2	1	2	3	11	16	0	1	TP
F	51	6	6	2	4	4	22	20	1	4	EC
F	51	7	7	5	5	6	30	32	5	5	EC
F	52	5	2	2	2	2	13	15	7	7	OF
F	52	4	2	5	5	2	18	12	3	3	DH
F	52	6	4	2	6	5	23	20	2	3	TP
F	53	3	3	4	4	3	17	20	5	2	OF
F	53	4	3	4	4	4	19	20	0	0	DH
F	53	6	4	4	5	5	24	23	4	5	EC
F	54	3	2	2	1	2	10	17	0	0	DH
F	54	8	8	8	8	8	40	38	16	19	OF
F	57	2	2	2	2	1	9	8	0	0	OF
F	57	3	2	3	2	2	12	11	1	2	EC
F	57	6	5	3	3	4	21	20	4	8	TP
F	64	5	3	2	4	4	18	23	6	7	OF
F	65	5	3	4	2	4	18	21	1	4	OF
F	67	2	1	1	1	1	6	7	0	0	DH
F	70	6	6	5	6	4	27	28	6	6	OF
F	75	7	5	1	1	1	15	18	3	5	OF

GENDER	AGE	SFQ1	SFQ2	SFQ3	SFQ4	SFQ5	SF TOT1	SF TOT2	TKTS LSTYR	TKTS CURYR	REASON
M	18	2	3	2	2	2	11	14	5	6	TP
M	18	6	6	6	6	6	30	29	11	15	EC
M	18	8	7	8	4	7	34	35	5	10	EC
M	19	3	2	2	2	1	10	16	3	2	EC
M	19	8	7	6	5	7	33	26	9	4	TP
M	19	6	6	5	5	6	28	27	6	13	DH
M	20	3	4	3	3	3	16	17	7	2	TP
M	20	7	5	5	4	5	26	19	2	4	OF
M	20	6	6	4	5	6	27	28	1	0	TP
M	20	6	7	5	5	5	28	30	3	7	OF
M	20	6	6	5	4	5	26	29	8	12	TP
M	20	8	8	7	8	8	39	39	9	12	TP
M	21	4	4	6	4	4	22	8	3	5	TR
M	21	3	2	4	3	3	15	18	13	12	EC
M	21	5	5	4	5	5	24	24	3	1	EC
M	21	6	6	6	6	4	28	29	2	5	TP
M	21	8	8	8	8	8	40	38	17	20	TP
M	22	4	4	4	2	4	18	17	8	12	TP
M	22	8	7	5	6	5	31	32	10	15	TP
M	22	8	8	7	8	7	38	29	12	14	DH
M	22	4	4	5	5	6	24	25	8	10	TP
M	25	5	6	4	6	2	23	24	5	4	EC
M	25	6	6	4	4	5	25	31	0	0	EC
M	26	8	8	8	8	8	40	38	9	5	OF
M	27	6	6	3	6	5	26	25	3	0	TP
M	30	8	8	6	4	6	32	30	12	16	EC
M	31	8	8	4	4	4	28	28	5	3	EC
M	31	8	8	6	6	6	34	33	4	2	TP

GENDER	AGE	SFQ1	SFQ2	SFQ3	SFQ4	SFQ5	SF TOT1	SF TOT2	TKTS LSTYR	TKTS CURYR	REASON
M	32	2	2	1	2	1	8	7	2	3	TP
M	33	6	6	5	6	6	29	30	1	6	OF
M	33	7	7	7	6	6	33	37	8	4	TP
M	33	8	8	8	8	8	40	36	14	16	VA
M	34	4	4	4	2	2	16	12	3	2	EC
M	34	4	5	4	6	5	24	22	9	5	TP
M	35	4	4	4	5	5	22	19	9	7	EC
M	36	4	4	3	4	3	18	16	0	0	TP
M	36	6	6	6	6	6	30	24	6	10	TP
M	37	4	4	4	2	3	17	23	5	9	EC
M	38	8	8	8	8	8	40	37	13	16	EC
M	39	5	6	5	6	5	27	29	8	5	TP
M	40	1	1	1	1	1	5	9	2	4	TP
M	41	8	8	8	8	7	39	31	6	7	OF
M	42	4	2	2	3	2	13	10	1	1	EC
M	42	5	6	8	3	5	27	24	12	16	DH
M	43	6	6	5	5	5	27	20	9	13	DH
M	48	6	5	5	6	4	26	32	2	0	TP
M	48	7	8	7	7	7	36	29	2	4	EC
M	48	8	8	7	7	8	38	40	11	8	DH
M	49	5	5	6	5	5	26	23	1	0	TP
M	49	7	8	6	6	7	34	29	3	7	EC
M	50	8	6	5	8	5	32	35	3	5	OF
M	50	8	8	6	6	6	34	36	11	9	EC
M	50	8	8	8	8	8	40	36	14	16	DH
M	52	8	7	7	7	7	36	37	5	6	TP
M	53	7	7	6	6	4	30	26	11	15	TP
M	54	5	5	4	5	4	23	22	4	6	OF

GENDER	AGE	SFQ1	SFQ2	SFQ3	SFQ4	SFQ5	SF TOT1	SF TOT2	TKTS LSTYR	TKTS CURYR	REASON
M	54	3	2	2	3	2	12	14	6	9	TP
M	54	6	6	4	5	4	25	26	12	16	EC
M	55	2	1	1	1	1	6	8	0	3	EC
M	55	4	4	4	3	4	19	13	8	9	DH
M	55	6	5	4	6	5	26	28	8	10	DH
M	55	7	7	4	7	6	31	32	10	12	TP
M	56	2	2	1	2	1	8	7	3	5	EC
M	57	4	4	2	3	3	16	13	6	5	EC
M	57	8	5	8	5	5	31	29	4	5	TP
M	57	6	6	7	6	8	33	37	5	10	EC
M	58	4	4	3	4	4	19	14	6	7	TP
M	59	5	4	4	4	4	21	13	5	7	DH
M	63	8	6	6	7	5	32	33	2	6	EC
M	65	4	4	3	4	4	19	24	3	4	TP
M	65	8	8	6	5	5	32	26	4	3	TP
M	67	6	7	2	6	4	25	21	1	1	EC
M	67	6	6	6	4	5	27	38	3	8	TP
M	72	6	4	1	1	2	14	15	2	2	EC
M	77	7	8	7	6	5	33	32	3	3	DH

Appendix B

SURVEY DATA: HEALTH CLUB SCENARIO II

GENDER	MARITAL STATUS	INCOME	OPHOURS	EXWEEKT1	EXWEEKT2	EXPECT
F	M	L	1	2	3	BE
F	M	L	1	1	2	ME
F	S	L	1	1	4	ME
F	S	M	1	2	2	ME
F	S	L	2	1	2	BE
F	S	L	2	2	4	EE
F	M	L	2	2	3	ME
F	M	M	2	1	2	ME
F	M	M	2	3	4	ME
F	S	M	2	3	4	ME
F	S	H	3	3	3	EE
F	S	H	3	4	4	EE
F	S	L	3	1	3	EE
F	M	M	3	2	3	EE
F	M	M	3	3	3	EE
F	M	H	3	3	3	ME
F	M	L	3	2	2	ME
F	S	M	3	3	3	ME
F	S	M	4	2	2	BE

GENDER	MARITAL STATUS	INCOME	OPHOURS	EXWEEKT1	EXWEEKT2	EXPECT
F	S	H	4	3	4	ME
F	M	H	4	4	3	ME
F	M	H	4	5	6	ME
F	S	L	4	5	5	ME
F	M	M	4	3	3	ME
F	M	L	5	3	3	BE
F	S	M	5	5	5	EE
F	M	H	5	4	4	ME
F	S	H	6	4	3	EE
F	M	H	6	5	5	EE
F	S	H	7	5	5	BE
M	M	H	1	3	4	BE
M	M	L	1	2	4	BE
M	S	L	2	2	3	BE
M	M	L	2	1	3	EE
M	M	H	2	4	3	ME
M	M	L	2	2	2	ME
M	M	M	2	3	3	ME
M	S	M	3	3	5	BE
M	M	L	3	2	2	EE
M	S	L	3	3	4	EE
M	S	H	3	3	3	ME
M	M	L	3	2	3	ME
M	M	M	3	3	3	ME
M	S	L	4	5	6	EE
M	S	M	4	5	5	EE
M	S	H	4	4	5	ME

GENDER	MARITAL STATUS	INCOME	OPHOURS	EXWEEKT1	EXWEEKT2	EXPECT
M	S	L	4	3	5	ME
M	S	L	4	5	4	ME
M	M	M	4	3	2	ME
M	M	M	4	3	4	ME
M	M	M	5	4	3	BE
M	M	H	5	5	6	EE
M	M	H	5	4	4	ME
M	S	H	5	6	7	ME
M	S	M	5	5	6	ME
M	S	H	6	6	6	ME
M	S	M	6	7	6	ME
M	M	H	7	5	5	EE
M	S	H	7	7	6	ME
M	S	M	7	6	7	ME

Glossary

action research See *field research*.

alpha (α) The level of probability, set by the researcher, that is used to control for committing a Type I error (usually 0.05 or 0.01).

analysis The exploration of data, especially through the use of statistics. We call the process by which data is explored *analytics*.

analysis of variance (ANOVA) A statistical technique used to examine the differences among multiple means on one dependent variable that is measured with an interval or ratio scale.

applied research Information collected that can be used in actual practice to solve problems.

bad instrumentation An obstruction to research resulting from use of a measurement instrument that is not valid and reliable.

basic research Information collected that is fundamental, essential knowledge.

bell-shaped curve See *normal curve*.

best fit line A line added to a scatterplot that best represents the set of data, used when two variables have a linear relationship.

beta (β) The level of probability, set by the researcher, that is used to control for committing a Type II error (usually 20%).

case study An in-depth examination of one aspect of a specific problem or question, in which the researchers gather extensive information based on observations or reliable reports.

categorical variable A variable that changes, that cannot be manipulated, and that can take on only a fixed number of values.

chi-square test A nonparametric statistical test used to examine the difference between observed and expected frequencies of data in two or more categories; the test statistic is χ^2.

chi-square test of goodness of fit A test of the observed and expected frequencies of data that fall within each category of a single variable; also called a *one-way classification*.

chi-square test of independence A test that compares the observed and expected frequencies of data based on two classifications, one for the column variable and the other for the row variable; also called a *two-way classification*.

classification variables Term used in descriptive research for independent variables.

closed-ended questionnaire Questionnaire in which respondents choose an answer for each question from a prepared list.

cluster random sampling A sampling method in which the target population is divided into clusters, a desired number of clusters is selected, and then subjects are chosen from the selected clusters.

coefficient of determination (r^2 or R^2) The percentage of variance in a dependent variable that is shared with independent variable (or a combined set of independent variables); the measure of meaningfulness for correlation and regression.

confidence interval (CI) A range of values that has a certain level of probability of containing the true population mean.

construct An idea, concept, or theoretical formulation that is typically unobservable.

construct validity A measure is considered to have construct validity when it is able to measure the construct it is intended to measure.

content validity Evidence for a measure's validity based on the fact that the measure adequately covers the breadth of a particular topic or area of study.

continuous variable A numerical variable that may take on several values within its range.

contract Funds awarded by an organization, usually a company or governmental agency, to support a project that will enhance its operations or a community.

convenience sampling In cases where access to the target population is restricted, instead of striving for a representative sample, the researcher simply works with the subjects who are available.

convergent validity Evidence for a measure's construct validity based on the measure's relationship to other variables to which it should theoretically be related.

correlation The degree of the relationship between two or more variables that are measured on an interval or ratio scale.

correlation coefficient (r) A measure of the strength of the linear relationship between two variables.

correlational study A study in which the researchers examine the extent to which two variables are related; also called a causal study.

Cramer's V A measure of meaningfulness for χ^2 that can be used when one or both classification variables have more than two levels.

criterion validity Evidence for a measure's validity based on its correlation to another measure, which is known to be valid (the criterion measure).

criterion variables Term used in descriptive research for dependent variables.

cross-sectional study A study in which the investigators examine different participant groups at a single point in time.

deductive methods Methods in which the investigators test a general theory by searching for specific facts; commonly used in qualitative research.

degrees of freedom (df) The number of values used in the final calculation of a statistic that are free to vary.

Delphi study A type of study in which the researcher acquires opinions from a group of subject experts, usually through rounds of surveys conducted until a conclusion is reached by consensus or a satisfactory answer is determined, for the purpose of forecasting or problem solving.

demographics Data about individuals' personal characteristics, such as age, gender, education level, and household income.

dependent t-test A t-test comparing the means from two samples that are related, commonly used for pre–post test studies.

dependent variables Variables that the researcher cannot control.

descriptive case study A case study that presents an overview of a condition in great detail, often reporting "insider"-type information.

descriptive research Research that simply describes characteristics and conditions of populations and phenomena, used for studying social situations and other aspects of human behavior and sometimes providing the factual foundation for other forms of inquiry.

descriptive statistics Statistics that describe the characteristics of a data set, including measures of central tendency (mean, median, and mode) and measures of variability (standard deviation, variance, and range).

discrete variable A variable limited in the values it can take on; its value must be a whole number.

discriminant validity Evidence for a measure's construct validity based on the measure's lack of relationship to other variables to which it should not theoretically be related.

dummy coding The assignment of a quantitative value to each category for categorical-scaled or nominal-scaled variables, such as 1 for male and 2 for female.

effect size The standardized difference between two means as a function of the pooled standard deviation; a measure of meaningfulness for a *t*-test; also called *Cohen's d*.

empirical research Information collected that stands the test of repetition and time.

error variance A fluctuation of measures that is attributable to chance.

eta-squared (η^2) The proportion of total variation of a dependent variable that is accounted for (or explained by) an independent variable; a measure of meaningfulness for one-way ANOVA that tends to overestimate slightly.

evaluative case study A case study that assesses existing information and generates judgments about the information.

experimental research Research in which the investigators make predictions about how participants might react to the introduction of a variable, determine a procedure to test the predictions, conduct the experiment, and determine whether the variable affected the outcome.

external validity When research results can be generalized to a population, they have external validity.

extraneous variable A variable that emerges during the study that is unrelated to the study's purpose, resulting in a discrepancy in results traceable to unwanted effects.

***F* distribution** A probability distribution based in inferential statistics, especially ANOVA, that we use when examining the ratio of the variances for two normally distributed populations.

face validity Evidence for a measure's validity based on the fact that the measure seems to be or "looks" like it is measuring what it is supposed to be measuring.

factorial ANOVA An ANOVA that compares the effects of two or more independent variables on one dependent variable, often preferred over one-way ANOVA because it allows the analyst to examine the effects of multiple independent variables simultaneously.

feasibility study A study that indicates whether it is possible to manufacture a product, build a facility, host an event, or provide a service.

field research Research carried out according to an experimental method in which there may be no control or randomization, but instead the investigators study a real situation with specific treatments.

financial analysis An analysis that indicates whether a profit is likely to exist for a product, facility, event, or service by determining the costs of the project, such as manufacturing, construction, management, advertising, and sales costs, as well as revenue projections and potential for investments.

heteroscedasticity Exists when the variability of one variable is *not* consistent or uniform across the values of the other variable.

histogram A graphic illustration of the frequencies in a data set, such as a bar graph.

historical research Research that examines existing information, such as news accounts or eyewitness reports, in such a way as to address questions or test hypotheses and draw conclusions about past experiences, incidents, and trends.

history An obstruction to research referring to the fact that the longer a problem or specific participants are studied, the more likely it becomes that extraneous variables might affect the outcome of the study.

homoscedasticity Exists when the variability of one variable is consistent or uniform across the values of the other variable.

hypothesis A theory or predicted outcome of a relationship or lack or relationship between variables; the result investigators expect to find.

independent *t*-test A *t*-test comparing the means from two independent (different) sample groups.

independent variables Variables that the researcher controls.

inductive methods Methods in which the investigators make specific observations and uncover facts that lead to broader realities; commonly used in quantitative research.

inference The process by which the results obtained from a sample are generalized or applied to the target population.

interaction effect In a factorial ANOVA, the effect of the interaction of the independent variables.

internal consistency Evidence for reliability based on the correlation between several items or questions that are designed to tap into the same construct.

interpretative case study A case study that describes a single individual circumstance or a set of trends and goes on to evaluate the subject, explain the facts based on a theory, or attempt to generate new ideas.

inter-rater reliability Evidence for reliability based on the correlation between ratings performed by multiple raters or observers of the same participants and trials.

inter-tester reliability See *inter-rater reliability*.

interval scale A measurement scale in which the distances between the units of measurement are the same, but there is no absolute zero point on the scale, such as a judge's ratings of athletic performance.

kurtosis The flatness or peakedness, relative to a bell-shaped curve, of a data distribution that may not be distributed normally.

leptokurtic Describes a curve that is more peaked than the normal curve (kurtosis > 0).

line fit plot Scatterplot of the actual and predicted scores of a dependent variable for each value of an independent variable, providing visual evidence of a linear relationship.

longitudinal study A study in which the investigators examine the same participants at different ages.

main effect The calculated effect of each independent variable in a factorial ANOVA.

market analysis An assessment of the present and potential consumer market for a product, facility, event, or service, often addressing distribution channels, general trade practices, and market comparables.

maturation An obstruction to research referring to the fact that subjects can experience personal changes over time.

mean (*M*) The arithmetic average of a data set (the sum of all scores or values in the data set divided by the total number of scores or values in the set); a measure of central tendency.

meaningfulness See *practical significance*.

measure of central tendency A single score that represents all the scores or values in a set of data, allowing the analyst to describe a collection of scores or values quickly and to evaluate how any one particular score or value compares with the middle (or central) scores in a set of data.

measurement The process for collecting data through the use of instruments, tests, questionnaires, or other types of measures.

median The middle point in a set of data, where 50 percent of the scores fall above it and 50 percent fall below it, or, if the middle point falls between two scores, the value that is halfway between these two scores; a measure of central tendency.

mesokurtic Describes a curve with a kurtosis value of 0; a bell-shaped curve.

mixed-design study A study in which the investigators use both longitudinal and cross-sectional methods.

mode The most frequently occurring score (or scores) in a set of data; a measure of central tendency.

mortality An obstruction to research referring to the fact that subjects may drop out of a study over time.

multiple regression A regression that uses two or more independent variables.

naturalistic inquiry See *qualitative research*.

needs assessment An assessment of the resources that an organization possesses and the new resources it might acquire to improve its position.

negative skew Describes a distribution that is skewed in the direction of negative values; the tail of the curve is drawn out to the left.

nominal scale A measurement scale in which the data fall into mutually exclusive categories, such as gender or ethnicity.

nonparametric tests Statistical tests that may be used when the assumptions for using parametric tests cannot be met, including tests for data that are measured on nominal or ordinal scales.

normal curve A curve representing a data set with an equal distribution of scores on either side of the measure of central tendency; also called *bell-shaped curve*.

normal distribution The distribution associated with a normal curve, in which the mean, median, and mode are all equal.

omega-squared (ω^2) The proportion of total variation of a dependent variable that is accounted for (or explained by) an independent variable; a measure of meaningfulness for one-way ANOVA that is more accurate than η^2.

one-group method of pre- and post-testing Experimental research design in which the same group is tested before and after a treatment so that the investigator can judge the effects of the treatment.

one-tailed statistical test A test for statistical significance in which we look to only one tail of the distribution to find the level of significance; the analyst is hypothesizing that the relationship between the variables lies in one direction only (either positive or negative).

one-way ANOVA An ANOVA that compares the means from two or more independent sample groups on one dependent variable, examining only one independent variable (or factor).

one-way ANOVA with repeated measures An ANOVA that compares the means from two or more samples that are related, such as when one sample group is measured two or more times on the same dependent variable.

one-way classification See *chi-square test of goodness of fit*.

open-ended questionnaire Questionnaire in which respondents answer questions in their own words, without prompting.

ordinal scale A measurement scale in which the data are organized in rank-ordered categories, such as ratings of agreement on a Likert scale.

outlier An extreme value in a data set, which may cause measures of central tendency and other statistics to represent the entire data set inaccurately.

p value The probability that a test statistic of a size indicating a finding of significance would emerge from the data, assuming the null hypothesis is true; the p value is compared to the alpha level and used to establish the level of significance.

parallel-forms reliability Evidence for reliability based on the correlation between two different measures of the same construct.

parametric tests Statistical tests that may be used for interval and ratio scales, including *t*-tests, correlation, regression, and analysis of variance (ANOVA).

partial eta-squared (η_p^2) The proportion of total variation of a dependent variable that is explained by an independent variable; a measure of meaningfulness for a one-way ANOVA with repeated measures.

phi coefficient (ϕ) A measure of the strength of association (correlation) between two classification variables; the measure of meaningfulness for χ^2.

philosophical research Research whose purpose is to address facts and values and examine the meaning of phenomena from a conceptual perspective.

pictorial questionnaire Questionnaire that presents drawings, photos, or graphics from which respondents choose.

platykurtic Describes a curve that is flatter than the normal curve (kurtosis < 0).

pooled variance The weighted average of sample variances.

population The group of all individuals that are of interest or relevant to the particular problem or issue in a study.

positive skew Describes a distribution that is skewed in the direction of positive values; the tail of the curve is drawn out to the right.

power The probability that a test will detect a real or statistically significant difference that exists in the population.

practical significance Measures of practical significance take into consideration the power of the study to determine whether the relationship between variables is meaningful, whether or not it is statistically significant. Also called *meaningfulness*.

predictive validity Evidence for a measure's validity based on how well the new measure predicts the results of a criterion measure, which is developed/administered at a later time.

primary data Data that are original and collected firsthand by researchers, through focus groups, interviews, surveys, field trials, and so forth.

probability The likelihood that an event will occur.

profitability study A study that provides information about the marketability of a product, facility, event, or service.

psychographics Information about individuals' behavior and preferences.

purposive sampling A type of sampling commonly used in qualitative research, when the investigators wish to study a specific group to learn about explicit realities in their surroundings.

qualitative research Research in which the investigators assume that there are multiple realities, collect data in a natural setting, employ inductive methods, and allow their personal values to play a role in the investigation.

quasi-experimental design Research methods in which the investigators study a problem without having total control of the procedure.

random assignment The assignment of subjects to experimental groups or conditions through a random process.

random sampling Sampling in which all participants within a population have an equal opportunity to be selected for a study.

random variance See *error variance*.

range The difference between the highest and lowest scores in a set of data; a quick but crude estimate of the variability in a data set, typically reported in conjunction with the median.

ratio scale A measurement scale in which the distances between the units of measurement are the same, and there is an absolute zero point on the scale, such as age, distance, time, and weight.

raw score A measurement acquired in a study, before any standardization.

regression A statistical technique for arriving at a prediction formula that allows us to predict the change in scores on one dependent variable based on changes in or information about a single independent variable or a group of independent variables.

reliability A measure is considered *reliable* if it consistently provides the same output or answers.

research The systematic collection of data and study of materials to address a question or make a decision.

research grant Funds awarded to investigators in order to add to the knowledge base of a topical area; the results of the research are submitted to the funding agency and may be published or presented through a scholarly forum.

residual The absolute value of the difference between a raw score and the sample mean.

residuals plot A scatterplot with each independent variable on the X-axis and the residuals on the Y-axis, providing visual evidence as to whether homoscedasticity exists.

sample A smaller group of individuals selected from a target population.

scientific method A systematic, controlled process of information gathering and problem solving.

secondary data Data that are previously gathered and made available, free or for purchase, by research houses, government organizations, or commercial agencies, such as chambers of commerce and local/regional business journals.

selection bias Lack of randomness in selection of a study's participants.

service grants Funds awarded in order to accomplish a practical objective for the agency or an institution, and/or to make a contribution to society as a whole.

simple correlation A statistic that assigns a quantitative value to the degree to which two variables are linearly related.

simple regression A regression that uses only one independent variable.

skewness A measure of the dispersion of scores around the mean, when one side, or "tail," of the distribution is more drawn out (skewed) than the other side; a perfectly symmetrical distribution has a skewness value of 0.

$SS_{Between}$ The sum of squares between groups; a measure of the variability between comparison groups.

SS_{Total} The sum of squares total; a measure of the total variability in observed data.

standard deviation The amount of difference that exists between each of the individual scores in a data set and the mean, symbolized by s or SD for a sample or by σ for a population; a measure of variability.

standard error of kurtosis A statistic that allows us to determine whether a data set has a mesokurtic distribution; if the absolute value of the kurtosis is more than twice as large as the standard error of kurtosis, then the distribution may not be mesokurtic.

standard error of measurement (SEM) A measure of the error associated with a measured score, allowing the researcher to calculate a range of scores in which the true score lies with a given level of confidence.

standard error of skewness A statistic that allows us to determine whether a data set is skewed; if the absolute value of the skewness exceeds twice the standard error of skewness, the distribution will be either positively or negatively skewed.

standard error of the mean (SE_M) An estimate of the variability (standard deviation) of multiple sample means drawn from the same population.

statistical significance A relationship between variables determined through statistical analysis has statistical significance when it is large enough to be considered to exist in the population.

statistics A way to interpret a collection of observations or data that is obtained from research.

story-type case study A case study that describes a situation, either fictional or fact-based, often accompanied by questions and used as a teaching tool.

stratified random sampling Sampling by selecting individuals who possess important key characteristics that are present in the target population or are believed to be particularly relevant to the issue being studied.

structured interviews Interviews that employ a rigid technique in which many respondents are asked the same questions in the same order; the questions are usually closed-ended, and data are collected under exact conditions.

systematic sampling Sampling by selecting every nth person from a listing of the population.

systematic variance An inconsistency in a measure caused by known or unknown influences that skew the results in one direction or another.

technical analysis An analysis that identifies the technology needed to produce or provide a product or service, such as equipment, materials and methods, time lines and schedules, essential facilities, and labor needs.

test statistic The final calculated value of a statistical test.

test–retest reliability Evidence for reliability based on the correlation between administrations of the measure on separate days (or trials) within a specified time period, such as the next day, a week later, or perhaps a month later.

theory A prediction for a set of facts.

T-score A score that has been standardized so that the data set will have a distribution with a mean of 50.00 and a standard deviation of 10.00.

t-test A statistical technique for studying the difference between two means measured on interval or ratio scales; the test statistic is t.

two-tailed statistical test A test for statistical significance, typically used when little research exists on the variables of interest, in which we look to both tails of the distribution to find the level of significance; the analyst is hypothesizing that the relationship between the variables may lie in either a positive or negative direction.

two-way classification See *chi-square test of independence*.

type I error The error of rejecting the null hypothesis when the null hypothesis should not have been rejected; concluding that a significant difference or relationship exists when the difference or relationship does not really exist in the population.

type II error The error of not rejecting the null hypothesis when the null hypothesis should have been rejected; concluding that there is no significant difference or relationship when the difference or relationship really does exist in the population.

unstructured interviews Interviews conducted with a flexible technique, where the same initial questions are asked of respondents, but the questions may be asked in any order, the interviewer may ask follow-up questions, and the respondents can then expand on their responses.

validity A measure is considered valid when it measures what it is supposed to measure.

value-bound inquiry Research in which the investigators believe that biases cannot be removed and, thus, allow their personal values to drive the inquiry.

value-free inquiry Research in which the investigators attempt to remove as many biases as possible that would interfere with an impartial conclusion.

variability A measure of how widely dispersed scores are in a data set—whether they are clustered together (low variability) or spread across the entire scale (high variability).

variables Features or characteristics that can take on different values and can be measured.

variance (s^2) A measure of the dispersion of data away from the mean; a measure of variability.

Z-score A score that has been standardized so that the data set will have a distribution with a mean of 0.00 and a standard deviation of 1.00.

Index